Simply Austen

Simply Austen

JOAN KLINGEL RAY

SIMPLY CHARLY
NEW YORK

Contents

Praise for *Simply Austen*

"*Simply Austen* is simply a must for anyone just starting off their Janeite journey or for those wanting a quick refresher course. Jam-packed with biographical facts and contexts, this smart pocket tutorial offers a fast-paced and accessible distillation of what scholars and biographers have pieced together about an enigmatic author so beloved that many readers refer to her solely by her first name—as if a close personal friend."
   –Janine Barchas, Professor of English at the University of Texas, Austin

"Joan Klingel Ray has written an admirably thorough, balanced, and accessible introduction to Jane Austen for new readers, while its subtle readings and judicious discussions of critical debate will also profit confirmed Janeites."
   –Elaine Bander, President of Jane Austen Society of North America (Canada) and Regional Coordinator for the Montréal region

"Joan Klingel Ray's gift for communication runs through this enticing and informative new biography all about Jane Austen. Blending key scenes from Austen's novels with essential contextual information about her life and times, this book will inspire you to read or reread her brilliant works and look further into a fascinating period in history."
   –Dr. Mary Guyatt, Curator, Jane Austen's House Museum, Chawton, UK

"Joan Klingel Ray's splendid new book, *Simply Austen*, introduces general readers to key issues about Austen's historical context, to the most important events in her life, and of course to the sweep of her career. In addition to covering Austen's youthful and unfinished works, Ray treats us to fresh and full-scale readings of the major novels that prove that "simple" reading is not to be confused with simplistic reading. This enviably clear book is informed by the kind of knowledge, nuance, and insight that can only come from decades of reading and re-reading her beloved Jane. Newcomers to Austen as well card-carrying Janeites will read this book with instruction and delight. In short, *Simply Austen* is simply marvelous!"

–Claudia L. Johnson, Murray Professor of English Literature, Princeton University

Other *Great Lives*

Series Editor's Foreword

S imply Charly's "Great Lives" series offers brief but authoritative introductions to the world's most influential people–scientists, artists, writers, economists, and other historical figures whose contributions have had a meaningful and enduring impact on our society.

Each book provides an illuminating look at the works, ideas, personal lives, and the legacies these individuals left behind, also shedding light on the thought processes, specific events, and experiences that led these remarkable people to their groundbreaking discoveries or other achievements. Additionally, every volume explores various challenges they had to face and overcome to make history in their respective fields, as well as the little-known character traits, quirks, strengths, and frailties, myths, and controversies that sometimes surrounded these personalities.

Our authors are prominent scholars and other top experts who have dedicated their careers to exploring each facet of their subjects' work and personal lives.

Unlike many other works that are merely descriptions of the major milestones in a person's life, the "Great Lives" series goes above and beyond the standard format and content. It brings substance, depth, and clarity to the sometimes-complex lives and works of history's most powerful and influential people.

We hope that by exploring this series, readers will not only gain new knowledge and understanding of what drove these geniuses, but also find inspiration for their own lives. Isn't this what a great book is supposed to do?

Charles Carlini, Simply Charly
New York City

Preface

In Karen Joy Fowler's 2004 best-selling novel, *The Jane Austen Book Club*, the opening line is, "Each of us has a private Austen" (NY: G.P. Putnam's, 2004: 1). It stands alone as a sentence. Of course, every reader of Austen's novels creates a personal perspective on the author. This is what I have called in talks dating back to the late 1990s and in my 2006 trade book, *Jane Austen for Dummies* (Wiley), "Jane the friend." By this I mean her narrative voice: the voice and attitude a writer assumes to relate the events of the text. Her voice is frequently so appealingly affable, comforting, wry, or ironic that it draws each of us into her world in a different, personal way—so much so, that writers about and readers of Austen have been known to call her "Jane." What other author do we call by his or her first name?

But there is another way that each of us has our own Austen: *what did she look like?* We have professional likenesses of Shakespeare (portraits) and Dickens (photographs) taken in their lifetimes. But no professional images of the world-beloved Austen.

The second youngest in a family of eight children, Jane Austen (1775-1817), the most famous of the Austens, is one of three Austen siblings who never sat for a professional portrait: the other two are her elder sister Cassandra and their brother George (Jr.), the second eldest of the Austen siblings.

For most of his life, George (1766-1838) did not live with the Austen family. Suffering "fits," possibly indicative of epilepsy, and being deaf and mute, George may also have been mentally ill, as was his mother's younger brother, Thomas Leigh (1747-1821). So the Austens sent little George to live with the family of Francis Culhum, the parish clerk at All Saints Church in the village of Monk Sherborne, about eight miles from the Austen family home in the village of Steventon. The Culhums also cared for the child's maternal uncle, Thomas. Boarding a child in Thomas's or George's condition outside the immediate family was not unusual in this period and was, in fact, comparatively kind–given the heartless way such persons were treated at large. But neither was George the beloved, albeit troubled son who regularly joined the Austen family at church, as the 2007-film *Becoming Jane* depicts him. In his hefty, scholarly biography, *Jane Austen: A Life* (NY, 1997), Professor David Nokes (late of King's College, London) writes, "Neither the Austens nor the Leighs cared to be reminded of the existence of [their] imbecile relatives" (522). So it is not surprising that the Austens never had George sit for a professional portrait.

But the Austen sisters? The only images of them are by amateurs: a homemade silhouette of Cassandra (on display at the Jane Austen House Museum); two silhouettes said to be of Jane Austen (not authenticated), one, a hollow-cut silhouette, in the National Portrait Gallery (item 3181) pasted into the second volume of *Mansfield Park* with the handwritten words "L'aimable Jane" above it, and another at Winchester Cathedral bearing the words on the back "Jane Austin [sic] done by herself in 1815" in an unidentified handwriting (again, unauthenticated); and two watercolors of Jane Austen painted by her sister (1804 and 1810). In the earlier painting, owned by an Austen family descendant and frequently reproduced, Jane Austen is sitting outside, turned sideways with a large bonnet blocking her face–no help there! Cassandra's 1810 pencil and watercolor sketch (just 4 1/2 in. x 3 1/8 in.) is at the National Portrait Gallery (item 3630), but the fingers of Austen's crossed arms are somewhat claw-like, giving the portrait an amateurish look.

Austen's nephew, James Edward Austen-Leigh, had his Aunt Cassandra's portrait of her sister revised as the frontispiece for his *Memoir of Jane Austen* (published 1869, but dated 1870). Mutton-chopped Victorian that he was, Austen-Leigh presents his aunt on the delicate female pedestal where Victorian gentlemen typically placed beloved fine ladies: a gentle, sweet "dear Aunt Jane," as he calls her on page one, whose inexplicable "genius" led to her writing. This frontispiece matches the Victorian ideal for womanhood: in place of Cassandra's sharp-faced, sharp-eyed Jane Austen with her arms folded and a determined look on her face as she glances sideways, Austen-Leigh substituted a round-faced, doe-eyed woman with her hands folded in her lap in a most lady-like pose (not cross-armed as Cassandra captured her sister) as she sweetly gazes at us. The latter is the most widely reproduced "face" of the author—the one that launched thousands of mouse pads, mugs, T-shirts, and book covers—because it is not under copyright.

The Memoir's engraved frontispiece, a copy of a copy, shows a softened image of Jane Austen (photo by Isobel Snowden, Jane Austen House Museum).

Cassandra Austen's pencil and watercolor portrait of her sister, Jane, was taken from life (reproduced by permission of the National Portrait Gallery, London).

But Austen was a Georgian (the period in England from 1714 to 1830, under the reigns of King George I, II, III, and IV, followed by the brief reign of George IV's younger brother William IV, all of the House of Hanover), not a Victorian: Austen died twenty years before Victoria ascended the throne. And Georgian England was the great age of satire and rollicking humor.

In 2011, biographer Paula Byrne claimed to have found another portrait of Austen, but its authenticity is again questionable, and its pictorial awkwardness suggests that the painter was an amateur. Prominent Austen expert Deirdre Le Faye calls it an "imaginary" likeness. A few others think it is of Austen. (I do not.) So we all visually imagine our own Jane Austens.

That the Austen sisters were never given professional portrait sittings reminds us of the marginalized role of women in Jane Austen's world, even with Austen as a popular, admired, though deliberately anonymous, novelist. She lived and wrote, as noted, during the English Georgian era (1714-1830), which subsumes a period (1811-1820, during which her six novels were published) called the Regency because King George III, deemed mad (likely suffering from undiagnosed porphyria), was removed from rule and replaced by his eldest son, The Prince of Wales. The future George IV headed the monarchy as the Prince Regent: a regent is the person appointed to rule because the ruler is incapacitated. Austen's books, for all their charm as "courtship novels," present marginalized females in a patriarchal society where the gentlemen cannot always be trusted to do well by the ladies under their care.

As Margaret Oliphant observed in her shrewd *Blackwood's Magazine* review of the first edition of Austen-Leigh's *Memoir*, while "Mr. Austen-Leigh . . . disarms us" with a "passing gleam of light" on his aunt, her actual novels reveal the "fine vein of feminine cynicism which pervades his aunt's mind" (vol. 107, March 1870, 290-305 *passim*). Just think how *Sense and Sensibility* begins with Austen's bluntly describing the patriarchal and fraternal marginalization—the very gentlemen who are supposed to look after the ladies in a patriarchal society that gives females virtually neither legal nor financial rights—of the Dashwood women. Like Mary Wollstonecraft, with whose strident *Vindication of the Rights of Woman* (1792) Jane Austen was certainly familiar, our novelist knew what depending on the kindness of brothers meant.

Modern researchers investigate Austen's six brothers (and occasionally even poor George). Of course, they study Austen's male siblings not so much because they were especially remarkable–though two, Francis (Frank) and Charles, served bravely as Royal Naval officers, and Frank, by virtue of living very long, became Admiral of the Fleet at age 89–but because they are brothers of the great novelist Jane Austen, never professionally painted, sketched, or sculpted.

So how did Jane Austen become one of the most revered and popular novelists in the world, the "prose Shakespeare," as the Victorians George Lewes and Lord McCauley described her? It starts with her family: their personalities, their professions, their tastes, and their encouragement of her as a young writer. For in her novels we see the world as she knew it.

Joan Klingel Ray
Colorado Springs, CO

Abbreviations for Novels

NA *Northanger Abbey*
SS *Sense and Sensibility*
PP *Pride and Prejudice*
MP *Mansfield Park*
E *Emma*
P *Persuasion*

1. Introduction: Jane Austen and her Culture–The Context of her Novels

B efore her death at only 41, Jane Austen (1775-1817) completed just six novels–all still popular with readers of all generations. They are taught in schools; discussed in book clubs; deconstructed by scholars; and adapted into films. Furthermore, her works have been updated with Internet trolling and drugs in a Harper Collins project, "Jane Austen Re-imagined," where six current best-selling authors like Alexander McCall Smith and Joanna Trollope adapt her novels for the 21st-century world. I believe, however, that there is no need for such modernization because Austen's works, although set in Georgian England, transcend time and place. She wrote about human nature, which, by definition, never changes: whether in bonnets, corsets, and bloomers of the 1800s, or the fashions of later centuries, her protagonists exhibit "timeless" character traits: boastfulness (John Thorpe); naiveté (Catherine Morland); impertinence (Elizabeth Bennet); over-indulgent emotionalism (Marianne Dashwood); over-confidence (Emma Woodhouse); male sexual carelessness, narcissism, and greed (Willoughby); and sexual jealousy (Fanny Price), among other characteristics.

Janeites of all ages exist around the world. Janeites or Janites is a word coined in 1894 by George Saintsbury in his "Preface" to an illustrated edition of *Pride and Prejudice*. Writing of Austen's growing readership, he stated:

> And in the sect–fairly large and yet unusually choice of Austenians or Janites, there would probably be found partisans of the claim to primacy of almost every one of the novels.

He repeated the word two years later in his *History of English Literature*:

> It did not apparently occur to this critic that he (or she) was in the first place paying Miss Austen an extraordinarily high compliment—a compliment almost greater than the most enthusiastic "Janites" have ventured.

In that sense, Jane Austen was and is unique. We don't hear of Williamites who love Shakespeare or Rowlingites who adore Harry Potter books. But Janeites are an active and vocal community, sharing, as they do, their views on Austen's books, characters, life, imaginary houses, actual houses, and characters on innumerable blogs.

Despite the depth and breadth of her novels, Austen's works can be enjoyed for their basic storyline and character appeal. While her satire is often subtle and her style and characters are frequently complex, many readers first come to her novels for one simple thing: their love stories. But that is not the main reason that this book is called *Simply Austen*. Rather, the title refers to the concise, yet comprehensive, format of the book, meant to provide an insightful introduction to the life and works of one of England's—and the world's—favorite authors.

Written for anyone who wants a crisp refresher on or introduction to Jane Austen, her culture, and her writing, *Simply Austen* provides just that. My many years of teaching Austen at the university (years before we saw Darcy in the wet shirt in the 1995-television series), writing about her and her novels in articles and books, as well as my six years as President of the Jane Austen Society of North America (www.jasna.org) went into this book's creation.

Because of my classroom experiences and public speaking to JASNA groups across the U.S. and Canada, I introduce this book with the context of Austen's cultural background, which may be as foreign to you, the reader, as it sometimes was to my students and many audiences. One such moment occurred during a classroom discussion of *Pride and Prejudice*, when a career Marine veteran impatiently griped that "Darcy and Bingley are just a couple of bums who ride around the countryside, but who should get jobs." Austen naturally expected her readers to understand the social conventions and mores of her day. While commentators have long praised her characters for their lifelikeness, these same characters live in a world of specific class distinctions and expectations. This is why my Marine vet student misinterpreted Darcy and Bingley. Though an intelligent man and a good reader, he simply did not know the culture in which these two characters lived: they were members of the gentry, a social class that did not hold jobs in a conventional sense, but rather derived their income from their land.

In fact, in Austen's time, the main standard of wealth was land. The gentry class (from which the word "gentleman" derived) was comprised of male landowners who had at least 300 acres, which they did not farm themselves. Instead, tenant farmers did the actual labor. As Mrs. Reynolds, Pemberley's housekeeper, proudly tells Elizabeth and the Gardiners of Darcy, "'He is the best landlord. . . . There is not one of his tenants or servants but what will give him a good name'" (PP 3:1).

The breadth of this class appears in *Pride and Prejudice*. An incensed and interfering Lady Catherine tries to discourage Elizabeth from marrying Darcy, whose annual income is five times Mr. Bennet's: "'If you were sensible of your own good, you would not wish to quit the sphere in which you have been brought up.'" Elizabeth calmly and correctly replies, "'In marrying your nephew, I should not consider myself as quitting that sphere. He is a gentleman; I am a gentleman's daughter; so far we are equal'" (3:14)—to which Lady Catherine, who normally loves the sound of her own voice, can initially utter just a one-word reply, "'True.'" (Then, of course, Lady Catherine reaches for Elizabeth's non-gentry relatives, a country attorney and a man in trade in London.) Although Elizabeth's father, with an income of £2,000 annually, does not own property as extensive as Darcy's Pemberley, he stays home, reads in his library, is served by a household staff that includes a butler, housekeeper, maids, and cook, and makes memorably snide remarks about his wife and five daughters. His tenant farmers do the actual farming, which readers know about because Mrs. Bennet remarks that the horses "'are wanted in the farm'" (1:7). Mr. Bennet is a "gentleman," which even the hyper-class-conscious Lady Catherine understands.

Gentlemen earned their wealth the truly old-fashioned way: they inherited it. The primary recipients of inherited titles and property were the eldest sons in a system called *primogeniture* (first born). Inherited property and title (if there was one) legally went to the eldest son and then to his male child, thus keeping property in the paternal name and line. But by Austen's day—and she recognized this—newly wealthy persons who earned or inherited their fortunes in the early years of the Industrial Revolution and its accompanying commercial enterprises aspired to buy estates that would raise them to the gentry as first-generation members. In *Pride and Prejudice*, Charles Bingley "inherited property [cash] to the amount of nearly an hundred thousand pounds from his father, who had intended to purchase an estate, but did not live to do it." Charles "intended it likewise, . . . but . . . it was doubtful to many of those who best knew the easiness of his temper, whether he might not . . . leave the next generation to purchase." His socially ambitious, catty sisters, who conveniently forget that their fortunes and their brother's "had been acquired by trade" in the north of England and snicker at Elizabeth's uncle's living "within view of his own warehouses" in London (2:2), "were very anxious for his having an estate of his own," obliterating the taint of trade and conferring on them gentry status (1:4).

Austen was a sharp satirist, relentlessly exposing vulgar social climbers, such as the Bingley sisters, *Emma's* Mrs. Elton, and Mrs. Elton's in-laws, the wonderfully named Sucklings who have owned Maple Grove for only 11 years—while Darcy's Pemberley is "'the work of many generations.'" (The Sucklings' neighbors are the equally cleverly named Bragges.)

Austen was also aware of the slowly changing social climate of her times: a gentleman was coming to be recognized as a man of excellent manners, good sense, and education, who may not own any land, rather than just being a landowner. Elizabeth's Aunt and Uncle Gardiner, who live in the commercial area of Cheapside, London, are a lady and gentleman, despite Mr. Gardiner's being in trade. Elizabeth even observes that when Darcy meets the Gardiners at Pemberley, he "takes them for people of fashion" (3:1).

If *Persuasion's* Naval hero, Captain Wentworth, was not of the gentry class when he first courted Anne Elliot of Kellynch Hall six years before the novel opens, he returns in 1814 as a wealthy Napoleonic War hero with the money and stature to socialize with the gentry and marry Anne. The fully established self-made gentleman had to wait until the Victorian period [1837-1901], during which the term "gentleman" underwent complex redefinition. But Austen saw the early stages of this transformation in her own day.

As Austen's father, George, was a clergyman, which was considered a respectable and "gentlemanly" occupation, the Austens mingled with the gentry. Being a clergyman in the Church of England was virtually a passport to the gentry's world. In *Emma*, the Rev. Mr. Elton pays social calls on the Woodhouses and considers himself a potential husband for the wealthy Emma Woodhouse of Hartfield, heiress to £30,000. *Northanger Abbey's* hero Henry Tilney, the younger son in a gentry family, is a clergyman, as is *Mansfield Park's* hero, Edmund Bertram, who is in similar familial circumstances. As the owner of the Mansfield Park estate, Edmund's father is a baronet and a member of the gentry. Baronets, though titled, are commoners, as are knights, whose titles end with their current holders. From highest in rank, the nobility still consists of duke, marquis, earl, viscount, and baron (remember this with a simple mnemonic: "Do Men Ever Visit Boston"). The Duke of Devonshire in Austen's day owned so much property that his income was 10 times that of the wealthy hero Darcy, whose £10,000 annual income is the gossip of the Meryton Assembly within minutes of his arrival.

Austen's father, maternal grandfather, two of her brothers (James and eventually Henry), and several cousins, were Anglican clergy. With the gentry populating Austen's fictional world, readers of her novels frequently encounter clergymen and talk of *church livings*. *Pride and Prejudice*'s obtuse Mr. Collins boasts of the church living, Hunsford, bestowed on him by Lady Catherine de Bourgh. But near the end of the novel, when Elizabeth and Darcy are engaged, Mr. Bennet facetiously advises Collins, who always curries Lady Catherine's favor, to "stand by the nephew [Darcy]. He has more to give," meaning he is wealthier with more church livings than Lady Catherine has (3:18). Sir Thomas Bertram must sell the profitable Mansfield Park church living to The Rev. Dr. Grant because of his elder son's extravagant expenses and give the less profitable church living, Thornton Lacey, to Edmund. As Sir Thomas chastises the careless Tom:

> "I blush for you, Tom," said he, in his most dignified manner; "I blush for the expedient which I am driven on, and I trust I may pity your feelings as a brother on the occasion. You have robbed Edmund for ten, twenty, thirty years, perhaps for life, of more than half the income which ought to be his. It may hereafter be in my power, or in yours (I hope it will), to procure him better preferment; but it must not be forgotten that no benefit of that sort would have been beyond his natural claims on us, and that nothing can, in fact, be an equivalent for the certain advantage which he is now obliged to forego through the urgency of your debts."
> (1:3)

The church living involved a patronage system enabling a would-be clergyman to become the rector of a church, accompanied by a house (rectory, parsonage, or vicarage) and land with an income based on tithes (tythes) and glebes: tithes were a 10th of the increase in the tenant farmers' crops, flocks, woods (lumber), and herds. Tithes formed a major part of clerical incomes; vicars (*Emma*'s Mr. Elton) had lower incomes than rectors (*Sense and Sensibility*'s Colonel Brandon gives Edward Ferrars the Delaford "rectory," meaning Edward will have a higher income than if he were a vicar). A glebe was a plot of land that provided profit to the parish clergyman. Church livings could be purchased and sold, and they could also be bestowed, as Sir Thomas gives the lesser church living in his care to Edmund. In Collins's obtuse and not very Christian behavior, as when Collins advises Mr. Bennet never to see or mention Lydia and Wickham after they live together out of wedlock, to which Mr. Bennet sneers "That is his notion of Christian forgiveness!" [3:17]), Austen slyly demonstrates the drawbacks in this system of patronage: not every clergyman was able or suited to lead a religious life. The same is true of Austen's treatment of Mr. Elton, who never forgives Emma or Harriet Smith and, along with his wife, displays mean-spirited behavior toward Harriet at the Crown Inn Ball.

One of Austen's favorite poets, William Cowper, satirically wrote about the Anglican practice of church livings in his poem *The Task* (1785), "Preserve the church! And lay not careless hands/On skulls that cannot teach and will not learn" (lines 393-394). But church livings were simply a fact of clerical life in Austen's day. And while an Oxford or Cambridge degree was required for ordination, a formal study of theology was not.

Other gentlemanly occupations for those who had to work—such as younger sons in a gentry family—were army officer (even the elder son, Captain Frederick Tilney, in *Northanger Abbey*, has his "'profession'" because his father advises "'employment'" for all young men [2:7], and Colonel Brandon in *Sense and Sensibility* is the younger son at the Delaford estate); naval officer (less prestigious because, as *Persuasion*'s snobbish Sir Walter Elliot complains, the navy, where promotion to officer rank was based more on merit than purchase as it was in the army, is "'the means of bringing persons of obscure birth into undue distinction, and raising men to honours which their fathers and grandfathers never dreamt of'" [P1:3]); and lawyer (law is one of the few careers Edward Ferrars's status-conscious family would have permitted him in SS 1:19).

A final point to emphasize when reading Austen's novels is that women had neither legal nor financial rights. Women's education was limited, and they were not admitted to universities. Mrs. Bennet's nervousness about getting her five daughters married is not as silly as her husband thinks because the Bennet estate, Longbourn, is entailed on the nearest male heir, Mr. Bennet's distant cousin Mr. Collins. An *entail* was a common custom–though not a law–to keep an estate in the paternal name, similar to primogeniture. But as Lady Catherine announces to Elizabeth, "'I see no occasion for entailing estates from the female line.–It was not thought necessary in Sir Lewis de Bourgh's family'" (2:6). Lewis de Bourgh's family is unusually forward in its thinking. [In PP, we see both de Bourgh and De Bourgh.]

In Austen's novels, the only heroine who does not have to marry for financial reasons is Emma Woodhouse, who has her own fortune of £30,000. So the husband-hunting in Austen's novels is a very serious proposition for gentlewomen, who had no other choice for future financial security. As Austen shows in *Sense and Sensibility*, the Dashwood sisters could not count on the financial help of their half-brother, John, although he had promised their father on his deathbed that he would assist them. He winds up giving them nothing, prompting Austen to satirize the patriarchal system where gentlemen were supposed to support the ladies in their families.

For a gentlewoman who had fallen on hard times, the only acceptable occupation was being a governess, as Jane Fairfax plans to become in *Emma*. "Hard times" had a specific meaning for gentlewomen of Austen's day. Like church livings, *marriage settlements* or *articles* explicitly or implicitly appear in Austen's novels. In *Pride and Prejudice*, for instance, the author spells out the marriage articles between Mr. Bennet and his fiancée, Miss Gardiner (the future Mrs. Bennet), "Five thousand pounds was *settled* by *marriage* articles on Mrs. Bennet and the children" (3:8). Where did that sum come from? The novel states that before her marriage, Miss Gardiner inherited £4,000 from her father (1:7); so, Mr. Bennet brought £ 1,000 to the settlement to "settle" on his future wife and children, for the total £5,000. Mr. Bennet also had the Longbourn estate and its income. A marriage settlement (aka, articles) was a legal document determining the financial fortunes (cash, land, and/or property) of the couple and their children. Understanding marriage articles explains how *Sense and Sensibility's* John Dashwood "was amply provided for by the fortune of his [late] mother, which had been large, and half of which devolved on him on his coming of age" (1:1). Mrs. Ferrars demands that son Edward marry Miss Morton, who is worth £30,000. And in the first paragraph of *Mansfield Park*, the narrator tells us that Miss Maria Bertram, with a mere £7,000, was said to be £3,000 short of an adequate marriage settlement with a baronet.

Orphaned as a child, Jane Fairfax inherited only a "very few hundred pounds" from her father, "making independence impossible" (E, 2:2). Although raised to be a lady by the kindly Campbells, Jane is "brought up for educating others": to "provide for her otherwise was out of Colonel Campbell's power; for though his income . . . was handsome, his fortune was moderate and must be all his daughter's." So while Miss Campbell has sufficient funds for the bride's side of the marriage settlement with her fiancé, the Irish estate owner Mr. Dixon, Jane Fairfax does not. Thus, she trained to be a governess, the only career appropriate for a gentlewoman. A governess lived in a kind of limbo: raised as a lady, she nevertheless was a servant to a lady, gentleman, and their children. No wonder Jane Fairfax calls the offices that find employment for governesses, "'Offices for the sale—not quite of human flesh—but of human intellect'" (2:17). The marriage of Emma's governess, Miss Taylor, to Captain Weston of Randalls is far more of a fairytale than Elizabeth's marriage to Darcy, for Darcy is a gentleman, and Elizabeth is a gentleman's daughter.

With major points about the cultural context of Austen's life and novels summarized and explained, we now turn to her life and her family of "novel-readers." Subsequent chapters will deal with her novels, other writings, reputation, and legacy.

2. Jane Austen and Her Family of Readers

Although she never attended a creative writing course–females in the late 18th and early 19th century England were given little formal education and no entry to college–Jane Austen came from an intelligent, chatty, and well-educated family: her father, George, and two of her brothers were Oxford-educated; her mother, Cassandra, was so clever that her uncle, an Oxford don, deemed her at age six, "the poet of the family"; and her beloved older sister (also named Cassandra) was her confidant and first reader. But even more important to young Austen's development into an intellectually groundbreaking novelist was that she came from a *reading* family; her letters reveal that books were discussed at home. In a letter of December 18-19, 1798 that Jane wrote to her sister about a recent notice encouraging the Austens to join a circulating library, the 23- year-old future novelist commented:

> As an inducement to subscribe, Mrs. Martin tells us that her Collection is not to consist only of Novels, but of every kind of Literature &c &c–She might have spared this pretension to *our* family, who are great Novel-readers & not ashamed of being so.

The novel-reading Austens were an affectionate and supportive family. When Austen wrote in *Mansfield Park* (1:2) of Edmund making "reading useful by talking to [Fanny] of what she read," she was possibly reflecting on her own youthful reading experiences with her family. Austen's letters and novels mention a wide variety of reading material that was deep and broad across genres: novels, biographies, poetry, sermons, and social and political history. By learning about her family's reading habits, we can better understand how Austen's own talent took shape and how she became one of the most popular novelists of all time, keeping in mind that the English novel only developed in the 18th century.

Jane Austen's family tree

George Austen (1731-1805), the author's father, was the son of a surgeon in Tonbridge, Kent; his mother, Rebecca, died when he was only a toddler. Mr. Austen remarried but died when George was six, leaving him and his sisters, Philadelphia (seven) and Leonora, about five, under the care of their stepmother, Susannah, who certainly ran a close second to the wicked stepmother of fairy tales. Indifferent towards her young stepchildren, she dispatched them to London to their paternal Uncle Stephen. But he was as disinterested in the children's welfare as their stepmother and soon shipped his young charges off to other persons, separating the siblings.

While parting from his sisters was difficult for young George, his luck changed for the better back in his native Tonbridge. He lived with a kind aunt and at age 10 began attending the Tonbridge School, where a generous uncle, the prosperous solicitor Francis Austen of Seven Oaks, supported his education. Diligent, gentle, and smart, George excelled as a student and at age 16 (in 1747) entered St. John's College, Oxford, through a fellowship established by a St. John's founder, who was a Tonbridge alumnus as well.

George earned his BA in 1751, and aspiring to become a clergyman in the Church of England, he pursued divinity studies, earning his MA and receiving ordination as a Deacon (a clergyman who assists the priest) in 1754. He returned to his home county of Kent and was ordained a priest on May 25, 1755; at 23, he reached the minimal required age for priestly ordination in the Church of England. Though only a poorly paid curate (a priest who assists the rector), Rev. Austen would eventually get help from his uncle Francis and a distant cousin by marriage, Thomas Knight I, who would secure church livings for him.

Meanwhile, George returned to St. John's College in 1757 to pursue a Bachelor of Divinity degree, which he received in 1760. But a year earlier, he became Junior Proctor of the College, where he was called "The Handsome Proctor" because of his tall stature and good looks. He certainly was attractive to Miss Cassandra Leigh (1739-1827), to whom he was introduced while she was visiting her uncle, Dr. Theophilus Leigh, Master of Balliol College.

Rev. George Austen surely was a "handsome proctor," as seen in this painting (photo by Isobel Snowden, courtesy Jane Austen House Museum).

Cassandra was the daughter of Rev. Thomas Leigh, rector of Harpsden near Henley-on-Thames, Oxfordshire. Her Greek mythological name came from the second wife (Cassandra Willoughby—yes, Willoughby, like the character in *Sense and*

Sensibility!) of her great-uncle, James Brydges (1673-1744), 1st Duke of Chandos, giving Miss Leigh noble connections.

During the early 1760s, while young Rev. Austen still resided at Oxford and courted Cassandra Leigh, his second cousin Jane Monk Knight's husband, Thomas Knight I, arranged for George to succeed to the livings at Shipbourne, near Seven Oaks in Kent, or Steventon in North Hampshire when the incumbents vacated them; he would take whichever living became available first. (The Knights' son, Thomas II, will later play an important role in the life of George Austen's son, Edward, and daughter Jane.) Rev. Austen's solicitor-uncle Francis of Seven Oaks also helped by purchasing for him the church livings of Ashe and Deane, neighboring the Steventon living; again, he would take whichever became available first.

Attractive, clever, humorous, and witty in conversation—in many ways like her Uncle Theophilus who was, however, rather unattractive—Cassandra's friendship with the handsome proctor grew. So did George's fortunes. In 1761, a Rev. Henry Austen, a member of Mrs. Knight's family, resigned as rector of the Steventon parish in Hampshire; Henry was living elsewhere (called "non-resident clergy," about which Sir Thomas complains in *Mansfield Park* 2:7), and left all the priestly duties to a curate, Rev. Thomas Bathurst. This made the Steventon living available for Thomas Knight to give to George, who officially became Steventon's rector on November 11, 1761. However, he usually remained at St. John's College (so George, too, was a non-resident clergyman) as classics tutor and assistant chaplain, while the same Rev. Thomas Bathurst performed the Steventon duties for George.

During these years, the handsome, quiet, scholarly, and devout George and the good-humored, lively, attractive, and practical Cassandra courted in Oxfordshire, as well as in Bath, where her family moved in 1762 because of her father's ill health. Rev. Leigh died there in January 1764.

On April 26, 1764, the couple married at St. Swithin's Church in Walcot, Bath. The new Mrs. Austen demonstrated her practicality in her choice of bridal attire: she wore a red woolen dress to her wedding and then traveled in it to Steventon, Hampshire, to her husband's church living. (Brides wearing white only became popular after Queen Victoria wore it to wed Prince Albert in 1840.) Cassandra's red dress saw many years of wear, as money was needed for other necessary items. Eventually, the red dress was cut and sewn into a coat for her son Frank's horseback-riding adventures. In the month before the wedding, Miss Leigh brought into her marriage a settlement leasehold property in Oxford; later, after the death of her mother in August 1768, she received £1,000 in cash.

The 100-year-old Steventon Rectory was a mess and in an entirely unlivable condition. Fortunately, the clergyman for the nearby Deane parish preferred to live in an attractive Georgian mansion called Ashe Park. So George was able to rent, reside at, and bring his bride to the Deane parsonage house, just two miles from Steventon. He could go by horseback to attend to his Steventon clerical duties, which he faithfully executed.

Mrs. Austen's widowed mother Jane (1704-1768) soon joined her daughter- and son-in-law at Deane. Accompanying Mrs. Leigh was a sickly child, George Hastings, the seven-year-old son of Warren Hastings, Governor-General of Bengal. The young couple had connections with East India on both sides of the marriage. Rev. George Austen's sister, Philadelphia (1730-1792), who had worked in London as a milliner's apprentice, sailed to India in 1752 to find a husband among the British colonials there. This was a common practice of the day for young women of good birth but insufficient money to secure marriage at home: recall those financially based marriage settlements and articles mentioned in the Introduction.

Within a year of arriving in Bengal, the attractive Philadelphia married an East India Company surgeon, Tysoe Hancock, 20 years her senior and once Warren Hastings's business partner. Their only child, Eliza, would greatly influence her younger cousin, Jane Austen. Warren Hastings also had connections with the Leighs of Aldestrop, Oxfordshire, Mrs. Austen's cousins. Because British colonials in India frequently sent their children, especially sons, home to England for their education, the widowed Warren Hastings sent four-year-old George to England to prepare for future entrance to Oxford or Cambridge. Young George Hastings lived with the Leighs until Mrs. Leigh brought him to the Austens at Deane. Unfortunately, shortly after arriving at Deane, young George died, likely of diphtheria—a death that Warren Hastings did not blame on his Leigh or Austen friends. The still-childless Cassandra Austen mourned young George's death with profound maternal grief.

Soon, however, the happy sounds of children would erupt from the Austens' home at the Deane Parsonage. Sons James (1765-1819), George (1766-1838), and Edward (1767-1852) arrived in rapid succession. In 1765, Rev. Austen's sister Philadelphia, her husband, and their little daughter Betsy, later called Eliza (1761-1813), came home from India and eventually visited the Austens. Mr. Hancock hoped to make money in business that would enable his family to live stylishly in England. But by 1768 his hopes vanished, and he returned to India, leaving his wife and daughter behind; they soon moved to France, where they could live well for less money than in London. (Mr. Hancock died in Calcutta in 1775.)

In the summer of 1768, the five Austens and Mrs. Austen's mother moved from Deane to the Steventon Rectory, now repaired, enlarged, and ready to welcome the young family. Mrs. Austen, who was ill at the time, made the journey on top of a feather bed loaded onto a wagon. Though razed in 1824 because of water damage, the rectory was a beloved and picturesque home. Drawings of it from the period, as well as verbal descriptions by those who knew it well, still exist. With three stories and many windows, the brick rectory had seven bedrooms, a study for Rev. Austen and his growing library, a dining room, four sitting rooms, as well as a kitchen; a charming trellis divided its façade. Elms, firs, meadows, a kitchen garden with potatoes and wildflowers, farmed fields (the glebe of three acres), and grassy hills surrounded the property. Through Thomas Knight, George also had additional farmland at nearby Cheesedown. Rev. Austen, who frequently borrowed money but paid back his debts, presided over his parish as a gentleman farmer and dutiful priest. Steventon's St. Nicholas Church was just across the road from the rectory. It was a charming place for a family to grow up in, and Jane Austen would spend her first 25 years there.

The Steventon Rectory, from the front, is shown in this painting (photo by David Smith, courtesy Austen family scrapbook).

In 1814, Jane Austen's niece, Anna Austen Lefroy (married Benjamin Lefroy in November 1814), sketched the back of the Steventon Rectory, where she lived for many years before her marriage (photo by David Smith, courtesy Austen family scrapbook).

But a serious problem soon arose for the young couple. Little George, their second son, began having fits between the ages of three and four; he also showed signs of deafness, speech difficulties, and the inability to care for himself. He may have also been mentally ill, as was his mother's younger brother, Thomas. By the time he was about 13, George was sent to live with the family of Francis Culhum, the parish clerk at All Saints Church in the village of Monk Sherborne, about eight miles from the Austen family's rectory. The Culhums also cared for the boy's uncle, Thomas. Sending a child like George or Thomas to live with another family, known as private custody, was a kind move, especially when compared with the cruel asylums of the day. After George's parents died, his wealthy brother Edward paid for his care.

Anna also sketched the side of the Steventon Rectory (photo by David Smith, courtesy Austen family scrapbook).

The firstborn at Steventon Rectory, Henry (1771-1850), would become Jane's favorite brother, her literary "agent," and eventually her literary executor. Like his father, Henry was tall, optimistic, and witty. Two years later, the first Austen daughter, Cassandra (1773-1845) arrived. In the same year, Rev. Austen became rector of neighboring Deane, a living purchased by his uncle Francis of Seven Oaks, along with Ashe. The additional income from Deane helped reduce the family's financial problems.

Soon thereafter, Uncle Francis sold the Ashe living to a Mr. Benjamin Langlois for nearly £1,000. The wealthy Benjamin gave the Ashe living to his nephew, Rev. George Lefroy who, along with his wife Anne, moved to Ashe in 1783. The Lefroys would play an important part in the life of young Jane Austen.

Beginning in 1773, with five children to support, Rev. and Mrs. Austen took in young boys as boarding students. For the next 13 years, Mr. Austen taught them Latin and other subjects in preparation for the University, Oxford or Cambridge. Mrs. Austen wrote poems for the boys and treated them as if they were her own sons—mending their clothes, treating their scrapes and cuts, and soothing their sorrows.

The Austens' next son (1774-1865) was Francis (Frank), the one who would get a red coat made out of his mother's wedding dress. At age 12, in April 1786, Frank entered the Royal Naval Academy at Portsmouth; on December 23, 1788, he left the Academy to sail with the Royal Navy and begin a distinguished naval career, eventually becoming Admiral of the Fleet (1863). If 14 seems a young age for Frank to go to sea, remember scenes in the film *Master and Commander* showing uniformed young boys scurrying about the ship.

Jane Austen's early years

On December 17, 1775, Rev. Austen announced in a letter that "a plaything for her sister Cassy" was born on the previous day, December 16; her name was Jane.

The Austen sisters were so close in a family of boys that their mother later said of her two girls, "If Cassandra's head had been going to be cut off, Jane would have hers cut off too." The sisters shared jokes and emotions, confided in each other, and were best friends. They called the youngest Austen child, Charles (1779-1852), "our own particular little brother" (Letter, JA to CA, Jan. 21, 1799). Charles would follow Frank's career, studying at the Royal Naval Academy between 1791 and 1794. And, like Frank, Charles had a distinguished career at sea.

With the seven Austen children and the boarding students, the Rectory resounded with young voices, giggles, laughter, and pounding feet. Mrs. Austen taught her daughters penmanship, some French, and reading, as well as "work," meaning sewing. (Austen's heroines receive similar educations.) As a result of this home-based education, Jane Austen would display a fine hand for the needle, mending her brothers' collars and cravats, and sewing little gifts for friends and family; she could also sew her own dresses. At about 10, Jane learned to play the piano—something she enjoyed for the rest of her life.

As a child, Jane followed Cassy everywhere. *Northanger Abbey*'s Catherine Morland plays baseball in Chapter One; this is the first place the *Oxford English Dictionary* (OED) found the word "baseball" in print. Catherine also enjoys rolling down the grassy hills near her father's rectory. We have every reason to believe that young Jane also enjoyed these same activities, especially in the household of little boys, both boarders and brothers. Frank saved for a pony and would speed by the rectory on it in his red coat; his family called him Fly. As the baby of the family, Charles was probably a plaything for his sisters. Meanwhile, the eldest child, James, left for St. John's College, Oxford, at this time.

Mrs. Austen had a unique way of caring for her children. After nursing the babies for a few months, she sent them off to a woman from a nearby farm or the village to be nursed, weaned, and raised until they were manageable at home—maybe 18 months or two years. We don't know whether any of the little Austens were traumatized by this separation from their mother.

In May of 1779, two visitors arrived at the rectory: The son- and daughter-in-law of Rev. Austen's previous benefactor, Thomas Knight II of Godmersham Kent, and his bride Catherine. Thomas Knight also owned the Chawton estate, located 20 miles from the rectory. But as the young couple preferred to live in Kent at their Godmersham estate, the Knights rented out the Chawton Great House, which would eventually figure as an important part of Jane Austen's adult life and writing activities.

During this visit, the Knights met Edward, who was about 12 at the time. Knowing they would be childless, they took Edward with them. While his father fretted that his son would miss his Latin studies, required for University entrance, Mrs. Austen calmed her husband, reminding him of the Knights' wealth, kindness, and generosity.

Four years later, Thomas and Catherine formally adopted Edward, naming him heir to their two extensive estates in Kent and Hampshire; after Mrs. Knight's death in 1812, he assumed the surname Knight. In adulthood, Edward provided for his widowed mother and two sisters the cottage in Chawton where Jane Austen wrote her novels: it was there that she revised two earlier works begun at Steventon, wrote and published three more, and revised one earlier work (*Northanger Abbey*), but placed it "on the shelf."

Beginning in December 1782, the Austens and their student boarders started performing contemporary plays in the barn under the direction of the eldest sibling, James, when he was home from Oxford for the holidays. The Austens viewed James as the writer of the family; he had literary pretensions as a poet—though nowadays his poetry is read not on its own merits, but mainly because he was Jane Austen's brother. While young Jane was too little at the time to participate in these productions, she watched and listened, clearly absorbing dramatic structure and the use of dialogue that would later characterize her novels. Such performances became customary Christmas events and included Richard Brinsley Sheridan's famous comedy of manners, *The Rivals*, in 1784. Comedies of manners satirize social classes, especially the fashionable world, and use witty, fast-paced dialogue, such as we find exchanged between Darcy and Elizabeth in *Pride and Prejudice*.

While Mrs. Austen was teaching her two young daughters at home, her elder sister, Mrs. Jane Cooper, decided to send her daughter, also named Jane, to Mrs. Cawley's school in Oxford. Mrs. Cawley was the widowed sister of Mrs. Cooper's husband, Rev. Cooper. Seven-year-old Jane Austen insisted on accompanying her sister Cassandra (age 10), who was going to the school as a companion for her cousin Jane. Off went Cassandra and two Janes to continue their reading, sewing, and French classes. But a measles outbreak in Oxford prompted Mrs. Cawley to move her school to Southampton—a bad idea, as it turned out, because Southampton was a harbor town.

In 1783, troops sailing home from the American Revolutionary War brought typhoid fever. Soon the girls were ill, and Jane Cooper, at 12 the eldest of the trio, wrote her mother about the sickness in a letter. The Leigh sisters–Mrs. Jane Cooper and Mrs. Cassandra Austen–headed to the rescue, nursed the girls, and brought them home. Unfortunately, Mrs. Austen's sister contracted the fever and died a few months later.

Back at the Steventon Rectory, the three girls–Cassandra and the two Janes–continued their education under Mrs. Austen and possibly Rev. Austen's tutelage; they may have joined his boarding students. The girls read children's books, but in time Rev. Austen's growing library provided them with more options. They read or heard read aloud Shakespeare's and other plays, novels, geography, history, poetry, and periodical literature. A year later, in 1784, the three girls again went off to boarding school, the Abbey House School in Reading, run by a Madame La Tournelle, who was actually named Sarah Hackit (Hackett), spoke no French (but employed a teacher who did), and walked with a wooden leg. Mme. La Tournelle regaled her charges with stories about the theater and also gave them plenty of free time to read, play, and perform plays. Jane may have taken piano lessons there, too. Recalling their schooldays to Cassandra, she wrote to her sister, "I could die of laughter at it, as they used to say at school" (September 1, 1796).

Brother Edward visited his sisters and cousin Jane and took them out for treats, as did Jane Cooper's brother Edward, who was studying at Eton. Austen's charming description of Mrs. Goddard's boarding school in *Emma* likely reflects her memories of the Abbey House School:

> a real, honest, old-fashioned Boarding-school, where a reasonable quantity of accomplishments were sold at a reasonable price, and where girls might be sent to be out of the way, and scramble themselves into a little education, without any danger of coming back prodigies. (1:3)

In 1786, when the Austens and Rev. Cooper removed their daughters from the Abbey House School, one of the students, Jane Austen, likely did return home a prodigy—though not because of any specific training she received at Mrs. Cawley's school. The 11-year-old continued her writing and reading, chatting about those activities with her family, particularly her clever and increasingly educated elder brothers, James and Henry. And a year later, in 1787, Jane, still only 11, began writing "novels"—short fictional works known as "juvenilia" and created as gifts for family and friends. But luckily she also copied them in three notebooks, which she elaborately titled *Volume the First* (held at The Bodleian Library), *Volume the Second*, and *Volume the Third* (both held by the British Library). These early texts reveal the young author's sense of how a novel is structured: how characters evolve and interact, and how a plot works. She had clearly been absorbing the books she read and the plays she saw. There are many indications that Jane Austen was, indeed, precocious.

In addition to writing, the teenager was also enjoying the usual activities of other adolescent girls of her age and class. Jane and her siblings visited the Chute family at their nearby magnificent estate, The Vyne, where they played cards and games, her brothers rode and hunted, and she danced with young Tom Chute, three years her senior. As young ladies (the marriageable age for gentry girls was 16), the Austen sisters went to assemblies or dances at Basingstoke and Alton. Like the Meryton Assembly in *Pride and Prejudice* or the balls held in the Bath Assembly Rooms attended by Catherine Morland in *Northanger Abbey*, the assemblies the sisters attended were dances for which tickets had to be purchased. The young women also danced at many private balls held in gentry mansions, giving Austen a sense of what life at grand country estates (such as the fictional Pemberley or Mansfield Park) was like; she also saw this kind of life at her brother Edward's grand estate, Godmersham, Kent, where the mansion is a truly stately home.

The Vyne is among the country estates she frequently visited (photo by Crystal Dussart taken from Wiltshire Archaeological and Natural History, Devizes: H.F. Bull, 1884: facing p. 392, courtesy Coe Library, University of Wyoming).

Jane Austen frequently visited friends, and one of her most valued ones was Anne Lefroy, the wife of Rev. George Lefroy, rector of Ashe. The Lefroys arrived at Ashe in 1783, and Madam Lefroy, as she was known for her sophistication and elegance, invited the eight-year-old younger daughter of the rector of the neighboring parish, to visit as a playmate for her daughter Lucy, four years Jane's junior. But the friendship planned for the two young girls soon turned into a friendship between Madam Lefroy and Jane. A writer herself, Madam Lefroy saw and appreciated her young neighbor's talent and perspicacity, giving her access to the fine library at Ashe Rectory.

A budding novelist

At 16, Austen began writing an unfinished "novel" in Volume Three of her juvenilia, Catharine, or the Bower. It marked an important point in the development of the young novelist because it was her first prose text with a realistic setting and plot about a young lady encountering society, social rank, and potential courtship—all aspects of her later, adult novels. Characters are developed, and their dialogue is sustained in a mature and realistic way. Austen may have abandoned this work because she wrote herself into a corner. But it was a wonderful learning experience for her as a writer. (More about *Catharine*, as well as Austen's other juvenilia, appears later on in this book.)

For the 2003 Annual General Meeting of the Jane Austen Society of North America (www.jasna.org), The British Library kindly loaned Austen's mahogany writing desk to sit on the small table at the Jane Austen House Museum (photo by Joan Ray).

On June 2-3, 1793, when she was 18½, Austen copied her final text in the juvenilia volumes. A poem, "Ode to Pity," which ironically and perhaps intentionally never refers to pity, appears in *Volume the First*, reminding us that the fair copies in her juvenilia were not entered chronologically. The poem alludes to odes by William Collins and Joseph Wharton, showing us that she knew the work of those two 18th-century English poets well.

Leaving her juvenilia stage of writing behind, Austen was preparing to write more mature fiction. And in time for either her 19th birthday or Christmas of 1794, her father purchased for her at Ring Brothers in Basingstoke a portable mahogany writing desk for 12 shillings. It is a sloped (ergonomically correct) box with a drawer for storing writing implements. The top is hinged, allowing the box to open, with a glass inkstand at the top. The desk provides a nice surface for writing. Joan Austen-Leigh, Jane's great-great-grandniece through the novelist's eldest brother James, donated this desk to London's British Library on October 29, 1999; it is now among "The Treasures of the British Library" on display, along with Shakespeare's First Folio, The Gutenberg Bible, and other invaluable artifacts, in the Library's Sir John Ritblat Gallery.

In 1794, Austen wrote all or part of her unfinished epistolary (told in letters) novel *Lady Susan*, on her writing desk. She left the work untitled, but when James Austen-Leigh published it in 1871 as an appendix to the second edition of his *Memoir* of his aunt, he titled it, *Lady Susan*.

Between late 1795 and early 1796, the Lefroys' Irish nephew, Thomas (Tom) Lefroy, a law student at Lincoln's Inn, London, danced with 20-year-old Jane while he was visiting his aunt and uncle for the Christmas school recess. Austen mentions him pertly in some letters. At the time of his visit to Hampshire, Tom was actually pre-engaged to the sister (Mary) of his college roommate at Trinity College, Dublin (the two eventually married). Tom returned to Dublin as a member of the Irish Bar in 1797, beginning a brilliant legal career that culminated in being appointed Lord Chief Justice of Ireland in 1852. Jane may have been charmed by him, and he by her, but that was as far as it went. However, years later, as an elderly man, Lefroy recalled his "boy's love" for the young novelist.

The 2007 film, *Becoming Jane*, imagines a reckless, flirtatious, and impetuous Tom Lefroy, who was very much in love with and about to elope with Jane Austen. The real Tom was quite different—devout, studious, and ambitious for a distinguished legal career, which he would achieve. The film ends with a fictional reunion between an older Tom, Austen (looking like George Eliot and doing a public reading, which she never did), and his teenage daughter Jane—implying the girl is named for Jane Austen. Tom and Mary's daughter was actually named after her grandmother, Jane. (See my "The Truth About Jane Austen and Tom Lefroy," *Notes and Queries*, 2006, 53: 311-314.) So *Becoming Jane* is a totally fictional account of the relationship.

Austen's writing continued. Other than a few occasional poems and one short play (*Sir Charles Grandison*, dated around 1790-93), she now focused on writing novels. At age 19, she began writing "Elinor and Marianne," the epistolary (told in letters) forebear of *Sense and Sensibility*. Epistolary novels were still popular in the 1790s, and Austen's favorite novel, Samuel Richardson's *Sir Charles Grandison*, which she had attempted to turn into the aforementioned short play, was in the epistolary format.

Cassandra Austen's "memorandum," a small sheet of paper on which she recalled and scrawled the chronological order of composition of her sister's novels, is now at NYC's Morgan Library. As Cassandra noted, "Sense & Sensibility begun Nov. 1797 / I am sure that something of the / same story & characters had been / written earlier & called Elinor & Marianne." Unfortunately, the world has no known letters written by Jane Austen in that year, but she clearly kept this manuscript to revise once she settled in Chawton on July 7, 1809. After the publication of *Sense and Sensibility* in 1811, she apparently destroyed the earlier epistolary manuscript. Scholars suggest that Cassandra's allusion to "something written earlier" may refer to Austen starting to pen "Elinor and Marianne" in 1795.

Jane's eldest brother James lost his wife on May 3, 1795, and sent their toddler daughter Anna to live with his parents and sisters at Steventon. Meanwhile, over the 1795-96 Christmas and New Year's holidays, Austen danced and flirted a bit, as noted earlier, with Tom Lefroy. She also witnessed the widowed James flirt unsuccessfully with their visiting "French" cousin, Eliza de Feuillide, whose husband had been guillotined in 1794, and comforted Cassandra when her fiancé Tom Fowle, who had joined William Craven, 1st Earl of Craven, on his West Indian campaign as his private chaplain in autumn 1795, sailed for the West Indies in January 1796, and died of tropical fever in San Domingo. He was buried at sea.

According to Cassandra's recollection in her memorandum, her sister began a novel, *First Impressions*, in October 1796: Jane Austen was the same age as her heroine, Elizabeth, who tells the inquiring Lady Catherine, "'I am not one and twenty'" (P&P, 2:6). Written in the epistolary format, the manuscript was completed in August 1797. The Austen family clearly enjoyed and admired this novel, for, on November 1, 1797, Rev. Austen wrote to Cadell, the publisher of English novelist and playwright Fanny Burney, offering a novel "about the length of Miss Burney's *Evelina*." The publisher returned George's letter, writing on it "declined by Return of Post" at the very top. The Library of his Oxford College, St. John's, holds his letter.

In spite of Cadell's flat rejection, the manuscript was still of intermittent interest to the family. On January 8-9, 1799, writing to Cassandra, who was staying at Godmersham, the Knight estate in Kent, Jane comments, "I do not wonder at your wanting to read *first impressions* again, so seldom as you have gone through it, & that so long ago."

While Jane Austen was working on her socially realistic courtship novels, a less realistic type of fiction, the Gothic, had taken hold of readers' imaginations. The Gothic novels combined the emotions of sensibility (i.e., a belief that strong feelings were a guide for behavior and that valued the sympathetic tear) with horrors, mysteries, eerie noises, threatening villains, fainting heroines, and haunted crumbling castles. Such terror was pleasing to readers. As *Northanger Abbey*'s (1:14) Henry Tilney jokes, "'The Mysteries of

Udolpho, when I had once begun it, I could not lay down again;—I remember finishing it in two days—my hair standing on end the whole time." The best-selling *The Mysteries of Udolpho*, for which author Ann Radcliffe received a whopping £500 from her London publisher, was published on May 8, 1794. Mrs. Radcliffe practiced what has been called "the rationalized Gothic," wherein her mysteries have rational explanations: the eerie noises turn out to be burglars talking in a nearby room, and the wraithlike figure who seems to haunt the grounds is actually the demented, guilt-stricken, perambulating nun, Signora Laurentini di Udolpho.

Jane Austen clearly read Radcliffe's bestseller with a critical eye, for she wrote a true parody of it in the novel we know as *Northanger Abbey*: a parody means "a song sung beside," and knowing what she brilliantly parodies enriches the reading. According to Cassandra's memorandum, "North-hanger abbey was written about the years '98 & '99." Austen first titled this manuscript, *Susan*. Internal evidence (i.e., evidence within the text itself) from *Northanger Abbey* suggests that she continued to work on *Susan* after the 1799 date given by Cassandra. For example, *Northanger Abbey* mentions a novel, *Belinda*, which did not appear until 1801.

By the end of June, Austen probably finished *Susan*, and in the spring of 1803, she sold the copyright for her novel to the London publisher Crosby for £10. Her manuscript sat with the publisher, who had promised publication but failed to do so.

In a letter dated April 5, 1809, she attempted to retrieve the still unpublished *Susan* from Crosby; she signed the letter using a pseudonym, Mrs. Ashton Dennis, i.e., M.A.D.—obviously showing her feelings about the book's non-publication. Richard Crosby replied that she could have her manuscript back for the same £10 that he paid for it. The timing of Austen's M.A.D. letter coincided with the appearance of a now-forgotten novel published in 1809 also called *Susan*; its authorship remains unknown. After the success of *Emma* in 1816, Jane's brother Henry retrieved the manuscript for the stipulated amount. Austen retained and worked a little on the manuscript, changing the heroine's name from Susan to Catherine, likely because of the appearance of the 1809 novel *Susan*.

The unreliable family story handed down by Austen's niece Caroline (James's younger daughter) reports that when Jane returned home from visiting her friends Mary and Martha Lloyd and heard that her father was planning to retire in December 1801, move his wife and two daughters with him to Bath, and turn over the Steventon Rectory to his eldest son, the clergyman James Austen, our shocked aspiring novelist fainted. One fact is sure: upon moving to Bath, Jane Austen did not write much.

We don't know whether her writing petered out because Jane, in her early 20s by then, was so busy socially that she had no time, or because, like Anne Elliot, the heroine of *Persuasion*, she disliked the crowded, sun-drenched Bath. But that fashionable city certainly provided Austen with knowledge about the theater, Assembly Rooms, Pump Room, and other locations that would later appear in *Persuasion*, her last completed novel. Bath was, of course, a familiar location for Austen's parents: they courted and married there. Mrs. Austen's brother (James Leigh-Perrot) and his wife lived there as well.

To escape the summer heat of Bath, the four Austens went to the seaside, visiting Sidmouth in Devonshire, where Mr. and Mrs. Austen's former boarding student, Richard Buller, was now a vicar and newly married. According to conflicting and uncertain family recollections of this visit in 1801, Jane Austen met a charming, good-looking, nameless young clergyman, and over the period of several weeks, the two became strongly attracted to each other. Cassandra was said to have approved of the young man as a husband for her sister. As one story goes, he was called away on business, but promised the Austen family that he would return. However, his brother soon wrote that the young clergyman had been stricken with a sudden, fatal illness. With no letters from this period, we cannot ascertain the truth of this account.

During 1802, in addition to time spent in Bath and Devonshire, the two sisters, escorted by their brother Charles, returned to their

Steventon neighborhood. On November 25 of that year, Jane and Cassandra visited with some of the sisters in the Biggs-Wither family at their estate, Manydown. All the girls were great, longtime friends. The eldest Austen brother, Rev. James, likely escorted his sisters to Manydown. (Notice, by the way, how the young gentry ladies were always escorted when they traveled. And this is why when General Tilney sends Catherine packing from Northanger Abbey without an escort, it is such a terrible thing for him to do). Rev. James now occupied the Austen Rectory with his second wife, Mary Lloyd, and two children: Anna from James's first marriage, and James-Edward, who would later become his Aunt's biographer.

During this visit to Manydown, Harris Bigg-Wither, heir to the estate, proposed to Jane Austen, and she accepted. She had known Harris, six years her junior, for years, and she knew that in marrying this kind, shy, stammering young man, she would join a family she had long known and become the lady of a grand house with extensive property. On a previous visit two years earlier, (November 8-9, 1800), Jane wrote to Cassandra, "Harris seems still in a poor way, from his bad habit of body; his hand bled again a little the other day and Dr. Littlehales has been with him lately." What "his bad habit of body" was is unclear. Harris must have been very comfortable around Jane, a good friend of his sisters, especially Elizabeth, Catherine, and Alethea, who would remain friends with Jane Austen for the rest of her life.

MANYDOWN IN 1790.

Razed in 1965, Manydown Park, Hampshire, is shown as it appeared in 1790, during Austen's lifetime (photo by Crystal Dussart from Reginald Fitz Hugh Bigg-Wither. Materials for a History of the Wither Family. Winchester, England: Warren and Son, 1907: between pages 108-109).

But after accepting his proposal, Jane ended the engagement the next day. Harris's sisters drove the Austen ladies back to Steventon, from where they soon left for Bath. On November 18, 1814, Jane Austen would write to her beloved niece, Fanny Austen Knight (Edward's eldest child), "I love you too well not to tell you without hesitation what I think and feel . . . . Anything is to be preferred or endured rather than marrying without affection." Perhaps we can apply that remark to Jane's decision to break her engagement at Manydown more than a decade earlier.

The Austens enjoyed summer holidays in Lyme Regis in 1803 and again in 1804, but without Cassandra, who was in Weymouth with their brother Henry. Jane would later set major sections of *Persuasion* in Lyme Regis, including Louisa Musgrove's momentous and careless jump down the old steps called "Granny's Teeth" that lead from the Cobbe to the beach.

Although she never visited Weymouth, a fashionable seaside resort, Jane Austen had negative impressions of it from Cassandra's report. While at Lyme Regis on September 14, 1804, Jane wrote to her sister:

> Weymouth is altogether a shocking place I perceive, without recommendation of any kind and worthy only of being frequented by the inhabitants of Gloucester [i.e., Gloucester House and the Royal Family]. I am really very glad that we did not go there.

Jane Austen's pejorative comments about Weymouth may account for placing certain characters of questionable morality or sense there in later novels. In *Sense and Sensibility*, the fatuous Mrs. Palmer has been in Weymouth with an uncle. In *Mansfield Park*, the irresponsible, spendthrift heir to the estate, Tom Bertram, meets in Weymouth the Hon. John Yates, who brings the acting infection to the Bertram home. In *Emma*, Jane Fairfax meets Frank Churchill in that same town, where the two form their secret engagement. Austen would also ridicule the growing mania for seaside resorts as a cure in *Emma* and especially in her final, incomplete novel, *Sanditon*, the name she gave to one such fictional place.

Interspersed with visits to Godmersham (the Edward Austens), Ashe (the Lefroys), and other places, Jane Austen began an unfinished short (under 18,000 words) novel, *The Watsons*, on paper watermarked 1803 and 1804. The public first saw this text in the second edition of James Edward Austen Leigh's *Memoir of Jane Austen* (1871): he gave it the title by which we now know it.

On December 16th, 1804, Jane's 29th birthday, her dear friend and mentor from Ashe, Madam Lefroy, died in a riding accident. A little over a month later, on January 21, 1805, her father Rev. George Austen, died suddenly at their Bath home. Because an Anglican rector's pension died with him, the three bereft Austen women vacated their larger No. 4 Sydney Place lodgings and moved to less expensive rooms at 25 Gay Street. Biographers suggest Jane ceased writing *The Watsons* after her father's sudden death because her fictional Old Mr. Watson was ailing and near death.

Austen, the published novelist

We have no compositions from Jane Austen after *The Watsons* until after she settled back in Hampshire at the Chawton Cottage in 1809. Mrs. Austen relied on the financial help of her sons, especially Edward and Henry, to support herself and two daughters–though Cassandra had funds from her late fiancé's will, in which he made her his beneficiary. Before the Chawton move, the three Austen ladies did a lot of visiting, including to Manydown, Steventon, and Godmersham. In the summer of 1805, Martha Lloyd, the spinster sister of Mary Lloyd who had married the widowed James Austen, joined the Austen ladies' household. In January 1806, the three Austen women left Gay Street for Trim Street in Bath, while Martha lived nearby. But on July 2 of that year, the Austens left Bath for good to head to Clifton. In late July, Mrs. Austen and her daughters paid an extended visit to her cousin, Rev. Thomas Leigh, at his rectory in Aldestrop. There they saw the "improvement" made to Aldestrop House by Humphry Repton, the great English landscape gardener whom Mr. Rushworth wishes to hire to "improve" his Sotherton house and estate in *Mansfield Park*. Improvement of one's estate was quite *au courant* in this period. On August 5, the three Austens and Rev. Leigh went to the magnificent Stoneleigh Abbey, Warwickshire, which Rev. Leigh would inherit; they spent 10 days there. Along with Stoneleigh Abbey, Jane Austen visited and lived in other great English houses as well (mansions of at least 25 rooms) to be able to write about them knowingly in her novels.

Meanwhile, Frank Austen married Mary Gibson in July 1806, and by October 10th, 1806, Frank, Mary, the three Austen ladies, and Martha Lloyd took lodgings at Castle Square, Southampton. This was helpful to Mary Austen, as Frank was returning to active duty at sea as a Royal Navy officer. In November 1806, Mr. and Mrs. Edward Austen had their fifth daughter and tenth child, Cassandra Jane, at Godmersham. So in December, Cassandra left Southampton to help care for her nieces and nephews at the beautiful Kent estate.

The two Austen ladies and Martha were in Southampton to help Mary Austen (Frank's wife) in April 1807, when she gave birth to a daughter she named Mary Jane Austen. Frank came home and then headed back to sea on June 22 of that year, sailing on HMS *St. Albans*. He left from nearby Portsmouth, a major dockyard for the navy, where the sea-going Prices live in *Mansfield Park*. With Southampton as their home base, the Austen ladies traveled, visiting their expanding family and old friends. While they were at Southampton, 14-year-old niece Anna Austen, James's elder daughter by his first wife, visited her aunts and grandmother in the spring of 1808. Amidst travels, visits, and guests, shocking news arrived: on October 10, 1808, Elizabeth Austen, Edward's wife, died suddenly, 12 days after giving birth to her 11th child, Brook John, born September 28, 1808. Cassandra was at Godmersham to help her brother, nieces, and nephews. Edward's two eldest sons, who were at Winchester College (a public boarding school, pre-University), the devastated Edward (age 14) and George (not yet 13), "sobbed aloud" when they arrived at the Castle Square House to be comforted by their Aunt Jane, grandmother, and old family friend Martha Lloyd.

It is interesting that Jane Austen wrote to Cassandra on October 24-25, 1808, just two weeks after Mrs. Edward Austen's death, about her plan, suddenly underway, to move to Chawton Cottage. The cottage, with its six bedrooms, was the former bailiff's house on Edward's Chawton estate, a few miles from Steventon, in their native Hampshire. One might speculate that, just as Mrs. John Dashwood in Chapter 2 of *Sense and Sensibility* convinces her husband not to assist his half-sisters despite their father's deathbed wish, Elizabeth Austen was not forthcoming in helping Jane and Mrs. Austen. Biographers have observed that it was usually Cassandra who went to Godmersham when a new baby was born or when help was needed. Perhaps Jane's tongue might have been a little too sharp for her, or maybe a somewhat class-conscious Elizabeth (a daughter of the prominent Bridges family, baronets of Goodnestone Park, Kent) thought that Jane Austen lacked the refinement of her elder sister, Cassandra, about whom Jane once teasingly wrote, "I know your starched notions."

Leaving Southampton for a while, Mrs. Austen and her household arrived at Godmersham on May 15, 1809. Henry had been helping them with their Chawton moving plans before they left Southampton. Henry and his wife and cousin, the glamorous Eliza, also came to Godmersham to visit with the family. On June 30, Mrs. Austen and Jane went back to Southampton, where they were followed a week later by Edward Austen and Cassandra. And on July 7, 1809, Edward escorted his mother and sisters from Southampton to Chawton, where Martha Lloyd would join them at the cottage, which is now The Jane Austen House Museum.

Settled in a quiet country village in familiar surroundings and near lifelong friends, Jane Austen, now in her 30s, resumed writing on the mahogany writing desk purchased for her by her father in 1794. At Chawton, life settled into a routine that allowed her to have uninterrupted time to write. She practiced the pianoforte in the morning and prepared breakfast. Then her mother, sister, and friend Martha, keeping the novelist's doings a secret, gave her the freedom to write in a room of her own—with thanks for the phrase to Virginia Woolf, who admired Austen's craft.

Chawton Village. P.T.O.

A postcard from 1910 shows the Austens' former cottage, still with a duck pond at the front, in the village of Chawton. Behind the trees at the front of the cottage, one can discern the large window, now blocked, out of which Jane looked as she wrote (photo by David Smith of a postcard courteously shared from an Austen family descendant's scrapbook).

The cottage's front room had a large window, giving Austen a view of the main coach route. It also had a small table on which she set her writing desk. According to some accounts, the hinges on the door leading into the room were deliberately kept un-oiled so that she could hear them squeak when the door opened and quickly hide her manuscript. In his *Memoir* of his aunt, James Edward Austen-Leigh recounted that "she wrote upon small sheets of paper which could easily be put away, or covered with a piece of blotting paper." In fact, James Edward learned only at age 16 that his aunt was the author of the recently published *Mansfield Park* and other novels. He wrote about his newly acquired knowledge in a poem dedicated to Jane Austen, which begins:

> No words can express, my dear Aunt, my surprise
> Or make you conceive how I opened my eyes,

Like a pig Butcher Pile has just struck with his knife,
When I heard for the very first time in my life
That I had the honour to have a relation
Whose works were dispersed throughout the whole of the
nation.

Austen published her novels anonymously and never sought personal publicity. But she did keep careful accounts of the money her novels earned. She was a practical woman.

Her immediate family, of course, knew of her writing. She likely read her day's work to her sister in the evening in their shared bedroom. Henry assisted as her informal business agent. Austen first revised her Dashwood-sisters manuscript into *Sense and Sensibility*, leaving behind the epistolary format. She received a letter that her novel was accepted for publication in the winter of 1810, the same year that scholars believe Cassandra painted the portrait of her sister now housed at London's National Portrait Gallery, which has been the basis for her other likenesses. In it, her sharp eyes are looking to the side, as if suddenly attracted by something or someone *over there*, and the determined-looking face and folded arms suggest Austen's intellectual strength and skills in observation.

In her letter to Cassandra of April 25, 1811, Austen reported that she was proofreading the novel while staying at their brother Henry's home in London to be near her publisher, Thomas Egerton: "No, indeed, I am never too busy to think of S. and S. I can no more forget it, than a mother can forget her sucking child." She also mentioned that Mrs. Knight, Edward's adopted mother, was anxious to read the novel.

Published at the end of October 1811, *Sense and Sensibility* was advertised over several days in London's *Morning Chronicle* with small headlines reading "Extraordinary Novel" and "Interesting Novel." Both reviews, in *The Critical Review* (Feb. 1812) and *The British Critic* (May 1812), were lengthy (mostly plot summary) and favorable. The story goes that in May 1812, Jane Austen and her niece

Anna, about 19 at the time, were examining novels at the Circulating Library in Chawton. Anna picked up the first volume of *Sense and Sensibility* and said, "It must be nonsense with a title like that," and put it down as her bemused Aunt Jane silently watched her.

Austen's first novel was published on commission, meaning that the author pays the publishing expenses, retains the copyright, and after paying a commission to the publisher, keeps the profits. She earned £140 on the first edition, of which all 750 printed copies sold by July 1813. A second edition, which scholars use as the more reliable text, appeared a few months later. With the anonymous byline, "By a Lady," Austen was not only avoiding fame, but also escaping charges of assertiveness, traditionally seen as a male characteristic. The byline also gave potential readers expectations about what the novel would be about: after all, the authoress was a Lady who wrote about the manners of the gentry class. Yet lest we think that Austen was a prude, we need to remember that adultery, pre-marital sex, children born out of wedlock, injuries, and death all occur in her novels, though not necessarily acted out in the novels' pages.

With *Sense and Sensibility* accepted for publication near the end of 1810, the following year was very busy for the novelist. Cassandra recalled that her sister began *Mansfield Park* "sometime around" February 1811 and finished it "soon after June 1813"; this was the first novel she completely conceived and composed at Chawton. But as we've seen, by late March she was in London at Henry's correcting page proofs for her first published novel. Staying with Henry and Eliza at their Sloane Street home, she also enjoyed London's theater, shops, and art galleries, as well as parties and dinners, thrown both by her sister-in-law and other London friends.

By the end of May, Austen was back in Chawton. And towards the end of 1811, she started revising the manuscript written in her early 20s: *First Impressions*, under its new title *Pride and Prejudice*. If, as the timetable suggests, she was handling three novels at once—proofing *Sense and Sensibility* in time for its October 1811 publication date, starting her revisions of *First Impressions* into

Pride and Prejudice, and composing *Mansfield Park*—she could certainly juggle well. It may be no coincidence that her young nieces and nephews recalled not only her cheerfulness around them, but also her great skill playing games like spillikins (do you recall playing "Pick-Up Sticks"?) and ball and cup, both of which require excellent hand/eye coordination.

Austen likely changed the title of her early Darcy/Elizabeth manuscript because in 1800 *First Impressions; or, The Portrait*, by Margaret Holford appeared. *The Critical Review* (June 1801) said of this novel that "there is nothing reprehensible in First Impressions except its bulk." The cited "bulk" of Holford's novel is thought-provoking in comparison to Austen's revision of *First Impressions*. For if Austen's father was correct in saying in his letter of 1797 to the publisher Cadell that *First Impressions* was "about the length of Miss Burney's *Evelina*," then Austen made extensive cuts in her revised novel. While still in three volumes (known as the "triple-decker," a popular novel form through the Victorian period) as is *Evelina*, *Pride and Prejudice* is about one-third the length of Burney's book.

As with Austen's other completed novels, we have no manuscript of the original *Pride and Prejudice* that she sold in the autumn of 1812 to Egerton for £110. Egerton published it as "by the author of *Sense and Sensibility*" on January 28, 1813. Writing to Cassandra the next day, Austen told of having "lop't and crop't" her original manuscript, which accounted for its shortened length. She also changed it from the original epistolary form. But it is interesting to note how many letters conveying important information are still in the novel.

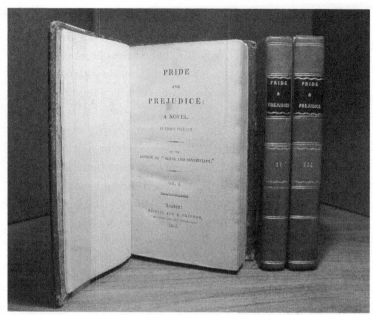

Publishers enclosed the pages of a book in "boards": they sewed the text block together and covered it with blue or grey paper pasteboards; it was up to the book buyer to have a book rebound. Edward Austen Knight's copy of Pride and Prejudice is bound in leather (photo by Isobel Snowden, courtesy Jane Austen House Museum).

Receiving her copy of the book on January 27, 1813, Austen wrote to Cassandra two days later, "I have got my own darling child from London." In this letter, she told her sister (who was at the Steventon Rectory with the James Austens at the time) about a visit at Chawton from their friend Miss Benn that same day. "In the evening we fairly set at it [the book]," she wrote, "and read half the first vol. to her, prefacing that having intelligence from Henry that such a work would appear," they asked him to send a copy. "It passed with her unsuspected," wrote the coy novelist, who desired public anonymity. Miss Benn, she continued, "really does seem to admire Elizabeth. I must confess that I think her as delightful a creature as ever appeared in print." The reviews for the second novel were laudatory:

"Written with Great Spirit As Well as Vigour," praised *The British Critic* (February 1813); "Very Superior," enthused *The Critical Review* (March 1813); "the Author's talents" were acclaimed by *The New Review* (April 1813). Lady Byron thought it "a very superior work" and called it "the *most probable* fiction I have ever read" (Letter to her mother, May 1, 1813). Flattered by the praise, Austen joked in a letter to Cassandra that "The work is rather too light, and bright, and sparkling" (February 4, 1813). To this day, it has not lost its luster.

With her second published novel a major hit, Austen plugged away at *Mansfield Park*, finishing it around July 1813. She was also occupied with family matters. On April 21, Edward Austen and his family came to Chawton House, just up the road from the ladies' cottage, for a four-month visit. But the next day, Edward escorted Jane to London to help their brother Henry care for his dying wife, Jane's glamorous, sparkling cousin, the former Eliza Hancock de Feuillide, who was in the final stage of breast cancer. Eliza died on April 25, with her adoring cousin/sister-in-law Jane at her bedside. Eliza was buried with her mother (also a breast cancer victim) and son Hastings at the St. John-at-Hampstead Churchyard in London on May 1; the novelist returned home the same day.

Mansfield Park is Austen's first published novel that was conceived and composed at the Chawton Cottage; however, she may have also written parts of it while visiting Steventon, London, and elsewhere. She consulted Frank about how the ships would dock at Portsmouth for scenes in the novel. Written by a published, well-received novelist now in her mid-30s, the novel emanates true confidence in presenting a heroine, Fanny Price, whose interior life we first observe when she is 10 years old, but whose adult personality lacks the zest we see in Elizabeth Bennet or Emma Woodhouse. Fanny's sad childhood forms the adult heroine, who has been as critically browbeaten as she is emotionally intimidated at Mansfield Park.

This novel was published in May 1814 "on commission," again by Thomas Egerton in a run of 1,750 copies; the byline reads, "By the Author of 'Sense and Sensibility,' and 'Pride & Prejudice.'" There are no known contemporary reviews in the press of the day, but Austen kept a written five-page record of "Opinions of Mansfield Park," now held by the British Library.

Next, she wrote *Emma* in a little over 14 months, between January 21, 1814, and March 29, 1815. Austen's extant letters give no clue about her progress on the novel. Having sent *Mansfield Park* to press with its heroine predominantly on the periphery of the action, she was now quickly producing a novel with the eponymous Emma at the center of her world: every action in the novel is either initiated by her or reverberating on her. Critics call it her masterpiece, written with energy and skill, especially in its use of free indirect discourse.

Emma is also the work of a mature and confident novelist in another way: she changed publishers from Thomas Egerton to John Murray, publisher of the most famous writers of the day, including Lord Byron and Sir Walter Scott. One reason for her leaving Egerton may be that when the novelist and her brother Henry went to London on November 30, 1814, to meet with the publisher about doing a second edition of *Mansfield Park*, he refused. Making the leap from Egerton to the very prominent John Murray was a significant move for Austen.

Murray sent the manuscript of *Emma* for review to his trusted friend William Gifford, the editor of the popular *Quarterly Review*, which boasted a grand roster of contributors. Gifford wrote back, "Of 'Emma' I have nothing but good to say." His commendation meant a lot. But according to Austen's nephew and biographer James Edward Austen-Leigh, his Aunt Jane, while "'very fond of Emma . . . did not reckon on her being a general favourite; for, when commencing that work, she said, 'I am going to take a heroine whom no one but myself will much like'" (*Memoir of Jane Austen*).

Fame and admiration

Austen went to London on October 4, 1815, and stayed longer than she had anticipated nursing her brother Henry, who was very ill. While she was at his home at Hans Place, Dr. Matthew Baillie, who also cared for the Prince Regent (later George IV), was called for a second opinion. Henry, immensely proud of his successful novelist sister, who was now a client of prominent publisher John Murray, tended to tell people who admired her books that their author was Jane Austen. As early as 1813, the word that Austen was the author of *Sense and Sensibility* and that year's literary hit, *Pride and Prejudice*, began spreading. Writing from Godmersham to her brother Francis on September 25, 1813, Jane complained:

> Henry heard P. & P. warmly praised in Scotland, by Lady Robert Kerr & another Lady; −& what does he do in the warmth of his brotherly vanity & Love, but immediately tell them who wrote it!−A Thing once set going in that way− one knows how it spreads−and he, dear creature, has set it going so much more than once.

So it is likely that Henry told Dr. Baillie that the books at his bedside were written by his sister when the doctor mentioned that the Prince Regent admired those same novels and had a set of them at each of his residences. Soon an invitation came for Jane to visit the Prince Regent's library at Carlton House, his London residence.

The Royal Librarian and Domestic Chaplain, Rev. James Stanier Clarke, conducted her tour on November 13, 1815. Clarke also told her that she could dedicate her forthcoming novel (to be published in December) to the Prince Regent. Austen, like so many of her countrymen, had been long disgusted by the Prince Regent's immoral antics: he was rumored to have had many mistresses and fathered several illegitimate children. Thus, she confided to her publisher that she did not want to do this. But the savvy Murray advised her that this invitation was a command and an honor. He suggested the correct wording for the dedication to the Prince Regent.

After a series of letters between Henry Austen and John Murray, the publisher met with Jane Austen and her brother at Henry's London home in November 1815. He offered £450 for *Emma*, along with the copyrights for *Sense and Sensibility* and *Mansfield Park*. The final agreement was that the author would retain the copyright and pay for the publication of *Emma* with a 10 percent commission going to Murray. In February 1816, Murray would publish her desired second edition of *Mansfield Park*.

Jane Austen left London to return to Chawton on December 16, 1815, her 40th birthday. *Emma* was published just days later, on December 23, 1815, although advertisements for the novel appeared as early as December 2 in the *Morning Post*. The year 1816 appears on the title-page of the first edition, "BY THE AUTHOR OF 'PRIDE AND PREJUDICE,' &c. &c."

As with *Mansfield Park*, Austen recorded the opinions of family and friends about *Emma*, but the novel was widely reviewed—indeed, far more than her other books when they appeared. The most important and longest review came from the most popular best-selling novelist of the day, Sir Walter Scott, to whom Murray suggested the project.

Published in *The Quarterly Review* (October 1815, though not actually distributed until March 1816), one of the most influential political and literary journals of the day (published by Murray), Scott's review discussed not only *Emma* in laudatory terms, but also *Sense and Sensibility* and *Pride and Prejudice*. And more than just reviewing *Emma*, Scott differentiated between the early novel and "the style of novel [that] has arisen, within the last fifteen or twenty years." The latter, wrote Scott, is more realistic, more probable, "presenting to the reader, instead of the splendid scenes of the imaginary world, a correct and striking representation of that which is daily taking place around him." He continued:

We, therefore, bestow no mean compliment upon the author

of Emma, when we say that, keeping close to the common incidents, and to such characters as occupy the ordinary walks of life, she has produced sketches of such spirit and originality, that we never miss the excitation which depends upon a narrative of uncommon events. . . . In this class she stands almost alone.

Considering that this complimentary review was written by the distinguished Sir Walter Scott and published in a wide-reaching and highly respected journal, Jane Austen–though still writing under an anonymous byline–was now a very important novelist, critically and popularly. *Emma* sold well, with sales likely boosted by Scott's commendatory review.

Back at the Chawton Cottage, Austen, frequently accompanied by her sister, made a busy round of visits. Over Christmas and New Year's 1814-1815, they went to see their longtime friends, Alethea Bigg and the widowed Elizabeth Bigg Heathcote at their home at 12 The Close, Winchester (Elizabeth's little boy, William, would become a lifetime friend of James Edward Austen-Leigh; the two met at Winchester College). They also visited the James Austens at Steventon; the Lefroys at Ashe; and the Portal family that made the paper for Henry's London bank at Laverstoke.

Jane's time in 1815 was interrupted by intrusive letters, which suggested plots and characters for future novels. The epistolary intruder was her host at Carlton House, Rev. James Stanier Clarke. These intrusions had begun the day after Austen visited Carlton House; while still at Henry's, she received a letter from Clarke, suggesting that her next novel be about a clergyman–just like him! His suggestions might well have made Austen recall the obtuse clergyman and letter-writer that she had previously created, Mr. Collins.

Clarke described the hero of his novel like this: with "the Habits of Life and Character and enthusiasm of a Clergyman," who "pass[ed] his time between the metropolis & the Country"; "Fond of, & entirely engaged in Literature," "affectionate tho' shy," and "no man's Enemy but his own." Clarke was as persistent as the fictional Mr. Collins: after Austen politely rejected his suggestion in a letter of December 11, 1815, writing in self-deprecation that she was not learned enough to depict such a clergyman, she heard from him again on March 27, 1816. He wrote suggesting, "an historical romance illustrative of the august House of Cobourg would just now be very interesting" with a dedication to Prince Leopold. She politely put an end to his suggestions, again in a self-deprecating manner, "I could no more write a romance than an epic poem" (April 1, 1816).

Possibly inspired by the relentless Clarke, Austen wrote a satiric "Plan of a Novel, according to hints from various quarters." Her favorite niece, the witty Fanny (now about 21), and her father, Edward, were visiting Chawton, and Fanny may have laughingly helped her aunt. "Plan of a Novel" clearly dates from the period of Austen's correspondence with Clarke, between November 1815 and April 1816. The manuscript is now at the Morgan Library in New York City.

Austen began writing *Persuasion* shortly after completing *Emma*. But in April 1816, she started to experience what was called in her day "a slow decline" in health. She suffered from backaches, headaches, fevers, mottled skin, and a general malaise. She was fortunate to have more family members living near her cottage: in August 1814, Frank Austen, home from the navy (after Napoleon was imprisoned at Elba), and his family moved into the Chawton Great House, just up the road from his mother's and sisters' cottage, and would remain there for two years. Henry arrived in December 1816 to live in Chawton because his London bank (Austen Maunde & Tilson) collapsed on March 15, 1816. The bank's failure reflects the uncertain economy of England after the Napoleonic Wars.

Cassandra had been to the Cheltenham Spa with Mary Lloyd Austen, James Austen's second wife, who often complained of being unwell: perhaps Mary Austen inspired Mary Musgrove's whining in *Persuasion*, "'My sore throats, you know, are always worse than anybody's'" (2:6). (When asked, Austen insisted that she never modeled a character on a particular person. As D.H, Lawrence once advised, "Never trust the teller; trust the tale.") Salutary effects of Cheltenham spring waters were later attributed to epsom and glaubus salts it contained, both used as mild laxatives.

Encouraged by reports of Mary's successful treatment, the two Austen sisters went to the Cheltenham Spa on May 22, 1816, seeking a cure for the ailing Jane. They stayed there for three weeks, but to no avail. Returning home, Jane finished her first draft of Persuasion on July 18, 1816. Dissatisfied, she revised the ending to the currently known version, completing it on August 6, 1816. Austen realized that her original ending failed to match the subtlety of the rest of the story. Her biographer nephew James Edward Austen-Leigh called it "too tame and flat." In the Memoir, he recalled, "This weighed upon her mind, the more so probably on account of her weak state of health." She would never recover her health to see Persuasion in print.

On March 23, 1817, the still ailing Jane Austen wrote to her beloved niece Fanny that she had "another [work] ready for publication": "You may perhaps like the Heroine, as she is almost too good for me." When the novel opens, Anne Elliot, whom the narrator calls "the elegant little woman," is 27, the age when ladies were very much at the end of their marriageability. Having given us, in Emma, the healthy, lively, and blooming Emma Woodhouse, in Persuasion, she created a heroine who had experienced "an early loss of bloom" (1:4), only to regain it.

Ever the optimist and not wishing to cause dissension, Austen often spent evenings at the cottage stretched out on three hard chairs so that her mother could use the sofa. When she did not have the strength to walk, she rode in a little donkey cart. When feeling well enough, she rode atop a quiet donkey, led by Cassandra and her nephew, James Edward. But Austen also returned to her writing desk when she could. On January 24, 1817, Jane wrote to Alethea Bigg that "I am more and more convinced that Bile is at the bottom of all I have suffered." Three days later, she must have been feeling sufficiently well to begin writing Sanditon, working on it intermittently through February. On March 23, 1817, she wrote to niece Fanny Knight about her fevers and "recovering" her "looks a little which have been bad enough, black & white, and every wrong colour." She added, though, "Sickness is a dangerous indulgence at my time of Life." Her niece Caroline (James Austen's youngest child) recalled her Aunt looking very pale and speaking in a weak voice at times.

Parts of her *Sanditon* manuscript, including some revisions, are in pencil—presumably because Austen was too weak to use a quill pen. The handwriting varies from a strong, clear hand to the nearly illegible hand of a frail person, reflecting the vagaries of her illness, which forced her to lay down her pencil on March 18th (dated in her hand on the manuscript). She had written 24,804 words on paper bound in three sewn booklets, but stopped in the middle of Chapter 12. It is the longest manuscript we have in the novelist's hand. King's College, Cambridge, owns the manuscript.

When asked by her brother James Edward Austen-Leigh how she remembered her ailing Aunt Jane when she visited her at age 12, Caroline Austen recalled that she was at first too ill to see anyone; so, Caroline stayed nearby with her half-sister Anna and her husband, Ben Lefroy. The following day Caroline and Anna walked to the Chawton cottage and found their aunt "quite like an invalid" and soon too weak to speak; the visit ended after 15 minutes. On Aril 27, Austen surreptitiously—so as not to distress her mother and sister—wrote her Will, naming her sister her main beneficiary and executrix.

While still at home, she was treated by the Alton apothecary, Mr. William Curtis. But by May, the family sought the help of a surgeon, the prominent Giles King-Lyford who practiced at the new County Hospital in Winchester. On a rainy May 24, the Austen sisters sat in Mary Austen's (James's wife's) carriage on the way to Winchester; their brother Henry and nephew William, Edward's son, accompanied them on horseback. The Austen sisters' old friends, Alethea Bigg and her sister Elizabeth, arranged for the Austens to stay at No. 8 College Street and provided as many comforts as possible.

Rallying now and then, Jane Austen could not fool her brother James who wrote to his son, the novelist's favorite nephew and future biographer, that Mr. Lyford described her condition as "desperate." He was writing around June 9, having escorted his wife Mary to join the Austen sisters a few days earlier. Jane Austen knew this, but tried, when she could, to give her family hope. Occasional visits from nephews, nieces, brothers, and old friends filled the time. Henry rode to Chawton and back to check on Mrs. Austen. Once, thinking the end was near, and while she could still speak, Jane told Mary, her sister-in-law, "'You have always been a kind sister to me, Mary.'"

On July 15, Austen felt up to writing a poem, "When the Winchester Races." But by that night, she was worse and slept a great deal. About half an hour before falling unconscious, she said, when asked, that she wanted "nothing but death, and some of her words were: 'God grant me patience, pray for me, oh, pray for me!'" The following morning, Thursday, July 17, at about 4:30 am, Jane Austen died in Cassandra's comforting arms. According to Mrs. Austen, Mr. Lyford, who was giving his patient palliative care, "supposed a large blood-vessel had given way."

Jane Austen was 41 years, seven months, and one day old.

Cassandra feelingly wrote to Fanny, "I have lost such a treasure, such a Sister, such a friend as never can have been surpassed—she was the sun of my life, the gilder of every pleasure, the soother of every sorrow." She snipped locks of her sister's hair as mementos for family members before the coffin was closed. Hair mementos were very fashionable in the first half of the 19th century, and there was nothing ghoulish about them.

Early on the morning of Thursday, July 24, Jane Austen was buried in the north nave of Winchester Cathedral in a service led by Rev. Thomas Watkins, Precentor of the Cathedral and Chaplain of Winchester College. Women did not normally attend funerals in this period: Cassandra and Martha Lloyd watched the procession as long as it was viewable from their College Street window. Three Austen brothers, Henry, Edward, and Frank, attended, as did James

Edward, "the youngest mourner," in place of his ailing father, the eldest Austen brother, James. Charles was too distant to come in time.

Henry wrote his sister's obituary notice for the *Salisbury and Winchester Journal*, July 28, 1817, in which he named her novels:

> On Friday the 18th inst., died in this city, Miss Jane Austen, youngest daughter of the late Rev. George Austen, Rector of Steventon, in this county, and the Authoress of "Emma," "Mansfield Park," "Pride and Prejudice" and "Sense and Sensibility." Her manners were most gentle, her affections ardent, her candour was not to be suppressed, and she lived and died as became a humble Christian.

Likewise, her obituary in *The Gentleman's Magazine* (August 1817) acknowledges Austen as the author of *Emma, Mansfield Park, Sense and Sensibility,* and *Pride and Prejudice.* In the posthumous edition of *Northanger Abbey* and *Persuasion,* published in December 1817 by Murray as a four-volume set, the date on the title page reads 1818. The by-line still reads as it did in *Emma*, "By the Author of 'Pride & Prejudice,' &c .&c." But Henry Austen's "Biographical Notice of the Author" that prefaces the 1818-*Northanger Abbey* and *Persuasion* dual-novel set, states in the first paragraph that Jane Austen wrote *Sense and Sensibility, Pride and Prejudice, Mansfield Park,* and *Emma,* as well as *Northanger Abbey* and *Persuasion*.

Austen's simple gravestone at Winchester contains 21 lines, composed by her beloved brother Henry, extolling her virtues and Christian principles, but with no mention of her writing. James Edward Austen-Leigh, who had attended his aunt's funeral, used the profits from his *Memoir of Jane Austen* to have a brass plaque placed on the wall by her grave; the plaque extols her writing. On February 21, 1898, a letter from Montagu George Knight, grandson of the novelist's brother Edward Austen Knight, joined by Lord Selborne, Lord Northbrook, and Hampshire MP Mr. William Wither Beach, appeared in the London *Times* announcing a subscription for a window of "painted glass in her memory" in the cathedral. The following month, across the Atlantic, Oscar Fay Adams, a Boston-based admirer of Austen, who met Montagu Knight during his trip to England to visit Austen sites in preparation for writing her biography, provided a cover letter for the subscription announcement that was reprinted in *The Critic, a New York Weekly Review of Literature and the Arts.* In 1900, the window honoring Jane Austen was unveiled in Winchester Cathedral. Today, one frequently sees flowers by the gravestone, usually placed by the Jane Austen Society. The cause of Jane Austen's early death had been a mystery. But the most accepted diagnosis comes from Dr. Zachary Cope, an endocrinologist, in his article, "Jane Austen's Last Illness" in the *British Medical Journal* of July 1964. Noting first that her illness presented itself symptomatically with severe back pain after she experienced "a severe shock"–the collapse of her brother's bank–Dr. Cope also examined Austen's other symptoms as described in her letters. The most salient symptom for him, however, was the discoloration of her face, which she mentions in several letters, but especially in the letter to Fanny Knight of March 1817, quoted earlier in this chapter: "There is no disease other than Addison's disease that could present a face that was 'black and white' and at the same time give rise to other symptoms described in her letters," Cope stated.

Addison's disease is named for its first diagnostician, a British physician at London's Guy's Hospital, Thomas Addison, MD, FRCP, who described it in a monograph, *On the Constitutional and Local Effects of the Suprarenal Capsules* (1855). In Addison's disease, the adrenal glands produce insufficient cortisol and aldosterone; nowadays it is treated with hormones. The most famous patient with Addison's disease was President John Kennedy.

3. Jane Austen's Family Enjoys Her Early Writing

J ane Austen began writing "novels" before she turned 12. I place the words "novels" and "novel" in quotation marks when discussing Austen's juvenilia because a *novel*, proper (for example, *Emma*), is defined in the *Oxford English Dictionary* as a "long fictional prose narrative . . . filling one or more volumes and typically representing character and action with some degree of realism and complexity" (definition 4 B). Jane Austen's juvenile "novels" are short, just a few pages, and frequently non-realistic. Much of her juvenilia mentioned in Chapter 1 parodied or satirized the popular literature of her day. Parody comes from the Greek word *paroidia*, which means a "song sung beside or against." Satire uses humor and irony to expose / correct folly (Horatian Satire) and or vice (Juvenalian Satire): Horatian satire is mild, while Juvenalian is angry. The mature Austen used both forms in her novels. As the definitions suggest, understanding parody or satire requires one to be familiar with the object(s) parodied or satirized. While sharing similarities, parody and satire serve distinct purposes. A parody is an imitative work that entertains, frequently through comedic elements, using as its skeleton the original work, which it aims to trivialize. Satire endeavors to correct flaws and expose shortcomings; it uses irony and frequently humor, but it has an instructive purpose. Austen's juvenilia is mainly comical, but one could also say that she was a young satirist as well, insofar as she is showing her readers how silly the faddish "novels of sensibility" were.

Sensibility means valuing emotion as the best guide to human behavior and viewing human beings as essentially benevolent. It is not to be confused with "sensible," which is synonymous with "practical" and "realistic." Sensibility was a strong theme in Austen's writing, even in her adulthood, because she showed its flaws and, therefore, satirized it. She was thoroughly familiar with the "The Age of Sensibility," spanning 1745-1785, which bridged the Enlightenment's (c. 1650-1750) emphasis on reason and early Romanticism's (1789/1798) emphasis on emotion, subjectivity, and vivid imagination in art and literature. Sensibility took such a strong hold on the mindset of young people of that era that it actually influenced how they behaved (think Marianne Dashwood in *Sense and Sensibility*).

Fundamental to the "sensibility" movement was *Characteristics of Men, Manners, Opinions, Times*, a three-volume book by Anthony Ashley Cooper, Third Earl of Shaftesbury (1671-1713). Its first edition was published in 1711, followed by several reprints. Cooper stated that benevolence or fellow feeling (empathy) is innate, that virtue is its own reward, and that emotion is the route to knowledge. Following these ideas, philosophers elevated emotion over reason as a guide to moral action. Even Adam Smith—yes, the same Adam Smith who wrote about economics in *The Wealth of Nations*—argued in his *Theory of Moral Sentiments* (1759) that a sympathetic response to distress and suffering is the foundation of moral judgment. (Beginning with Austen's incomplete manuscript *The Watsons*, written when she was about 25, readers see her economic concerns in relation to females in a patriarchal society.)

Literature of sensibility promoted what came to be called "the faculty of feeling." The cult of sensibility in literature and life was reflected in highly sensitive young women, so overwhelmed by emotion that they wept and fainted. Young gentlemen also wept, sighed, and empathized with sorrowful events. Scenes of pathos and virtue arousing sympathy for widows, orphans, and society's victims fill the pages of novels of sensibility, with titles like Henry Mackenzie's *The Man of Feeling* (1771) and Laurence Sterne's *A Sentimental Journey Through France and Italy* (1768). Sterne's hero, Parson Yorick, says he "generally act[s] from the first impulse," privileging emotion over reason, as a guide to conduct (chapter "The Remise Door. Calais").

A rather long scene in Sterne's book, abbreviated here, epitomizes the lachrymosity readers encounter in a novel of sensibility. Parson Yorick visits "that disorder'd maid," Maria of Moulines, whose elderly father has died "'of anguish, for the loss of Maria's senses'"–resulting from the loss of her goat, which affected her deeply: "Maria let me wipe [her tears] away as they fell, with my handkerchief.–I then steep'd it in my own–and then in hers–and then in mine–and then I wip'd hers again."

Here's an equally lachrymose example of the emotional Harley, the hero of *The Man of Feeling*: "The girl cried afresh; Harley kissed off her tears as they flowed, and wept between every kiss" (chapter 35). Recognizing the absurdity of the tear-filled pages of Mackenzie's novel, late Victorian scholar, Henry Morley, Professor of Literature at University College London, included a satirical index to "Tearful Scenes" (*"Chokings, &c., not counted."*) in his 1886 edition of Mackenzie's novel, which featured an advertisement for handkerchiefs at the end of the volume.

Morley's satirical index to Mackenzie's book would have amused the young Jane Austen. For while she recognized the sensibility cult and its excessive emotion, she also absorbed the satirical influences of the early 18th century that continued into her own day. Writers such as Alexander Pope and Jonathan Swift used Horatian and Juvenalian satire, respectively.

For example, Pope's comic-epic poem, "The Rape of the Lock" (1712), comically exposes the follies of the upper-class through the beautiful society-belle Belinda's hysterics as she suffers the "horrific loss" of a lock of hair at a Hampton Court party, where the Baron surreptitiously snips her favorite curl. But the poet slyly observes in Canto II of the poem:

> This Nymph, to the Destruction of Mankind,
> Nourish'd two Locks, which graceful hung behind
> In equal Curls, and well conspir'd to deck
> With shining Ringlets her smooth Iv'ry Neck.

Swift, on the other hand, in the ironically titled "A Modest Proposal" (1729), displays what he called his "savage indignation" at not only the way the British and its absentee landlords treated the Irish, contributing to Ireland's dire poverty, but also how indifferent the Irish seemed to their plight under British rule. Using the persona of a reasonable proposer (in a time when "Proposals" for various issues flourished), Swift's speaker calmly and reasonably leads up to his proposal for using babies for food and little children's skin for fine leather goods. The attuned reader can "hear" Swift's anger increase when his apparently "modest" proposer suggests what to do about "the vast number of poor people who are aged, diseased or maimed":

> I have been desired to employ my thoughts what course may be taken to ease the nation of so grievous an encumbrance. But I am not in the least pain upon that matter because it is very well known that they are every day dying and rotting by cold and famine, and filth and vermin, as fast as can be reasonably expected.

Swift's proposer sounds so reasonable as he leads up to these horrific solutions for Ireland's problems that many readers mistake Swift for his fictional persona, the proposer.

Satire continued and flourished into the late 18th century, sometimes called "The Golden Age of Satire," with the emergence of cartoons that mercilessly lampooned the royal family (especially the Prince of Wales's fat belly and his erstwhile wife Princess Caroline's scandalous conduct abroad), Napoleon, politicians (usually corrupt), fashion (especially ladies' BIG wigs), high society, celebrities, etc. There were no boundaries, and the more scurrilous and bawdy the visual satires were, the more popular they became. Libel laws were virtually non-existent at that time, giving free rein to the satirical impulse.

While Jane Austen was a parson's daughter, she and her family (possibly with the exception of Austen's beloved elder sister Cassandra, whom Austen teased for her "starched notions!") laughed heartily at the world around them. Prudery was a feature of the later Victorian era (1837-1901). But in Georgian England (1714-1830), or more specifically the Regency (1811-1820)–so called when the Prince of Wales ruled as the Prince Regent in place of his ailing father, King George III—the rules of moral conduct were more relaxed.

Austen's juvenilia

Jane knew 18th-century satire, and its use of irony and humor—even dark humor—to convey its point. She certainly read Henry Fielding's rollicking novel, the social and moral satire *Tom Jones* (1749). She applied her familiarity with satire to her early writing that began at age 12.

Some of her adolescent "novels" bear titles like "Jack and Alice," "Frederic and Elfrida," and "Edgar and Emma," parodying the use of names as titles for popular novels: for example, *Tom Jones*, *Joseph Andrews*, *Pamela*, or *Clarissa*. Most of her "novels" have dedications, sometimes elaborate, to the family member to whom she presented them as gifts; again, she parodied the wordy dedications in the novels of her day. Her dedication of "Jack and Alice" to her brother Frank, reads: "Jack and Alice Is respectfully inscribed to Francis William Austen Esq. Midshipman on board his Majesty's Ship the *Perseverance* by his obedient humble Servant The Author."

Because her juvenilia includes 29 texts and over 90,000 words, *Simply Austen* considers just a few of them, which are most representative of her youthful development as a writer. Austen wrote her juvenilia between the ages of 12 and 17 (1793). The works were read aloud to entertain the family, and fortunately for us, she kept neat and exact copies, called "fair copies." Her family clearly enjoyed her "novels," and her father so admired them that he purchased over time three notebooks for his daughter to record her writing—in a period when paper was expensive. Rev. Austen wrote inside the front cover of *Volume the Third*: "Effusions of Fancy by a very young lady Consisting of Tales in a style entirely new." He was clearly proud of his young daughter's talent.

The juvenile work reveals Jane's precocious understanding of how characters are presented, how dialogue is used to develop the action and character, and how plots evolve. And far from prissy, her "novels" (from a few paragraphs to several pages in length) feature cartoon-like violence that results in no permanent injury (a character's leg is caught in a bear trap, but within minutes, she can again walk; a child eats his mother's hand), shady morals (males and females live as husbands and wives, but without marriage), and drunkenness, as in the final sentence of Chapter the First of "Jack and Alice," her earliest "novel":

> The Masks were then all removed & the Company retired to another room, to partake of an elegant & well managed Entertainment, after which, the Bottle being pretty briskly pushed about by the 3 Johnsons, the whole party (not excepting even Virtue [Lady Williams's mask]) were carried home, Dead Drunk.

Readers can "hear" the 12-year-old Austen's ear for comic timing.

Again, listen to this line from "Jack and Alice": "In Lady Williams every virtue met. She was a widow with a handsome jointure & the remains of a very handsome face." Like Swift, she knows how to warm up the reader by moving along calmly and then dropping the proverbial other shoe. And again: "Charles Adams was an amiable, accomplished, & bewitching young Man; of so dazzling a Beauty that none but Eagles could look him in the Face." A few lines later, our clever young writer continues:

> Of the Males, a Mask representing the Sun was the most universally admired. The Beams that darted from his Eyes were like those of that glorious Luminary, tho' infinitely superior. So strong were they that no one dared venture within half a mile of them; he had therefore the best part of the Room to himself, its size not amounting to more than 3 quarters of a mile in length & half a one in breadth. The Gentleman at last finding the feirceness of his beams to

be very inconvenient to the concourse, by obliging them to croud [sic] together in one corner of the room, half shut his eyes, by which means the Company discovered him to be Charles Adams in his plain green Coat, without any mask at all.

She wryly observes in Chapter the Second:

> FOR three months did the Masquerade afford ample subject for conversation to the inhabitants of Pammydiddle; but no character at it was so fully expatiated on as Charles Adams. The singularity of his appearance, the beams which darted from his eyes, the brightness of his Wit, & the whole *tout ensemble* of his person had subdued the hearts of so many of the young Ladies, that of the six present at the Masquerade but five had returned uncaptivated.

She may have had trouble with the "i before e" spelling rule, as in "feirceness," but she knew the word "expatiate" at age 12. And she also knew how to deliver irony and a joke, including in the title: the Jack of "Jack and Alice" does not appear until the end and then immediately dies of drink.

R. Brimley Johnson reproduced as the frontispiece to volume one of his 1906-edition of The Novels of Jane Austen (London: J.M. Dent) the purported portrait of Jane Austen at age 12, painted in 1788 by Ozias Humphry. Known as "The Rice Portrait," it is discussed in detail by its owners, the Rice family, at their website (http://www.janeaustenriceportrait.com). The eminent Austen scholar, Princeton Professor Claudia Johnson, is currently working on a book about this controversial portrait, Her Picture in the Exhibition at Last (photo by Chrystal Dussart).

By the time Jane had turned 14, she had matured as a writer. Using the epistolary format (told in letters) of popular novels (e.g., her favorite Samuel Richardson's epistolary *Pamela, Clarissa,* and *Sir Charles Grandison*), she composed the lengthier *Love and Freindship,* but still had problems with the "i before e" spelling rule. The words "Finis June 13th 1790" are written on it. This "novel" is a deliberate send-up of sentimental novels or novels of sensibility. As an epistolary work, it required its author to maintain the characteristics of the different writers in their respective letters.

In this "novel," the shrewd teenage writer showed how the demonstration of sensibility could be a façade to hide dishonesty, ruthlessness, and greed. *Love and Freindship* is quite an authorial coup for a young teenager. Its subtitle, "Deceived in Freindship and Betrayed in Love," ironically and knowingly undermines the title. It is not surprising that in 1980, the late great scholar of 18th-century British literature, Jean Hagstrum (1913-1995), coined the phrase "Sex and Sensibility," for as will be shown in the discussion of *Love and Freindship,* sensibility led to female hysteria and sexual misconduct. (Jean Hagstrum. *Sex and Sensibility: Ideal and Erotic Love from Milton to Mozart.* Chicago: University of Chicago Press, 1980).

In *Love and Freindship,* Isabel asks, on behalf of her teenage daughter Marianne, that her friend Laura writes to Marianne about the "misfortunes and adventures" of her life; Laura does so in letters three through 15. The letters are meant to teach Marianne the dangers of obstinate fathers and thwarted love. Laura's story is summarized here: The teenage Laura lives with her parents; her father had prepared for the ministry, but is not ordained. Someone knocks on the door, and after a zany conversation among the family members about whether to open the door, her father opens it to reveal "the most beauteous and amiable youth"–a hero of sensibility–that teenage Laura has ever seen. His name is Lindsay, but he asks to be called Edward. He became lost running away from his father, who wants him to marry the lovely Lady Dorothea, whom he admits to loving. But because his father wants him to marry her, Edward / Lindsay believes it is best to resist and leave home. Defying his father is, he proudly announces, "his greatest boast." Edward and Laura, of course, experience love at first sight, which Austen parodies. Laura's father, who, as mentioned before, was never ordained, marries them. The two visit Edward's friend Augustus, who is married to Sophia. Laura and Sophia immediately become best friends, confide to one another their deepest secrets, and "faint alternately on the sofa." After a series of events, including being separated from their "husbands," the ladies coincidentally meet their grandfathers, lie to and pilfer from those who help them, and eventually become reunited with Edward and Augustus who, riding in a phaeton, suddenly overturn. Both men lay bleeding on the ground.

Sophia and Laura behave like true heroines of the sensibility genre: Laura runs around and shrieks, while Sophia repeatedly faints, causing her to be carried away by a "galloping consumption," from which she dies. This leads to the moral, "Run mad as often as you chose, but do not faint!" Numerous other coincidences and characters pop up, disappear, and re-surface.

Already as an adolescent, Austen parodied all the conventions that defined novels of sensibility: dramatic deaths, long-lost friends who are suddenly reunited, immediate friendships, demanding fathers, love at first sight, and extreme coincidences. Virginia Woolf greatly admired Jane Austen and wrote in *The Common Reader* (1925) about reading *Love and Freindship*:

> Brothers and sisters must have laughed when Jane read out loud her last hit at the vices, which they all abhorred. "I die a martyr to my grief for the loss of Augustus. One fatal swoon has cost me my life. Beware of Swoons, Dear Laura. . . . Run mad as often as you chuse, but do not faint. . . ." And on she rushed, as fast as she could write and quicker than she could spell, to tell the incredible adventures of Laura and Sophia. . . . . Undoubtedly, the story must have roused the schoolroom to uproarious laughter. And yet, nothing is

more obvious than that this girl of fifteen, sitting in her private corner of the common parlour, was writing not to draw a laugh from brother and sisters, and not for home consumption. She was writing for everybody, for nobody, for our age, for her own; in other words, even at that early age Jane Austen was writing. One hears it in the rhythm and shapeliness and severity of the sentences. "She was nothing more than a mere good-tempered, civil, and obliging young woman; as such we could scarcely dislike her–she was only an object of contempt." Such a sentence is meant to outlast the Christmas holidays. Spirited, easy, full of fun, verging with freedom upon sheer nonsense,–Love and Freindship is all that; but what is this note which never merges in the rest, which sounds distinctly and penetratingly all through the volume? It is the sound of laughter. The girl of fifteen is laughing, in her corner, at the world.

Writing in the epistolary format

By the time the 16-year-old Austen penned *Catharine, or, The Bower* (dated August 1792), which she transcribed into *Volume the Third*, she avoided the absurdity, exaggeration, and parody of her earlier "novels." In *Catharine*, which she dedicated to her sister Cassandra, Austen presents a realistic gentry heroine facing realistic familial, social, and economic situations, as do the heroines of her later, mature novels. The book's orphaned 16-year-old eponymous heroine is honest and good-natured. She is, however, socially inexperienced because her guardian, Aunt Percival, an older, wealthy, unmarried woman, suffers a "constant apprehension of her marrying imprudently" and a fear of "Young men." This, of course, prevents Catharine (Kitty) from mixing much with society (16 was the marriageable age for young gentry ladies in Georgian times). So

Catharine retreats to her bower, but the potential dampness of the place arouses Aunt Percival's fears.

Years ago, Catharine built the bower with her dear childhood friends, the Wynne sisters. But after Mr. and Mrs. Wynne died, their children faced separation and treatment similar to that experienced by Jane Austen's father and his sisters, notably Philadelphia:

> [The Wynnes] had been reduced to a state of absolute dependance [sic] on some relations, who though very opulent and very nearly connected with them, had with difficulty been prevailed on to contribute anything towards their support. . . . The eldest daughter had been obliged to accept the offer of one of her cousins to equip her for the East Indies, and tho infinitely against her inclinations had been necessitated to embrace the only possibility that was offered to her, of maintenance. Yet it was one, so opposite to all of her ideas of propriety, so contrary to her wishes, so repugnant to her feelings, that she would almost have preferred servitude to it, had choice been allowed her−.
>
> Her personal attractions had gained her a husband as soon as she had arrived at Bengal . . . a man of double her own age.

Austen, of course, heard the story of her Aunt Philadelphia going to India to marry the much older Mr. Hancock, an event that she obviously duplicated here.

With Catharine's situation set up, Austen needed to introduce new characters in order to arouse conflict. Enter Aunt Percival's distant relations, the Stanleys, who had long been hinting for an invitation to her home, but whom Aunt Perceval has been putting off because she thought they'd be accompanied by a young male member of their family, Edward. But with Edward safely in Europe, Mr. and Mrs. Stanley arrive with their daughter Camilla, a shallow society belle: for Camilla, all the young ladies she meets are "'either the sweetest Creature in the world . . . or horrid, shocking and not fit to be seen.'" Camilla's elaborate rhetoric anticipates Isabella Thorpe's in *Northanger Abbey*. Austen gave the two young ladies lively dialogue, pitting Kitty's straight talk, integrity, good sense, and innocence against Camilla's exaggerated language, egocentricity, worldliness, and inanity.

On the morning of the day of a much-anticipated ball at a neighbor's, the Dudleys', house, Kitty awakens with a toothache. Camilla violently bemoans this setback, which will prevent Kitty's attendance at the ball:

> "To be sure, there never was anything so shocking," said Camilla; "To come on such a day too! For one would not have minded it you know had it been at any other time. But it always is so. I never was at a ball in my life, but what something happened to prevent somebody from going! I wish there were no such things as teeth in the world; they are nothing but plagues to one, and I dare say that people might easily invent something to eat with instead of them; poor thing! what pain you are in! I declare it is quite shocking to look at you. But you won't have it out, will you! For Heaven's sake don't; for there is nothing I dread so much. I declare I have rather undergo the greatest tortures in the world than have a tooth drawn. Well! how patiently you do bear it! how can you be so quiet! Lord, if I were in your place I should make such a fuss, there would be no bearing me. I should torment you to death."

The teenage Austen had fully captured how dialogue could convey a character's personality.

With the departure of Aunt Percival and the Stanleys for the ball—and Camilla "more violent than ever in her lamentations over her Friend as she practiced her Scotch steps around the room" [nice touch!] just before leaving—Catharine begins to feel better. Soon a knock at the door reveals the handsome Edward Stanley: he was the first of the self-assured young men that Austen created, to whom the heroine became instantly attracted—think Wickham in *Pride and Prejudice*. Persuading Kitty against her better judgment (and she is correct) that the two should go to the ball, Edward escorts her to the Dudley house. Edward and Kitty are the first couple on the dance floor—a completely indecorous move on his part that angers Aunt Percival, because her niece is actually dancing with a man, as well as the ball's hosts, the Dudleys, because Edward had not been invited.

Edward flirts with Catharine, deliberately irritating Aunt Percival, especially when he suddenly "seizes" Catharine's hand in the bower, kisses it, and immediately speeds away. At first puzzled by Edward's rushed departure, Catharine sees her aunt coming towards the bower, where she over-reacts and scolds her niece for "profligate" conduct. The next day, Edward lightly tells Catharine that he only kissed her hand to shock and irritate her aunt, which, naturally, upsets Catharine. However, his charming behavior during the rest of the day convinces Catharine that he truly loves her. She goes to bed thinking of Edward, but awakens the next morning to learn that he has already left for France without even bidding her goodbye.

Sensibly questioning herself about how he could have fallen in love with her in the very short time they have known each other—she's questioning love at first sight—Catharine feels silly. But Camilla soon arrives in her room to tell her that Mr. Stanley forced Edward to leave to appease Aunt Percival and that her brother truly loves Catharine. A letter from Cecilia Wynne, now Mrs. Lascelles, says she and her husband will return to England from India, while a letter from Camilla Stanley tells her that Edward has left for France and has not even mentioned Catharine's name.

Austen had written herself into something of a dead-end. Kitty asks her aunt to go to Exeter with her to see some strolling players (a troupe of itinerant actors) and requests that Miss Dudley accompany them; however, they require "some Gentlemen" to escort the ladies. The end. How "some Gentlemen" will escort the three ladies to Exeter is a good question, since Aunt Percival is fearful of young men.

The text interests Austen scholars because it foreshadows her later novels in its use of dialogue to move the plot forward and reveal the characters (after all, people get to know us in real life by what we say and how we say it); its theme of the innocent heroine entering society (*Northanger Abbey*'s Catherine Morland, *Mansfield Park*'s Fanny Price); and creation of plot developments used in the later novels: family conflict (the Bennets in *Pride and Prejudice* and the Elliots in *Persuasion*), female education (Camilla's shallowness is like Isabella Thorpe's in *Northanger Abbey* and shown even more noticeably in *Emma*'s Mrs. Elton), and reading (Kitty reads widely but not deeply; *Northanger Abbey* pays great attention to reading). As observed, Edward Stanley pre-figures Wickham and even Henry Tilney, who, though admirable, is also a self-assured young man who teases the innocent Catherine in *Northanger Abbey*. The bower, itself, has been interpreted as having a sexual subtext, for Edward kisses Kitty's hand there: it is the place of her sexual awakening. At 16, Jane Austen had set a model for her mature writing.

About one or two years later, sometime between 1793 and 1795, Austen returned to the epistolary format in *Lady Susan*, which has 41 letters in 158 manuscript pages in the copy at The Morgan Library; two pages bear an 1805 watermark on the paper. With few corrections in Austen's hand, this fair copy, made sometime between 1805 and 1809, is likely her transcription of an earlier draft.

No one has been able to date exactly when Austen composed *Lady Susan*, but it serves as a transitional text because it not only looks back to the use of exaggeration, with its protagonist's nearly melodramatic villainy (the evil Susan's victimization of her daughter, Frederica) seen in her juvenilia, but it also anticipates her mature skill at adept and full characterization. Lady Susan, whose voice we hear in her letters, is clearly a manipulative and possibly sociopathic protagonist. The text is also a satire on the decadence of London's high society—just as the contemporary popular cartoons of the prominent James Gillray (1756-1815) were. Austen may also have been experimenting with creating a female libertine in Susan: a character type that appeared concurrently with the Age of Sensibility and included Daniel Defoe's eponymous *Roxana* (1724) and Henry Fielding's Lady Bellaston in *Tom Jones* (1749).

Austen's biographer nephew James Edward Austen-Leigh was the first to publish this text, to which he gave the title *Lady Susan*, in the second edition (1871) of his *A Memoir of Jane Austen*. As with *Catharine*, the teenage author wrote herself into a dead-end, concluding with an abrupt break from the letter-writing and offering a flat, brief narrative ending, as if she grew tired of this work and just wanted to end it. Whit Stillman's 2016 film, *Love and Friendship*, is his adaptation of *Lady Susan*, for which Stillman confusingly used the title of an earlier Austen work.

Here is the summary:

The beautiful recently widowed and now broke, 35-old Lady Susan, who looks far younger than her years, is forced to leave the home of the Mainwarings, where she has been staying, because Mrs. Mainwaring realizes that Susan has been carrying on with her husband. Susan has also managed to divert the attention of the wealthy young fop, Sir James Martin, who was to marry her daughter, the quiet and innocent Frederica, about whom her mother writes to her London confidante Alicia Johnson, "She is a stupid girl, and has nothing to recommend her."

Dropping her despised daughter off in London at a finishing school, Susan moves in with the Vernons: Charles, her late husband's brother, and his wife Catherine, whose marriage to Charles Susan had tried to prevent years earlier. When Catherine's brother, the 23-year-old Reginald de Courcy, learns from local gossip that the notorious Lady Susan, "the most accomplished coquette in England," is living with his sister, he decides to visit, because, as he writes, "by all that I can gather Lady Susan possesses a degree of captivating deceit which it must be pleasing to witness and detect" (Letter 4).

Of course, the self-assured Reginald not only fails to detect Susan's deceptiveness, but also falls in love with her and defends her against his sister Catherine's suspicions. As Catherine writes to their mother, Susan never "acted less like a coquette in all of her life" than when around Reginald (Letter 10), thus completely duping him. The hypocritical Susan's interest in Reginald is purely financial: the de Courcy estate is entailed on him. So the urgent pleas of his father to leave Susan are futile because Lord de Courcy cannot disinherit him. Lady de Courcy and her daughter, Catherine, write to each other, bemoaning Reginald's conduct and Lady Susan's amoral character.

Susan drops her hypocritically charming mask in her letters to her London friend Alicia, who has married the much older Mr. Johnson for his money. Mr. Johnson is a moral gentleman, whom both Susan and Alicia despise; he does not want Alicia to see or correspond with Susan, but Alicia secretly does.

Learning that her mother wants her to marry Sir James Martin "as a punishment," Frederica runs away from her school in London. Her uncle, Charles Vernon, retrieves her and brings her to the Vernons' home, Churchill. When Catherine and Charles see that Frederica is a lovely, shy, and innocent teen who enjoys reading, Susan grows even angrier with her. Unexpectedly, Sir James arrives at Churchill, which terrifies Frederica, who has fallen in love with Reginald. She writes to Reginald about her fear of being forced into a marriage with Sir James. Reginald tells Susan about Frederica's disinclination to marry Sir James, but Susan, of course, talks her way into Reginald's favor again. Various manipulations and machinations practiced by Susan seem to assure that she will capture Reginald as her husband.

However, Reginald meets Mrs. Mainwaring at the home of her guardian, Mr. Johnson, a nice coincidence; there he hears of Susan's true past, which convinces him to leave her. Desperate now that Reginald knows the truth about her, Lady Susan, marries the much younger Sir James–though she will also likely continue her affair with Mr. Mainwaring. Lady de Courcy and Catherine Vernon plot to have Reginald marry Frederica. The female plotting, now by Lady de Courcy and her daughter, suggests that women have the power to manipulate the gentlemen who appear helpless in dealing with them–even though the men control the money.

Austen abruptly ends the epistolary style with an intrusive narrator, who begins, "This correspondence, by a meeting between some of the parties, and a separation between the others, could not, to the great detriment of the Post Office revenue, be continued any longer." She concludes artificially:

Whether Lady Susan was or was not happy with her second choice, I do not see how it can ever be ascertained; for who would take her assurance of it on either side of the question? The world must judge from probabilities; she had nothing against her but her husband, and her conscience. Sir James may seem to have drawn a harder lot than mere folly merited; I leave him, therefore, to all the pity that anybody can give him. For myself, I confess that I can pity only Miss Mainwaring; who, coming to town, and putting herself to an expense in clothes which impoverished her for two years, on purpose to secure him, was defrauded of her due by a woman ten years older than herself.

After Austen-Leigh published *Lady Susan* in 1871, his Victorian readers wondered how a parson's teenage daughter, living in the country, could have created a character like Lady Susan. But as observed earlier in this chapter, Jane Austen lived in a well-read family that was not afraid to speak out about the shenanigans of their neighbors and London's upper crust. Moreover, she was likely familiar with the family history of her and her sister's dear friends, the Lloyd sisters, whose maternal grandmother, Lady Craven, led a notorious life on which Austen may have modeled Lady Susan.

Here is the story of Lady Craven. The beautiful Elizabeth Staples (1698-1773) first married the Hon. Charles Craven, with whom she had six surviving children. After her husband's death in 1754, she and her children moved to Sevenhampton, where, according to her granddaughter Caroline Austen (James and Mary's Lloyd Austen's daughter), Mrs. Craven's exploits began. Charming, courteous, and fully ladylike in society, she was a tyrant at home, treating her daughters as if they were servants and locking them in the house when she was away. Determined to be rich, she married, within a few months of her widowhood, the wealthy Jemmett Raymond of Kintbury, Berkshire, with whom she had been involved prior to her first husband's death. She seduced him into making her his heir. In 1756, she forced her only surviving son, John (1732-1804), an ordained Anglican priest, to marry Elizabeth Raymond, the half-sister of her second husband because Elizabeth had money in her own right. John took after his mother: he was charged in an adultery case in 1776.

One day, when their mother was away from home, the Craven sisters escaped, ultimately being able to take care of themselves. The daughter of most interest to this study of Jane Austen was Martha Craven, who in 1763 married the Rev. Nowis Lloyd; they became the parents of Martha, Eliza, and Mary Lloyd, close friends of the two Austen sisters. After Rev. Lloyd's death in 1789, Mrs. Lloyd and her three daughters first lived in the Deane rectory, owned by Rev. George Austen, while the Austen family lived at the Steventon Rectory. Then in 1792, when Rev. James Austen became his father's curate at Deane, the Lloyds moved to Ibthorpe, where the Austen sisters frequently visited and stayed.

The Lloyd sisters' grandmother, once Elizabeth Craven, used the legacy of her deceased second husband (d. 1767) to have a big marble tombstone built for him at St. Mary the Virgin Church, Kintbury, Berkshire. It included a large bust of herself, identified as "the widow of the Honbl. Charles Craven Esq. Governor of South Carolina In the Reign of Queen Ann" [sic]—hence, Mrs. Craven is known as Lady Craven. Jane Austen would have seen this monument in her visits to the church's vicarage, the home of the Rev. Thomas Fowle II, whose son, the Rev. Tom Fowle (1765-1797) had been a pupil at Rev. George Austen's Steventon Rectory school between 1779 and 1783, and later the ill-fated fiancé of Cassandra Austen. Jane could have learned about Mrs. / Lady Craven from both the Lloyds and the Fowles, for the Austens were close friends with both families. A literary source for Lady Susan might be the epistolary novel *Les Liaisons Dangereuses*, the story of a scheming woman, seduction, and adultery.

Austen's interruption and precipitous termination of *Lady Susan* may have been caused by her inspiration to begin "Elinor and Marianne," the epistolary original for *Sense and Sensibility*, which would become her first published novel in 1811.

4. Responding to Trends in Sensibility and Gothicism: "The Watsons" and *Northanger Abbey*

I n 1795, while still living at the Steventon Rectory, the nearly 20-year-old Jane Austen began writing "Elinor and Marianne," which would become the heroines' names of her future novel, *Sense and Sensibility*, published in 1811. If Cassandra's scrap of paper on which she more or less scribbled the dates of her sister's novels is correct, "Sense & Sensibility [was] begun Nov. 1797 / I am sure that something of the / same story & characters had been / written earlier & called Elinor & Marianne." The earliest Austen letter we have is dated January 9-10, 1796, and as there are no known letters written for 1797, we cannot trace epistolary allusions to the prototype of *Sense and Sensibility*. The manuscript of "Elinor and Marianne" seems not to exist. Scholars assume that after Austen had checked the proofs from the publisher, she burned her handwritten manuscripts when the novels appeared in print.

As noted in Chapter 3, the question of whether to behave according to sense or emotion was much discussed during Austen's lifetime. The Austens read periodical journals, which featured essays about sensibility, in particular, the dangers of too much sensibility–especially as this trait affected impressionable young persons.

In its issue of January 2, 1799, *The Lady's Monthly Museum, or Polite Repository of Amusement and Instruction*, a popular periodical magazine, published an allegory with characters named Sense and Sensibility. An allegory is a narrative, usually meant for instruction, in which characters and events stand for abstract ideas. The most famous allegory is John Bunyan's *The Pilgrim's Progress* (1678), in which the protagonist, Christian, meets characters with names like Obstinate, Pliant, Discretion, Flatterer, and Mercy and encounters places like The Slough of Despair and Difficulty Hill. In the allegory published in *The Lady's Monthly Museum*, Sensibility falls prey to Susceptibility and Pride—as do Austen's Marianne Dashwood and Edward and Laura in *Love and Freindship*.

Warnings about sensibility were rife. Ironically, 15 years after Henry Mackenzie wrote the 1771-hit novel of sensibility, *The Man of Feeling*, he published an anonymous essay with the heavily didactic title, "Sensibility and Virtuous Feeling Do Not Always Lead to Beneficence and Virtuous Conduct" in the July 22, 1786, issue of the periodical, *The Lounger*. Another prominent writer, Vicesimus Knox II, the Anglican priest and headmaster (1788-1812) of George Austen's alma mater, Tonbridge School, included in his three-volume book *Winter Evenings; or Lucubrations on Life and Letters* (1788) a chapter with the verbose title, "Of Sensibility as it appears in Piety to God and Benevolence to Man, distinguished from that false Tenderness which is described in many Novels, and which gives rise only to Gallantry and Affectation." Notice how the title portrays novels in a negative light. One can reasonably assume that Austen read Knox's popular *Family Sermons* (1799), for she enjoyed reading sermons and owned his *Elegant Extracts*, in which she wrote notes in the margin. George Austen gave 14-year-old Frank a copy of that book to take with him when he went to sea. So Jane Austen was certainly familiar with Knox and may well have read his verbosely-titled essay. These essays are reprinted in my edition of *The Dictionary of Literary Biography: Jane Austen's Life and Novels*, volume 363, found in most college and university library reference collections, call number PR 4036.J39.2011. For Austen's reading of sermons, see Laura Mooneyham White, *Jane Austen's Anglicanism*. Routledge: 2016.

Knox was not the only person targeting novels as dangerous to readers, especially young females. In April 1793, *The Gentleman's Magazine*, an extremely popular journal, published an essay, "Danger of Modern Novels," bemoaning "the modern novel" as "literary opium," which "lulls every sense in oblivious rapture," especially in the "young lady's mind." The article continued: "Novels according to the practice of the times are the powerful engines with which the seducer attacks the female heart" (GM, 63, pt. 1 [1793]: 293-294). This essay repeats sentiments presented in "Cursory Thoughts on the Modern Novel" that appeared in *The Lady's Magazine*, 11 (1780): 693. It is no coincidence that Marianne Dashwood, the victim of near-fatal sensibility in *Sense and Sensibility*, is an avid reader of novels; when this heroine is rescued by the handsome Willoughby, "His person and air were equal to what her fancy had ever drawn for the hero of a favourite story" (1:9).

As literacy increased, especially among women whose minds were considered impressionable, words like "panic," "addiction," "fever," and "mania" were applied to novel-reading. But young men were not exempt. The media blamed Johann Wolfgang van Goethe's novel, *The Sorrows of Young Werther*, first published in English in 1779, for a rash of young men's suicides that copied the self-inflicted death of the protagonist, the sensitive young artist Werther. He shoots himself in the head out of his desperate love for the beautiful Charlotte, whose grief is so excessive that her "life was despaired of": the copy-cat suicides were known as Werther-Fever, and male Werther-followers even wore yellow pants and blue shirts as does the character.

Literary influences and inspirations

The novel was a new type of fiction in 18th-century England: even the word *novel* means "new." Jane Austen brought the novel to maturity and even respectability in her adult writing. In the discussion of *Northanger Abbey*, below, her famous defense of the novel in Chapter 5 of that book will be considered.

Ridiculing sensibility as a teen-ager in *Love and Freindship*, Austen made a serious analysis of it in *Sense and Sensibility's*

Marianne Dashwood, showing more fully than she did in her juvenile work how emotional self-indulgence nearly kills her character. She returned to her 1795 manuscript, which she began to revise into *Sense and Sensibility* in 1797, for deep revision after moving to the Chawton cottage in the summer of 1809.

Austen interrupted her revision of "Elinor and Marianne," beginning, again according to Cassandra, the epistolary "First Impressions" in October 1796 and finishing it 10 months later. As observed in Chapter 1, Rev. Austen was so impressed with it that he sent it to Thomas Cadell publishers in a letter dated November 1, 1797; Cadell immediately rejected the offer, sight unseen. Readers can see this letter, owned by St. John's College, Oxford, online. Despite Cadell's rejection, Jane kept pen to paper, writing *Susan*, which would be published after her death and retitled *Northanger Abbey*.

According to Cassandra, "North-hanger Abbey was written about the years '98 & 99." Cassandra's hyphenated version of the title reminds us of the controversial pronunciations of the word by some scholars who insist on saying, "North-ANGER," insinuating that Jane Austen was an angry feminist—she was certainly a feminist and at times an angry one—and "**North**unJER" (just pretentiousness). A *hanger* is a small wood on steeply sloping land. In 2:7 of *Northanger Abbey* we learn about the Abbey's location with a hanger behind the house: "The remainder [of the building] was shut off by knolls of old trees, or luxuriant plantations, and the steep woody hills rising behind, to give it shelter." Austen also uses the word "hanger" in *Sense and Sensibility*: John Dashwood admires the plentiful timber "'in the Delaford Hanger'" (3:14). So one should pronounce the title "North-Hanger," as Cassandra indicated, because the abbey building is backed by the northern hanger, a slope with trees.

In the "Advertisement by the Authoress to *Northanger Abbey*" that usually prefaces even reasonably priced paperback editions of this novel, Austen wrote in 1816:

This little work was finished in the year 1803 and intended

for immediate publication. It was disposed of to a bookseller, it was even advertised, and why the business proceeded no farther, the author has never been able to learn. That any bookseller should think it worth while to purchase what he did not think it worth while to publish seems extraordinary. But with this, neither the author nor the public have any other concern than as some observation is necessary upon those parts of the work which thirteen years have made comparatively obsolete. The public are entreated to bear in mind that thirteen years have passed since it was finished, many more since it was begun, and that during that period, places, manners, books, and opinions have undergone considerable changes.

With a copy of her *Susan* manuscript in her possession, she changed the name of its heroine to Catherine after the appearance of a novel called *Susan* in 1809. But even after securing the manuscript from Crosby in 1816, she did not re-submit it for publication. Busy with *Persuasion* and feeling ill, Austen might have believed, as her "Advertisement" indicates, that the work was too dated to publish. On March 13, 1817, she wrote to her niece Fanny Knight, "Miss Catherine is put upon the Shelve for the present, and I do not know that she will ever come out." *Northanger Abbey* was published in December 1817 (1818 on the title page), at the same time as *Persuasion*. This extremely comical novel took a long and circuitous route to see print.

Austen's belief—as she pointed out in the "Advertisement"—that "places, manners, books, and opinions have undergone considerable changes" since the novel was written, reminds us that *Susan* was meant as a parody of the Gothic romances of the late 18th century, particularly Ann Radcliffe's best-seller, *The Mysteries of Udolpho* (1794). Austen's literary executors, Henry and Cassandra Austen, entitled their sister's book, *Northanger Abbey*, emphasizing its Gothic parody. Many Gothic titles included the words "abbey" or "castle," which are really the only Gothic elements in them, if we take Gothic to mean life in the Middle Ages: *The Horrors of Oakendale Abbey*, *The Castle Spectre*, *Nightmare Abbey*, and *The Children of the Abbey* are all real titles.

The full title of Radcliffe's most famous book is *The Mysteries of Udolpho; A Romance Interspersed with Some Pieces of Poetry*. Notice the word "Romance" in the title. There is a reason for this. Horace Walpole, the writer of the first Gothic "novel" in English fiction, *The Castle of Otranto* (1764), called his work a "romance" and explained it in his "Preface" to the second edition (1765) by differentiating between the "ancient" and "modern" romance, with "ancient" referring to tales of knights and their fabulous exploits. *The Castle of Otranto*, he wrote, was an attempt to blend the two kinds of Romance, the ancient and the modern:

> In the former, all was imagination and improbability: in the latter, nature is always intended to be, and sometimes has been, copied with success. Invention has not been wanting; but the great resources of fancy have been dammed up, by a strict adherence to common life. But if in the latter species Nature has cramped imagination, she did but take her revenge, having been totally excluded from old Romances. The actions, sentiments, conversations, of the heroes and heroines of ancient days, were as unnatural as the machines employed to put them in motion.

Walpole's reasoning led to Gothic fiction being called Gothic romances.

Although *Northanger Abbey* is more than a parody, Austen's satire on both the Gothic romance and the conventions of 18th-century novels is ingenious. While *Udolpho* is set in 1584, its characters behave according to 18th-century mores, and the heroine is a typical female literary protagonist of that era. When *Udolpho's* heroine, Emily, is fleeing from the Castle of Udolpho without her hat, she must cease her flight immediately to purchase a new one, because a decorous eighteenth-century lady never travels hatless. The Italian Catholics in *Udolpho* are depicted according to the pejorative view the 18th-century English had of them. The more familiar the reader is with *The Mysteries of Udolpho*, the more one admires Austen's satirizing and parodying it. Remember that parody is derived from the Greek *paroidia*, "a song sung beside," and must have an object that is imitated and ridiculed. So here is a summary of Austen's parodic object, *The Mysteries of Udolpho: A Romance Interspersed with Some Pieces of Poetry*, all 700+ pages of it.

Udolpho, like many Gothic romances, is a story of the power struggles between a young female who is coming of age and a villain, set in an eerie medieval abbey or castle. Living with her elderly, frail parents at their idyllic chateau and estate, La Valle or La Valle'e [sic], "on the pleasant banks of the Garonne, in the province of Gascony," Emily St. Aubert is the definitive gothic heroine, with 18th-century sensibilities—pretty, artistic, and sensitive:

> In person, Emily resembled her mother; having the same elegant symmetry of form, the same delicacy of features, and the same blue eyes, full of tender sweetness. But, lovely as was her person, it was the varied expression of her countenance, as conversation awakened the nicer emotions of her mind, that threw such a captivating grace around her (1:1).

Emily's frail mother dies. Traveling with her ailing father, she meets, amid great excitement, Valancourt, the handsome young man with whom she immediately falls in love. Their meeting occurs with a dramatic adventure: From their coach, Emily and Monsieur St. Aubert hear distant gunshots; Valancourt "springs from the bushes," "full of manly grace" in his hunter's attire. The three travel together for a few days, allowing Emily and Valancourt to share their admiration for the natural scenery and each other. When Valancourt goes his separate way, the St. Auberts travel through an area known for bandits and hear someone approaching their coach. Monsieur St. Aubert precipitously fires his pistol, wounding none other than Valancourt himself! (Readers should keep all of this in mind when reading *Northanger Abbey*.)

Soon Monsieur St. Aubert succumbs to his illness and leaves his now orphaned daughter under the care of his sister, the widowed, wealthy Mme. Cheron—a vain, greedy, and socially ambitious woman. She brings Emily to her estate in Toulouse, where our heroine, no longer in her idyllic family world of La Valle, faces new challenges. Initially encouraging Emily's marriage to Valancourt (who survived the gunshot wound), Mme. Cheron suddenly and secretly marries Signor Montoni, the tall, dark villain of the novel, and banishes Valancourt from Emily's life. Unknown to Mme. Cheron, Montoni married her to access her money to pay off his huge gambling debts.

Now forbidding Emily's marriage to Valancourt, who, it turns out, is not as wealthy and as socially well-connected as Mme. Cheron first thought, the Montonis sweep Emily off to Venice, where her beauty attracts many Italian men, including the determined Count Morano, Montoni's friend. The Montonis try to bully Emily into marrying Count Morano because he appears to have money. But learning that Morano has lost his fortune to gambling and that his enemies are after him, Montoni, who also has deep gambling debts, quickly packs to escape from Venice and Morano.

With his wife, Emily, and an army of retainers in tow, Montoni travels through the steep, dark forests, high into the Apennines, to his brooding, crumbling Castle of Udolpho, at which Emily gazes "with wondering awe." Radcliffe describes all this scenery in excruciating detail, paying tribute to Edmund Burke's extremely influential *A Philosophical Enquiry into the Origin of Our Ideas of the Sublime and Beautiful* (1757), in which he defines "the sublime" as "whatever is fitted in any sort to excite the ideas of pain and danger . . . whatever is in any sort terrible, or is conversant about terrible objects, or operates in a manner analogous to terror." The Apennines, the Alps, and the Canadian Rockies evoke sublimity, as does a thunderstorm. Emily experiences plenty of sublimity during her trip and especially at the Castle. Radcliffe personifies the power and threats of the Castle of Udolpho in her famous description: "Silent, lonely, and sublime, it seemed to stand the sovereign of the scene, and to frown defiance on all who dared to invade its solitary reign." Emily is isolated with her books (she's an avid reader), art supplies (she is a talented painter), and chronic curiosity. She will be faced with even more challenges at the Castle than she had at Mme. Cheron's estate in Toulouse or Montoni's villa in Venice.

Annette, Mme. Cheron's voluble maid, leads Emily to her bedroom on the far side of the castle, far away from everyone else's room; its door does not lock. En route to the bedroom, the two take a wrong turn and arrive in a suite of apartments, which, as Annette's lantern reveals, is hung with paintings, one of which is covered by a black veil. When Emily asks about it, Annette exclaims, "'Holy Virgin! this must be the picture they told me of in Venice. . . . There is something very dreadful about that picture.'"

The next morning, the curious Emily investigates on her own the scary suite of apartments. The rooms are filled with decrepit furniture and ragged tapestries; she lifts the black veil, only to "drop senseless on the floor." This is the first of Emily's many fainting spells. She believes that the moldering body of the former owner of the castle, Signora Laurentini di Udolpho, is behind the black veil.

At night, when Emily hears inexplicable wailing music and mysterious faint conversations and recognizes Montoni's voice, she finds her nerves and curiosity intensifying. She soon realizes that Montoni is a Captain of the Condottieri, guilty of war, plunder, and murder. Meanwhile, the undaunted Morano, who has followed Emily to Udolpho, arrives in the middle of night hovering over Emily's bed (remember, her bedroom door does not lock), sword drawn (yes, it's phallic), intent on kidnapping the sleeping young lady. But Montoni arrives and seriously wounds him in a duel; Morano then threatens revenge and departs.

Financially desperate, Montoni tries forcing his wife to change her will: instead of leaving her wealth to her niece, Emily, he wants to be the one to inherit. Mme. Montoni refuses, and so Montoni locks her away in a distant turret, where she dies of maltreatment. Meanwhile, Montoni brings his mistress to Udolpho, and we read of various debaucheries occurring, though off-stage. He threatens Emily to sign over her inheritance to him, to which she stoically replies, "'The strength of my mind is equal to the justice of my cause; and I can endure with fortitude when it is in resistance of oppression.'" To this Montoni sneers, "'You speak like a heroine; we shall see whether you can suffer like one.'"

While Montoni realizes he cannot overcome Emily's will, he recognizes his physical power over her. So he begins to threaten her with physical and sexual intimations, "'I have a punishment, which you think not of: it is terrible! This night, this very night.'" In Austen's parody, Northanger Abbey's hero Henry Tilney teases heroine Catherine, as they head to his family's abbey by creating a Udolpho-like story with Catherine as heroine and speaks of her "'*unconquerable horror of the bed*,'" indicating that Austen, too, interpreted Montoni's threat as sexual violation. With his armed banditti roaming the corridors of the castle and a bedroom door that does not lock, Emily, fearing bodily injury, including the implied rape, barricades the doors of the secret staircase to her room with furniture. But being continually terrorized, she finally relents and signs over the estate.

Emily thinks that Valancourt is also held prisoner at Udolpho, but running into his arms, she realizes he is not Valancourt, but a Monsieur du Pont. He helps Emily, Annette, and another servant, Ludovico (whom Annette loves) escape Udolpho. They get back to France, coincidentally near the convent where Emily's father is buried. They stay in this Languedoc neighborhood with Count de Villefort, his wife, and daughter Blanche, who immediately befriends Emily.

The Villeforts live in the Chateau Blanc that once belonged to the Marchioness de Villeroi, who died in her room there. At Emily's request, the Marchioness's old servant, the voluble Dorothée, who has now replaced the voluble Annette as the stock garrulous and superstitious servant character, leads Emily to the bedroom where the Marchioness died. There, Emily sees the Marchioness's portrait and notices the resemblance between the departed woman and herself; she also senses that the room is haunted. Meanwhile, the forests around the chateau also seem haunted by a spectral figure and mysterious music: it turns out to be the mad and frenzied Sister Agnes, who frequently escapes her convent cell and roams the forest at night, playing "her favorite instrument" and singing. Emily eventually visits Sister Agnes on her deathbed at the convent. The nun confesses to Emily that she was formerly Signora Laurentini di Udolpho, heiress to the House of Udolpho, before Montoni owned it. She had been the mistress of Marquis de Villeroi, who had promised to marry her once he was rid of his wife, the Marchioness, who turned out to be Emily's aunt (her father's sister); hence, Emily's resemblance to the portrait in her aunt's bedroom. The Marquis conspired with Signora Laurentini to poison the Marchioness. Suddenly guilt-ridden over murdering his wife, he leaves the Chateau, leading Laurentini to the convent as penance for her part in the murder.

Count de Villefort and Lady Blanche accompany Emily back to her parental home, La Valle, where Emily learns of Montoni's death in prison, likely murdered by his enemies. She is now a wealthy young woman and reunited with Valancourt, with whom she lives happily ever after. The figure behind the black veil at the Castle of Udolpho is explained to be a *memento mori*: a waxed figure that was used for penance.

At the instigation of Isabella Thorpe, Catherine, the heroine of *Northanger Abbey*, can barely put down *The Mysteries of Udolpho*.

Emily vs. Catherine–Austen's take on the Gothic novel

The opening sentence of *Northanger Abbey* alerts readers about Austen's intentions: "No one who had ever seen Catherine Morland in her infancy would have supposed her born to be an heroine." But by age 15, Catherine had "now the pleasure of sometimes hearing her father and mother remark on her personal improvement.

'Catherine grows quite a good-looking girl,—she is almost pretty today.'" The sly narrator continues, "To look *almost* pretty is an acquisition of higher delight to a girl who has been looking plain the first fifteen years of her life than a beauty from her cradle can ever receive" (1:1).

Unlike Emily and other talented 18th-century literary heroines:

> Catherine's taste for drawing was not superior; though whenever she could obtain the outside of a letter from her mother or seize upon any other odd piece of paper, she did what she could in that way, by drawing houses and trees, hens and chickens, all very much like one another. (1:1)

At age eight, Catherine started piano lessons:

> She learnt a year, and could not bear it;—and Mrs. Morland, who did not insist on her daughters being accomplished in spite of incapacity or distaste, allowed her to leave off. The day which dismissed the music-master was one of the happiest of Catherine's life. (1:1)

So much for Catherine's being like the talented, lute-playing Emily. And unlike heroines who were extremely sensitive to the natural world—again, Emily comes to mind—Catherine "had no taste for a garden; and if she gathered flowers at all, it was chiefly for the pleasure of mischief." But she is "not always stupid" and even reads now and again. Emily, in contrast, always has a book at hand.

Finally, unlike Emily, who was orphaned as a teen-ager, Catherine's:

> father was a clergyman, without being neglected, or poor, and a very respectable man, though his name was Richard—and he had never been handsome. He had a considerable independence besides two good livings—and he was not in the least addicted to locking up his daughters. Her mother was a woman of useful plain sense, with a good temper, and, what is more remarkable, with a good

constitution. She had three sons before Catherine was born; and instead of dying in bringing the latter into the world, as anybody might expect, she still lived on—lived to have six children more—to see them growing up around her, and to enjoy excellent health herself. (1:1)

Can you hear Austen laughing to herself as our overt narrator piles on her heroine distinctly un-heroine-like characteristics, deliberately undercutting Radcliffe's Emily, as well as other lovely, orphaned, and talented heroines of 18th-century novels?

Eighteen-year-old Catherine visits sunny and crowded Bath (not the sublime, majestic, and isolated Apennines) with the Morlands' pleasant neighbors, Mr. and Mrs. Allen. Attending a ball in the Lower Rooms, she meets the novel's hero, Henry Tilney, who "if not quite handsome, was very near it." Hero and heroine meet through a most proper introduction made by the Room's Master of Ceremonies—the typical manner in which young couples met in Bath's Assembly Rooms. While Mrs. Allen is interested solely in fashion, Mr. Allen "had early in the evening taken pains to know who her partner was, and had been assured of Mr. Tilney's being a clergyman, and of a very respectable family in Gloucestershire." Mr. Allen has behaved appropriately as a chaperone, and neither he nor his wife bullies Catherine the way the Montonis bullied Emily. The otherwise innocuous Mrs. Allen merely advises Emily, when visiting the Tilneys, to "'put on a white gown; Miss Tilney always wears white'" (1:12).

Soon the lonely Catherine has a female friend—at least an erstwhile one—in the form of Isabella Thorpe, whose mother Mrs. Allen recognizes as an old school friend. Hearing Catherine's surname, Morland, Isabella—"four years older than Miss Morland, and at least four years better informed"(1:4)—immediately befriends Catherine. She does, however, have an ulterior motive, which the ingenuous Catherine cannot perceive. The beautiful and cunning Isabella is romantically interested in Catherine's elder brother

James, who is a good friend of Isabella's brother, John Thorpe, as the two young men are at Oxford together.

Isabella's rhetoric is hyperbolic. "'My dearest creature, what can have made you so late? I have been waiting for you at least this age!'" exclaims Isabella, who has been waiting for Catherine in the Pump Room for all of five minutes. "'But, my dearest Catherine, what have you been doing with yourself all this morning?–Have you gone on with Udolpho?'" she asks, having introduced Catherine to Radcliffe's book and other Gothic romances. Catherine stays up at night reading it, terrifying herself: "'While I have Udolpho to read, I feel as if nobody could make me miserable. Oh! the dreadful black veil! My dear Isabella, I am sure there must be Laurentina's skeleton behind it.'" Exaggerating her waiting time, Isabella also exaggerates her capacity for friendship: "'There is nothing I would not do for those who are really my friends. I have no notion of loving people by halves; it is not my nature.'" The only veil, black or otherwise, in Austen's novel, is the veil of best-friendship that Isabella drapes over her reason for befriending "'dearest Catherine.'" She merely cultivates Catherine because she has her eye on Catherine's brother, James.

John Thorpe and James Morland soon arrive in Bath, and James pairs up with Isabella, while John, boastful, arrogant, deceitful, "stout," and of "middling height"–he is unattractive conversationally and physically–attempts to attract Catherine by bragging about his carriage, horse-driving abilities, and drinking. In this new environment of Bath, the sensible young Catherine begins to doubt if John Thorpe is as great a fellow as her brother insists he is.

Failing to encounter Henry Tilney for several days, Catherine sees him entering a ball, escorting a lovely young woman: she turns out to be Eleanor Tilney, Henry's younger sister. But when Henry asks Catherine to dance, she is unable to do so because she had promised to dance with John Thorpe–who immediately upon entering the ball had gone off to the card room to trade horses and dogs. Courtesy dictates that Catherine cannot dance with a man when she has earlier promised to dance with another man–even though the first fellow has abandoned her. So poor Catherine's greatest challenge in the world of a brightly-lit, crowded Bath ballroom is trying not to look like a wallflower:

> She could not help being vexed at the non-appearance of Mr. Thorpe, for she not only longed to be dancing, but was likewise aware that, as the real dignity of her situation could not be known, she was sharing with the scores of other young ladies still sitting down all the discredit of wanting a partner. To be disgraced in the eye of the world, to wear the appearance of infamy while her heart is all purity, her actions all innocence, and the misconduct of another the true source of her debasement, is one of those circumstances which peculiarly belong to the heroine's life, and her fortitude under it what particularly dignifies her character. Catherine had fortitude too; she suffered, but no murmur passed her lips. (1:8)

Catherine is suffering from the embarrassment of being partnerless at a dance, rather than being a prisoner in a remote Alpine castle. Meanwhile, her new best friend Isabella is too busy dancing with James Morland to care about her friend's isolation. From this experience, Catherine "deduced this useful lesson, that to go previously engaged to a ball does not necessarily increase either the dignity or enjoyment of a young lady."

Her hope to run into Henry or Eleanor the next day by going to the Pump Room is interrupted when John Thorpe, followed by his sister and James, insists that she join them in a carriage ride. During the ride, John asks about the Allens, intimating that they are wealthy: "'Old Allen is as rich as a Jew—is not he,'" insists the crude Thorpe, who also believes that because the Allens are childless, Catherine is their heir. Tired of Thorpe's talk about having money, drinking, and racing horses until their necks break, Catherine, "little as [she] was in the habit of judging for herself, and unfixed as were her general notions of what men ought to be . . . could not entirely repress a doubt, while she bore with the effusions of his endless conceit, of his being altogether completely agreeable." She is learning to judge people on her own, not according to what her elder brother or new best friend say. She also learns that had she remained home and then accompanied Mrs. Allen on her walk, she would have met Henry Tilney.

THE INTERIOR OF THE PUMP ROOM, BATH.

Now a crowded restaurant, the Pump Room is shown here as it looked at the end of the 19th century in a photograph from Oscar Fay Adams, The Story of Jane Austen's Life (Boston: Lee and Shepherd, 1897):98 (photo by Crystal Dussart).

Meeting the Tilneys the next evening at a ball, Catherine, who has learned her lesson and come disengaged, accepts Henry Tilney's invitation to dance. With the ladies and gentlemen standing in parallel lines as they await their turn to dance to the top of the line, Catherine faces Henry across from her. But suddenly she finds herself unpleasantly distracted by the persistent Thorpe, insisting, albeit untruthfully, "'Hey-day, Miss Morland!' said he. 'What is the meaning of this? −I thought you and I were to dance together.'"

While Catherine denies, and rightfully so, that he engaged her for the dance, Thorpe persists, "'That is a good one, by Jove!—I asked you as soon as I came into the room, and I was just going to ask you again, but when I turned round, you were gone! —this is a cursed shabby trick!'" Blah, blah, blah—and Thorpe changes the topic to horses. Catherine is as persecuted by him as Emily was by both Montoni and Count Morano, but Thorpe's bullying is based on lies about her standing him up for a dance, not threats to her person, which Emily faced.

Instead of using a bloody sword fight, like the one that rescues Emily from the persistent Count Morano, Austen wrote a wonderful dancing rescue from the persistent Thorpe: "This was the last sentence by which he could weary Catherine's attention, for he was just then borne off by the resistless pressure of a long string of passing ladies." Catherine is rescued from Thorpe's intrusive chatter by the line of dancing ladies who are moving up the set. Before parting for the evening, Catherine agrees to join the Tilneys for a walk at noon the following day, with the proviso that it does not rain.

Of course, it drizzles a bit, and the weather looks iffy. Determined to wait and see if the Tilneys appear at the Allens' home, she is interrupted by John Thorpe, Isabella, and James, who burst in, determined to convince her to join them on another carriage ride. This time, Thorpe promises to drive her to Blaize Castle, which he knows, but she does not, is a "folly," an ornamental structure made to look like a building, but uninhabitable. Thinking it will be like the Castle of Udolpho, Catherine enquires if there will be towers, ramparts, and galleries like the ones Emily St. Aubert roamed. "'By dozens,'" lies Thorpe.

Seeing that Catherine remains uncertain about whether to wait or join the carriage ride, Thorpe creates another lie, this time making it sound as if the Tilneys have ignored their walking engagement with her: "'As we turned into Broad-street, I saw them—does he not drive a phaeton with bright chestnuts?'" cries Thorpe. "'I do not know indeed,'" replies Catherine. "'Yes, I know he does; I saw him. You are talking of the man you danced with last night, are not you?'"

continues Thorpe; "'Well, I saw him at that moment turn up the Lansdown-road,–driving a smart-looking girl.'" "'Did you indeed?'" inquires the hesitant Catherine. "'Did upon my soul; knew him again directly, and he seemed to have got some very pretty cattle too,'" Thorpe blithely adds, trying to arouse Catherine's disappointment in Henry Tilney. With no help from the innocuous Mrs. Allen, Catherine, albeit with "unsettled" feeling, leaves in Thorpe's carriage.

Driving down Pulteney Street and through the Argyle Buildings (Street), Thorpe arouses Catherine from her contemplation about Eleanor and Henry, asking, "'Who is that girl who looked at you so hard as she went by?'" Turning around, Catherine spots Eleanor and Henry walking with their umbrella towards the Allen residence:

> "Stop, stop, Mr. Thorpe," she impatiently cried; "it is Miss Tilney; it is indeed. –How could you tell me they were gone?–Stop, stop, I will get out this moment and go to them." But to what purpose did she speak? –Thorpe only lashed his horse into a brisker trot; the Tilneys, who had soon ceased to look after her, were in a moment out of sight round the corner of Laura-place, and in another moment she was herself whisked into the Market-place. Still, however, and during the length of another street, she entreated him to stop. "Pray, pray stop, Mr. Thorpe. –I cannot go on. I will not go on.–I must go back to Miss Tilney." But Mr. Thorpe only laughed, smacked his whip, encouraged his horse, made odd noises, and drove on. (1:11)

Austen's parody is a clever inversion of Radcliffe's scene. Rather than being driven in Montoni's coach through the dark and secluded mountains to the brooding Castle of Udolpho, Catherine is captive in Thorpe's one-horse gig and raced through the crowded city of Bath on its now sunny main streets by the sneering Thorpe, who is also something of a Count Morano, for he has stalked Catherine and temporarily kidnapped her.

With the misunderstanding about the walk clarified with the

Tilneys, Catherine plans to walk with them on another day. However, the two Thorpes and James Morland plan yet another carriage ride. Strolling with the Thorpes and her brother on the busy Royal Crescent, Catherine learns that the carriage trip is planned for the same time as her walk with the Tilneys. She refuses to change her pre-arranged appointment. Seeing the Tilneys up ahead, John Thorpe goes after them, while Isabella and James attempt to persuade, cajole, reproach, and bully Catherine into canceling her walk. A self-satisfied John Thorpe returns to the trio, announcing that he has told Eleanor that Catherine had sent him to plead "'a prior engagement'" to go driving with the Thorpes and James. "'A pretty good thought of mine—hey'" says Thorpe.

Appalled by his lie, Catherine tries to run after Eleanor Tilney and explain the truth. But again, on a busy Bath street, Catherine is held captive: "Isabella . . . caught hold of one hand, Thorpe of the other, and remonstrances poured in from all three. Even James was quite angry." Just as Emily St. Aubert was a prisoner at Udolpho, Catherine is now the captive of the Thorpe siblings on the busy Royal Crescent. Escaping at last, she is able to apologize to the Tilneys and meet Henry and Eleanor's father, General Tilney.

With James Morland off to see his parents about his planned marriage to Isabella, Captain Frederick Tilney, heir to Northanger Abbey, arrives in Bath. Isabella immediately spots a financially more lucrative catch than James. She is disappointed when James's letter arrives, informing her that his parents will be able to give them a church living of "about four hundred pounds yearly value, [which] was to be resigned to his son as soon as he should be old enough to take it" (2:1). Clearly, Isabella has been expecting more: "'It is very charming indeed,' said Isabella, with a grave face." She continues:

> "It is not on my own account I wish for more; but I cannot bear to be the means of injuring my dear Morland, making him sit down upon an income hardly enough to find one in the common necessaries of life. For myself, it is nothing; I never think of myself."

Of course, Isabella, like Mme. Cheron, thinks only of herself and is greedy to secure as high an income as she can. So Captain Tilney now looks even more attractive to Isabella, whose own family is not at all wealthy.

Meanwhile, Catherine, who is a welcome guest at the Tilneys' Bath residence, senses Eleanor's and Henry's "want of [i.e., lack of] spirits" around their father, General Tilney (2:1). But always hyper-ingratiating to Catherine, he invites her to join the family when they return to their home, Northanger Abbey, as a guest and friend for Eleanor.

Riding with Henry in his curricle at General Tilney's suggestion, Catherine is excited about going to an abbey. "'Is not it a fine old place, just like what one reads about?'" inquires "the well-read" Catherine. Henry teasingly regales Catherine by spinning a Gothic romance in which she is the heroine whose adventures follow Emily's in *The Mysteries of Udolpho*. As Henry says, "'*The Mysteries of Udolpho*, when I had once begun it, I could not lay down again;—I remember finishing it in two days—my hair standing on end the whole time.'"

Full of mysterious objects, suspicious rooms, and its own talkative Dorothée, Anglicized to Dorothy, Henry's Gothic romance arouses Catherine's fertile imagination with what she will find at his family's abbey. Although she begs him to continue the tale, "Henry was too much amused by the interest he had raised to be able to carry it farther; he could no longer command solemnity either of subject or voice." Poor Catherine does not share Henry's sense of irony.

Arriving at the Abbey, which is, of course, modernized and brightly lit, Catherine is disappointed at the difference between her expectations and reality: Northanger is as far from a gloomy abbey in a Gothic romance as John Thorpe's Blaize Castle is from the Castle of Udolpho. But with the help of a proverbial dark and stormy night, as well as an imagination primed by Henry's carriage story and her own reading of *Udolpho*, she finds overnight adventure when she spots in her room a seemingly mysterious cabinet that she cannot unlock. What a letdown when she finds out the next morning that the cabinet was actually unlocked and contained only a laundry list from a previous guest.

Still suspicious of the overly-solicitous General Tilney, who peculiarly boasts in a self-deprecating way about his china and furniture, she notices his angry outbursts, strictness about the dinner hour, authoritarian nature, lone walks, and the way Henry and Eleanor continue to appear more subdued around him. Catherine thinks that Mrs. Tilney is imprisoned somewhere in the Abbey and that the General is a guilty husband like Montoni. Fueled by these suspicions, she longs to inspect Mrs. Tilney's bedroom to look for clues, expecting that she may be suffering the way Mme. Montoni does in *Udolpho*.

When she has the chance to go sleuthing, she is embarrassed to be discovered by a returning Henry Tilney, who chastises her for her suspicions with his famous patriotic speech:

> "Dear Miss Morland, consider the dreadful nature of the suspicions you have entertained. What have you been judging from? Remember the country and the age in which we live. Remember that we are English, that we are Christians."

Although she is ashamed of her suspicions about the General's murdering his wife, she is correct in wondering about his personality and its peculiar effects on Eleanor and Henry. Something is rotten at Northanger Abbey: greed. For when General Tilney returns unexpectedly from a trip to London, he angrily orders Eleanor to banish Catherine from the Abbey early the next morning. (Notice that the General sends his daughter on this mission.) He has arranged for Catherine to go on her 70-mile trip home without an escort by public post-chaise: a chaise, which carried four passengers, was a carriage with no seat for the driver, but rather had a post-boy riding the left-hand horse. Going by post meant traveling from one post station to the next, about 10 to 15 miles apart; a person traveling by post could get on and off anytime. Sending a young lady alone on a trip like this was an insult: decorum dictated that she should have traveled in General Tilney's private carriage with a male servant escorting her.

The General is angry and vengeful, though his target of anger should not be Catherine, but John Thorpe because he fell for his lies in Bath and then in London. In Bath, Thorpe, thinking he would marry Catherine, lied to the General, exaggerating her wealth through both the Morlands and the Allens:

> Thorpe's vanity induced him to represent the family as yet more wealthy than his vanity and avarice had made him believe them. With whomsoever he was, or was likely to be connected, his own consequence always required that theirs should be great, and as his intimacy with any acquaintance grew, so regularly grew their fortune. (2:15)

Then in London the General again met John Thorpe, now angry and vengeful because not only had Catherine disappointed him in his self-created "engagement" to her, but her brother, James Morland, broke his engagement with Isabella because of her outrageous flirtation with Captain Frederick Tilney, who has since gone his own way, leaving Isabella without any marriage prospects. The susceptible General believes Thorpe's next round of lies that slander the Morlands as "a necessitous family" and scheming social climbers, a description that ironically fits the Thorpes. John Thorpe is a buffoon villain.

While General Tilney is neither a wife-torturer nor a murderer, he is as financially greedy and manipulative as Signor Montoni. And the General is even more gullible than Catherine about John Thorpe's stories, for he cannot see through Thorpe's bluster, while she can.

Catherine's experiences have given her more confidence in her own judgment because her intuition about the General proved true. She marries Henry, whose father relents after Eleanor marries the young man who left his laundry list in the guest room; he is suddenly and unexpectedly elevated to a viscountcy with all the prestige and wealth that General Tilney desires. (So much for Henry's assertion that "'we are English, that we are Christians.'") Greed, bullies, lies, hypocrisy, and revenge are as rife in Catherine's England as they were in the 16th-century Italy imagined by Ann Radcliffe.

Besides parodying *The Mysteries of Udolpho*, *Northanger Abbey* contains Austen's overt, spirited, and much-discussed defense of the novel–reminding us that 18th-century novels, with their crumbling Gothic castles or tear-covered pages of sensibility, were viewed with suspicion. In her famous defense (1:5), Austen presents a scenario about a young woman caught in the act of reading a novel:

> [T]here seems almost a general wish of decrying the capacity and undervaluing the labor of the novelist, and of slighting the performances which have only genius, wit, and taste to recommend them. "I am no novel reader–I seldom look into novels–Do not imagine that I often read novels–It is really very well for a novel." Such is the common cant. "And what are you reading, Miss?–" "Oh! it is only a novel," replies the young lady; while she lays down her book with affected indifference, or momentary shame.–"It is only Cecilia, or Camilla, or Belinda;" or, in short, only some work in which the greatest powers of the mind are displayed, in which the most thorough knowledge of human nature, the liveliest effusions of wit and humour, are conveyed to the world in the best-chosen language. (1:5)

Austen condemns "that ungenerous and impolitic custom so common with novel-writers, of degrading by their contemptuous censure the very performances, to the number of which they are themselves adding." For example, Fanny Burney in *Camilla* presents a character, Mrs. Berlinton, who has been misled by reading "some common and ill selected novels and romances, which a young lady in the neighbourhood privately lent her to read." Maria Edgeworth wrote at the beginning of *Belinda*, "The following work is offered to the public as a Moral Tale–the author not wishing to acknowledge a Novel. . . . [So] much folly, error, and vice are disseminated in the books classed under this denomination. . . ." These are novelists apologizing for their novels.

Austen also defends the novel by the very act of writing one, in which "the most thorough knowledge of human nature, the liveliest effusions of wit and humour, are conveyed to the world in the best-chosen language." In this youthful work, Austen domesticates the Gothic romance and empowers the un-heroine-like Catherine, who is an ordinary English teenager of the gentry class, but one who also has an "innate principle of general integrity," as Henry recognizes (2:12).

Austen's defense of the novel in Chapter 5 does not interrupt the flow of the plot. Rather, it reminds us how to read this text. Her five subsequent works epitomize what the novel is critically defined to be: a fictional narrative of considerable length with characters and events that are more or less representative of reality. This is what differentiates the novel from the romance, with the latter allowing its author greater latitude of imagination. Sir Walter Scott praised Austen's ability to create a new kind of fiction, for "copying from nature as she really exists in the common walks of life, and presenting to the reader, instead of the splendid scenes of an imaginary world, a correct and striking representation of that which is daily taking place around him" in his famous review of *Emma*.

Mystery behind an unfinished manuscript

Between the completion of *Susan* in 1803 and her return to Hampshire in 1809, Austen wrote only one incomplete text, "The Watsons," sometime during 1803 and 1804, or possibly as late as 1807. While visiting Bath in 1799, Austen saw on June 22 the Theatre Royal's production of *Die Versöhnung* by the popular German playwright August von Kotzebue. It was adapted (and altered) for the English stage by Thomas Dibdin and performed as *The Birth-Day*; Dibdin's version of Kotzebue's play was popular among British audiences. She may have also seen the play when it was reprised in Bath in May 1803. (Jane Austen's letters skip from May 27, 1801, to September 14, 1804). *The Birth-Day* includes characters named Bertram (as in *Mansfield Park*) and Emma. Austen may have been taking mental notes for future writing. But Dibdin's adaptation also likely gave Austen some ideas for "The Watsons." Author Margaret Kirkham has shown how *The Birth-Day*'s heroine, named Emma, and her elderly, ailing father—among other similarities—influenced Austen's writing of both "The Watsons" and *Emma* (*Jane Austen, Feminism and Fiction*. London and NY, 1997).

Austen's unfinished text presents the lovely Emma Watson, the youngest of four daughters of Rev. Watson, an ailing, elderly widower. Her rich aunt has raised Emma to be a well educated, graceful, and refined young lady. However, when the aunt remarries the ne'er do well Captain O'Brien, Emma returns to the Watson home. There she is appalled at the conduct of two of her vulgar, husband-hunting sisters, especially the way they run after Tom Musgrave, social-climbing friend of the local aristocrat, the socially awkward and snobbish Lord Osborne. Emma also has two brothers, Robert, who is a solicitor and has a vulgar wife (likely a forerunner of *Emma*'s Mrs. Elton), and Sam, a surgeon, who has been in love with a Miss Edwards for two years, but does not have the money to marry her. Although differing in views about comfort (for example, going to a ball in a carriage, to which Emma is accustomed from her wealthy upbringing) versus expense (walking to the ball, as her eldest sister advises), Emma enjoys her older sister Elizabeth, who cares for their father and runs the Watson home economically. Elizabeth considers the sensible and gracious Emma "'like nobody else in the World.'" Emma also has a unique sense of integrity. Thus, Elizabeth cannot understand why Emma would say that she "'would rather teach at a school . . . than marry a Man I did not like.'"

The central action is a ball, where Emma meets the highly agreeable Rev. Howard, a gentleman clergyman; his pleasant widowed sister Mrs. Blake, and her 10-year-old son, Charles Blake,

Austen's only charming child creation. Lord Osborne, who arrives fashionably late with his mother and sister, finds Emma attractive. But he is too insecure, despite his wealth and rank, to approach her. Little Charles loves to dance and even has the proper gloves for a young gentleman; he is eagerly anticipating the dance that Miss Osborne, Lord Osborne's sister, has promised him for a week. But she unexpectedly makes her excuses to the child and goes off to dance with the dashing Colonel Beresford. Poor little Charles is mortified: "he stood the picture of disappointment, with crimson cheeks, quivering lips, and eyes bent on the floor." "Emma did not think or reflect—she felt and acted.—'I shall be very happy to dance with you sir, if you like it,' said she, holding out her hand with the most unaffected good humour." The now delighted Charles and Emma dance, passing Miss Osborne who says to him, "'Upon my word, Charles, you are in luck . . . you have got a better partner than me'; to which the happy Charles answered 'Yes.'" The wonderful scene shows us that Austen has mastered the skill of showing her characters in action through dialogue and presenting dramatic irony and irony of situation. She also demonstrates the realistic, harsh situation faced by Elizabeth and Emma Watson, as well as their sisters, because their family lacks the money to put into good marriage settlements. As gentlewomen fallen on hard times, the Watson sisters need to marry (and their choice of men is not especially attractive!) in a society where marriage is a financial negotiation as much as a romantic attachment.

According to the second edition (1871) of James Austen Leigh's *Memoir* of his aunt,

> When the author's sister, Cassandra, showed the manuscript of this work to some of her nieces, she also told them something of the intended story; for with this dear sister—though, I believe, with no one else—Jane seems to have talked freely of any work that she might have in hand. Mr. Watson was soon to die; and Emma to become dependent for a home on her narrow-minded sister-in-law

and brother. She was to decline an offer of marriage from Lord Osborne, and much of the interest of the tale was to arise from Lady Osborne's love for Mr. Howard, and his counter affection for Emma, whom he was finally to marry. (364)

Austen-Leigh included the text of "The Watsons," to which he gave this title, in this second edition of his Memoir.

Why Austen left the manuscript unfinished at 17,500 words is not known. Was she reluctant to complete it because having worked hard on Susan, she was disappointed that it was not published after sitting six years with the publisher? Or was she depressed because her own father was ailing, as was Rev. Watson? George Austen died on January 21, 1805. In 1942, literary critic Q.D. Leavis postulated that Austen simply used "The Watsons" as a precursor to Emma. Other authors, dissatisfied with its lack of development, took it upon themselves to complete "The Watsons": L. Oulton (1923), Austen's great-grandniece Edith Hubback Brown (1928), John Coates (1958), Joan Aiken (1966), and the anonymous Another (1977).

If 1807, not 1805, is the work's date of composition, as some scholars state, Austen was then living a rather nomadic life with her widowed mother and sister, moving around to various brothers' and friends' homes; this life gave her no sustained time to write. When she finally was able to settle in Chawton in 1809, early manuscripts came out and were revised, and new novels were penned: all were published. But she did not return to The Watsons.

5. Two Revisions Become Classics: *Sense and Sensibility* and *Pride and Prejudice*

O n July 9, 1809, Jane Austen settled in a roomy cottage on the Chawton estate in her native Hampshire, not far from the Steventon Rectory in which she had spent the first 20 years of her life. She was near her friends and family, no longer leading the nomadic life of the past eight years. In a letter she wrote to her brother Frank on July 26, she poetically expressed her joy about not only the recent birth of Frank and Mary Austen's son, Francis William, but also the Austen ladies' new "Chawton home." Here is the relevant excerpt from that letter:

> As for ourselves we're very well;
> As unaffected prose will tell.–
> Cassandra's pen will paint our state,
> The many comforts that await
> Our Chawton home, how much we find
> Already in it, to our mind;
> And how convinced, that when complete
> It will all other Houses beat
> That ever have been made or mended,
> With rooms concise, or rooms distended.
> You'll find us very snug next year,
> Perhaps with Charles & Fanny near,
> For now it often does delight us
> To fancy them just over-right-us.

Jane and her housemates established a routine that allowed her uninterrupted writing time. Practicing the pianoforte in the morning, she then prepared breakfast. Her household, keeping the novelist's doings a secret, gave her the freedom to write in "a room of her own"—with thanks for the phrase to Virginia Woolf who admired Austen. The cottage's front room had a large window, now bricked over, giving Austen a view of the main coach route. The hinges on the door leading into the room were reportedly kept unoiled so she could hear them squeak when the door opened and quickly conceal her manuscript. According to her nephew James Edward Austen Leigh's *Memoir* of his aunt, "she wrote upon small sheets of paper which could easily be put away, or covered with a piece of blotting paper."

In fact, James Edward, who often sat in the drawing room with his aunts and grandmother, only learned in 1814 at age 16 that his aunt Jane was the author of the recently published *Mansfield Park* and two other published novels.

Austen published her novels anonymously and never sought personal publicity. But as a practical woman, she kept careful accounts of her earnings and was conscious of her finances. As she wrote to her friend Martha Lloyd, "P&P is sold. —Egerton gives £110 for it. —I would rather have had £150, but we could not both be pleased" (Nov. 29-30, 1812). One wonders if Mary Crawford's comment in *Mansfield Park* that "A large income is the best recipe for happiness I ever heard of" was something Jane Austen seriously considered herself (MP 2:4).

Cassandra's memorandum about the novels' composition states that in November 1797, her sister began revising "Elinor and Marianne," initially drafted two years earlier. James Edward Austen-Leigh wrote in his *Memoir* that his aunt's first year at Chawton, 1809-1810, was "devoted to revising and preparing for the press" her epistolary versions of *Sense and Sensibility* and *Pride and Prejudice*, dating from the mid to late 1790s (101). However, James Edward's youngest son and grandson, William Austen-Leigh (1843-1921) and Richard Arthur Austen-Leigh (1872-1961, William's nephew), respectively, make a convincing point in their *Jane Austen: Her Life and Letters. A Family Record* (1913):

It has been usual to dwell on the precocity of intellect shown in the composition of the first two of these works by a young and inexperienced girl, and no doubt there is much justice in the observation; but we venture to think that it is in *Northanger Abbey* that we get the best example of what she could produce at the age of three-or- four-and-twenty.

They further observe that in *Northanger Abbey*, completed in 1803 according to Jane's own advertisement of the work,

> she has not quite shaken off the tendency to satirise contemporary extravagances; and it is not until several chapters are past that she settles herself down to any serious creation of characters (96).

Taking the Austen-Leighs' points seriously, I believe that Austen substantially revised "Elinor and Marianne" when she settled at Chawton. The sophistication in her handling of the second chapter's conversation between Fanny and John Dashwood, in which Fanny convinces her husband to convince himself to break his deathbed promise to his father to care for his half-sisters, is dazzling. Austen demonstrates through John and Fanny Dashwood's conjugal dialogue her mature understanding of how a shrewd wife can manipulate an irresolute spouse, allowing him to think her ideas are his. This psychological insight is not from a 20-year-old, no matter how brilliant her parody and satires are. It is clear Jane had matured since her first attempts at writing.

Austen also confidently used free indirect discourse in the novels penned at Chawton. In these works, the omniscient narrator embeds the thoughts or viewpoints of a character into the text, thus moving between the narrator telling the reader what a character is thinking and letting the reader into the character's thinking. The voice we hear is the character's rather than the narrator's, enabling the character to reveal his or her personality to us instead of the narrator's telling us about that personality. As Fanny Dashwood prepares to work on her husband, who "had meditated within himself to increase the fortunes of his sisters by the present of a thousand pounds a-piece" (1:1), Austen gives Fanny free indirect discourse that reveals the author's mature and shrewd insights about husbands and wives:

> Mrs. John Dashwood did not at all approve of what her husband intended to do for his sisters. To take three thousand pounds from the fortune of their dear little boy would be impoverishing him to the most dreadful degree. She begged him to think again on the subject. How could he answer it to himself to rob his child, and his only child too, of so large a sum? And what possible claim could the Miss Dashwoods, who were related to him only by half blood, which she considered as no relationship at all, have on his generosity to so large an amount. It was very well known that no affection was ever supposed to exist between the children of any man by different marriages; and why was he to ruin himself, and their poor little Harry, by giving away all his money to his half sisters?

By applying free indirect discourse, Austen lets the reader slip into Fanny Dashwood's head to hear her thoughts from her; the voice we hear is the character's own voice. Austen was the first English novelist to use this technique consistently in her novels, allowing us to hear and see her characters' inner lives. As a narrative device, free indirect discourse allows for irony, especially dramatic irony, where the reader knows and understands what the character does not. In the passage quoted from Chapter 2 of *Sense and Sensibility*, Fanny Dashwood may think she is protecting her little son, but readers know that she is simply cold-hearted, manipulative, and greedy.

Furthermore, unlike the allegory of sense and sensibility that appeared in *The Ladies Magazine* in 1799, Elinor Dashwood, the so-called heroine of sense, is not a flat character, representing victorious sense, any more than Marianne, the beautiful sister with a highly wrought sensibility, represents pure emotion. Austen complicates Marianne, the nominal character of sensibility, writing that "She was sensible and clever . . . she was everything but prudent." And Marianne is only 16! Austen complicates Elinor even more, saying, "She had an excellent heart; –her disposition was affectionate, and her feelings were strong; but she knew how to govern them" (1:1). She's a sensible young woman who suppresses her strong feelings. Yet ironically, despite Elinor's control of her emotions, she suffers silently for two-thirds of the novel, as much as Marianne's sensibility leads her to suffer openly. Finally admitting to Marianne that the man she loves, Edward Ferrars, is engaged to Lucy Steele and plans to marry her, Elinor confesses, "'The composure of mind with which I have brought myself at present to consider the matter, the consolation that I have been willing to admit, have been the effect of constant and painful exertion'" (3:1). The nominal heroine of sense has kept her emotional pain to herself, keeping a game face, while silently suffering all the while.

When Edward, finally free of Lucy by a Robert *ex machina* ending, comes to ask for Elinor's hand, our heroine of sense "almost ran out of the room, and as soon as the door was closed, burst into tears of joy, which at first she thought would never cease" (3:12). Her "tears of joy" represent not the lachrymosity of a novel of sensibility, but a needed release of long pent-up emotions. Poor Elinor has forced herself to play the role of unaffected confidante to Lucy Steele, who hypocritically shares with Elinor her love for and secret engagement to Edward, as well as concerns about Mrs. Ferrars' disapproval of her, all as a warning to Elinor that Edward belongs to her: "'Pity me, dear Miss Dashwood!'" begs the two-faced Lucy.

Elinor's common sense also frequently misleads her: she believes Edward's ring is made from a lock of her hair, but it's Lucy's; she thinks that Edward and Lucy will be unable to marry because he has no chance of getting a church living, but Colonel Brandon owns one and even asks Elinor to offer it to Edward. So we are dealing with a far more sophisticated novel than 1803's Northanger Abbey. Sense and Sensibility was 15 years in the making and given its polish by a mature and confident writer.

Austen's first published novel

By winter 1810, publisher Thomas Egerton accepted *Sense and Sensibility* for publication. In this novel, we see how she delivers Elinor's and Marianne's stories in a tightly constructed linear plot. Many characters enter and exit the novel, but none is gratuitous. For example, actress Emma Thompson eliminated Lady Middleton, wife of Sir John Middleton, and the little Middleton children from her Oscar-winning screenplay of *Sense and Sensibility* (1995). Did Jane Austen overpopulate her novel? Hardly.

Lady Middleton and her spoiled young children serve Austen's purposes. The Steele sisters' bringing gifts for her little sons and daughters and constantly cooing over them feed Lady Middleton's insipid and prideful personality, which is highly susceptible to flattery about herself and her children. This tells us how Lucy was able to snag Edward and foreshadows how she will be able to insert herself favorably with the prideful Mrs. Ferrars and the John Dashwoods. Further, Lady Middleton is in her late 20s, while Sir John is about Colonel Brandon's age, the mid to late 30s. The Middletons' age difference reminds readers that in Austen's day, it was common for a gentleman to be considerably older than his wife because of his need to be financially secure entering marriage: Colonel Brandon, for instance, is nearly 20 years Marianne's senior. Finally, Lady Middleton, the daughter of a London tradesman, albeit a wealthy one, married a landed baronet, gained the title "Lady," and seeks to continue to climb socially. After Willoughby's engagement to Miss Grey is announced, she "determined . . . that as Mrs. Willoughby would at once be a woman of elegance and fortune, to leave her card with her as soon as she married" (2:10). Lady Middleton thus reveals the hypocrisy that Austen saw in society. To borrow the language of Aristotle from his *Poetics*, everything and everyone "is an organic part of the whole."

The novel likewise has "unity of action." It dramatizes how a reliance on only sense (Elinor, the nominal heroine of sense suffers silently) *or* sensibility (Marianne, the nominal heroine of sensibility, publically indulges herself so deeply in grief that she suffers a near-fatal depression) needs to be corrected by a healthy balance of the two (seen in Colonel Brandon).

Right at the novel's beginning, Austen presents the heroines' situations as young gentlewomen—they are "the daughter[s] of a private gentleman" (i.e., untitled)—in a patriarchal society. The narrator informs us about old Uncle Dashwood, who promised his nephew Henry Dashwood that he, his second wife whom he married after being widowed, and three daughters (ages 13, 17, and 19 when their father dies), who had cared for the elderly uncle for the past 10 years, would succeed to Norland Park, Sussex, upon the old gentleman's death.

But charmed by the antics of the toddler son of John Dashwood (John is the son of Henry Dashwood's late first wife) and his wife Fanny Ferrars Dashwood, the old uncle abruptly alters his will so that Henry has a life interest only in Norland. Tacitly, Austen implies that by doing this, the uncle ensures that the paternal name of Dashwood will continue to reside at Norland Park.

A year after the elderly uncle's passing, Henry Dashwood, himself, is on his deathbed, extracting a promise from his wealthy son John to care for his stepmother and half-sisters. But in the brilliant conversational scene in Chapter 2, Austen demonstrates how Fanny, "even more narrow-minded and selfish" than her spineless husband, slyly brings up their son's future to help sway John to do nothing for the Dashwood females. To assert their ownership of Norland, John, Fanny, and their little boy move into the mansion with undue haste, displacing the Dashwood women who had lived there for over 10 years.

By the end of Chapter 2, as Fanny assists John's conscience in feeling guiltless about giving his half-sisters nothing, Austen sets in motion—with her characteristic irony—the immediate and realistic complication for Elinor and Marianne: these two young ladies now face the gentlewomen's problem of securing husbands to support them. John Dashwood, the new family patriarch, marginalizes the very females he had promised to help. Juvenalian satire is delivered with a cashmere-gloved fist as Austen also mocks traditional family values, where the eldest male protects the women in his life: the Dashwood ladies, instead, are left to fend for themselves.

Clearly, Jane Austen was not the pious, proper, "dear Aunt Jane" that James Austen-Leigh portrayed in his *Memoir*. When Scottish writer Margaret Oliphant reviewed the *Memoir* in 1870, she focused mostly on Jane's novels, calling attention to "the fine vein of feminine cynicism" that runs through them (*Blackwood's Edinburgh Magazine*). But it took over a century more for readers to recognize Austen's Juvenalian satire.

With Norland Park now in the hands of John Dashwood (and to be passed on to his son), Mrs. Dashwood and her girls feel pressed to leave. Her distant cousin, Sir John Middleton, invites them to rent "on very easy terms" a small cottage on his estate, Barton Park in Devonshire. Hearing that the ladies will settle in Devonshire, Edward Ferrars, Fanny Dashwood's brother, who has had no direct speech since his entry to the novel two chapters earlier, utters "'Devonshire!'" "in a voice of surprise and concern" (1:5). Elinor is not surprised to hear his exclamation, for she has been spending time with the reticent and seemingly worried Edward since his arrival at Norland. Common sense dictates to her that he is sorry to see her moving so far away from Sussex. But as we learn by the end of the first volume, prior to attending Oxford, Edward was at school in Devonshire, where he entered a secret engagement with the schoolmaster's shrewd and pretty niece, Lucy Steele.

Edward allows Elinor to think as she wishes. Her sense also misleads her about the reason for "a want of spirits about him" that she sensibly, but erroneously, attributes to his mother's unpleasant behavior towards him and her demands that he strictly attend "to her views for his aggrandizement" in his career and marriage (1:4). Satisfied with her sensible conclusion, she will be shocked when the ungrammatical Lucy Steele informs Elinor about her engagement to Edward. Ungrammatical? Readers might notice Lucy's faulty usage as in her spiteful letter to Elinor: "I know your friendship for me will make you pleased to hear such a good account of myself and my dear Edward, after all the troubles we have went through lately. . ." (3:2). Austen keeps consistency of characters in their speech and letters.

Moving to Barton Cottage, the Dashwood ladies soon realize why Sir John Middleton invited them there: he hates to be alone and does everything he can to surround himself with company. With a family of women at the cottage, his hunting grounds are safe. Staying with the Middletons is Lady Middleton's vulgar but good-hearted mother, Mrs. Jennings, a London-based "widow with an ample jointure" (an estate settled on a widow); she enjoys teasing Elinor and Marianne about their beaux. With Edward Ferrars as Elinor's supposed beau, it's time to find one for Marianne.

Despite a threatening sky, Marianne, enamored with the natural world as a self-appointed person of sensibility, goes walking on the nearby hills, along with the youngest Dashwood sister, Margaret. Of course, a storm breaks. Running down the hill for shelter, Marianne slips on the wet ground, twisting her ankle. A "gentleman carrying a gun," accompanied by two hunting dogs, appears and immediately picks her up and carries her back to the cottage. This harkens back to Valancourt's first appearance in *Udolpho*. Austen emphasizes Marianne's novel reading: her "uncommonly handsome" "preserver," as Margaret dubs him, is John Willoughby, heir to the nearby Allenham estate, whose "person and air were equal to what [Marianne's] fancy had ever drawn for the hero of a favourite story."

As discussed in Chapter 4, 18th-century essayists cautioned about the dangerous influence that novels of sensibility had on young female readers. Marianne is one such young lady. While she will not act immorally because of Willoughby—though another teenager, Eliza Williams, did—she does fall into a situational depression over him that nearly causes her death. Marianne and Willoughby spend so much time together—he claims to love everything she loves—that Elinor concludes they are secretly engaged. This is another example of Elinor's "sense" or logic misleading her. Meanwhile, Elinor hears nothing from Edward and suffers in silence.

Soon Sir John Middleton's longtime friend, Colonel Brandon, arrives. Marianne dismisses him as "an absolute old bachelor, for he was on the wrong side of five and thirty." She and Willoughby cattily criticize Brandon for looking "silent" and "grave." Thoughtfully watching the two young persons, Brandon tells Elinor, who enjoys his intelligence and sensitivity, "'I once knew a lady who in temper and mind greatly resembled your sister, who thought and judged like her,'" but then he breaks off. While this "lady" remains a mystery until Volume 2, Chapter 9, Brandon receives a letter that prompts him to ride off hastily from Barton Park to London. Lady Middleton's mother, the gossipy Mrs. Jennings, speculates that his abrupt departure has to do with his "'little love-child,'" which sets an aura of sexual mystery around the colonel. His sudden departure will also reveal why he looks "silent" and "grave" during his time at Barton.

Soon and unexpectedly, Willoughby also leaves. He is pleading "'engagements'" in London on orders from his wealthy, much older cousin Mrs. Smith, the owner of Allenham Court, a country estate he will inherit; he claims that she has "'exercised the privilege of riches'" on "'poor, dependent'" him. Willoughby's departure leaves Marianne in utter despondency. She shows no interest in anyone or anything, isolating herself at the piano to play emotionally dramatic music, including a "magnificent concerto," and behaving with no social courtesy around visitors: when Marianne suffers, everyone suffers. But she perks up when Mrs. Jennings, around whom she has been anti-social and impolite, invites Marianne and Elinor to accompany her to London and live in her townhouse. For Marianne, this means she will be near Willoughby again!

The carriage ride to London, however, is characterized by Marianne's sitting "in silence almost all the way, wrapt in her own meditations, and scarcely ever voluntarily speaking . . . . To atone for this conduct therefore, Elinor took immediate possession of the post of civility which she had assigned herself."

Once in London, Marianne immediately writes to Willoughby—a major social *faux pas* as a young lady only wrote to a gentleman if they were formally and publicly engaged. When he doesn't reply or come to see her, Marianne grows more tearful and nervous. She insists on not leaving Mrs. Jennings' house in case he visits. When she finally agrees to go out, she finds upon her return Willoughby's card on the table. As Marianne continues to agonize about Willoughby's absence, her carelessness about her appearance, anti-social behavior, low spirits, and lack of appetite cause Elinor to fear "for the health of Marianne." Today, we recognize these signs as depression, which was referred to as melancholy or a nervous disorder in Austen's time. Meanwhile, the gossipy Barton Park set agrees that Marianne and Willoughby are engaged, but they, too, do not understand Willoughby's behavior, and so they turn Marianne into a weeping heroine of sensibility.

A few days later, Marianne, now nearly catatonic, goes with Elinor and Lady Middleton to a splendid London party. There she sees Willoughby "with a very fashionable looking young woman" (2:6). When Willoughby comes over to greet them, his behavior is formal, and he speaks mostly to Elinor, forcing Marianne, "her face . . . crimsoned over," to exclaim "in a voice of the greatest emotion, 'Good God! Willoughby, what is the meaning of this? Have you not received my letters? Will you not shake hands with me?'" An embarrassed Willoughby acknowledges knowing that the Dashwood sisters were in London with Mrs. Jennings, formally bows, and returns to his companion. Leaving the party with Elinor and Lady Middleton, Marianne retires to her bedroom, unwilling to speak with anyone.

The next morning at breakfast, which she does not eat, Marianne receives a letter from Willoughby, and immediately runs to her room. It is a cold and polite apology for leading her to think that he had feelings for her, explaining that his "affections have been long engaged elsewhere" and that he will soon be married. When he said before departing Barton Cottage that he had London "engagements," he was being quite literal. His bride-to-be is Miss Sophia Grey, an heiress with £50,000. Utterly grief-stricken, Marianne finally confesses to her sister that she and Willoughby were never engaged, which shocks Elinor, based on their behavior together at Barton. Unaware of the Lucy/Edward engagement, Marianne says her only happiness is in knowing that Edward is true to Elinor, who remains stoic and silent.

That evening, Colonel Brandon arrives at Mrs. Jennings' home. He shares with Elinor the story about the "girl" of whom Marianne reminded him, as well as the background on Willoughby. The girl was his orphaned cousin Eliza, who came to live at Delaford, the Brandon estate. The young Brandon and Eliza soon fell in love: her affection for him was as "'fervent as the attachment of your sister to Mr. Willoughby'" (2:9). But Brandon's father insisted that she marry his ne'er do well elder son, as the Delaford estate needed Eliza's money to stay afloat. Planning to elope, the young couple are caught and stopped. Brandon's father forced the 17-year-old Eliza (same age as Marianne) into a loveless marriage with her elder male cousin, the heir to Delaford, and Brandon, the younger brother, was sent away. He joined a regiment in the East Indies, trusting that Eliza's love for him will enable her to endure her forced marriage. But soon young Eliza, pressured by her husband's faithlessness, also committed adultery, leading to shameful divorce proceedings brought against her by her husband just two years after their marriage. (In Austen's day, when a woman was guilty of adultery, her husband divorced her, took all her money, and even prevented her from ever seeing their children. The divorcee was an outcast, while an adulterous husband was guiltless.) "'It was *that* which threw this gloom'" on him, confessed Brandon. He had expected more of Eliza. His sensibility is genuine and causes his silence and gravity.

Three years after the divorce, Brandon returned to England and found Eliza, dying in a sponging house with her little girl, also named Eliza, whom we will call Eliza Jr.: a sponging house, usually the bailiff's residence, was where debtors were placed before being sent to jail. Brandon took care of Eliza Jr., placing her at school. After the death of his debauched elder brother, Brandon assumed ownership of Delaford, where Eliza Jr. visited him on school holidays, arousing suspicion in the gossipy world that she was Brandon's "'little love child.'"

When Eliza Jr. turned 14, Brandon placed her with a respectable woman in Dorsetshire who also looked after other young ladies. (This is what Darcy does with Georgiana in *Pride and Prejudice*, and it was common practice.) He berates himself for granting Eliza's request to accompany a girlfriend to Bath, where the friend's father was staying for his health. There she met Willoughby, and the result of their relationship was the reason Brandon hurriedly left Barton Park in October. For "eight long months," Colonel Brandon heard nothing from his ward, until her letter arrived, informing him that she was pregnant by Willoughby, about whom Brandon says:

> "he had already done that, which no man who *can* feel for another would do. He had left the girl whose youth and innocence he had seduced, in a situation of the utmost distress, with no creditable home, no help, no friends, ignorant of his address! He had left her, promising to return; he neither returned, nor wrote, nor relieved her."

Notice how Austen has Brandon impugn Willoughby's false show of sensibility: "'he had already done that, which no man who can feel for another would do.'"

After Eliza Jr. had delivered her baby in London, the Colonel arranged for her and the child to live in the country. To Elinor's horror, the Colonel and Willoughby dueled, but neither was wounded. In having a sexual relationship outside of marriage, Eliza Jr. had replicated her mother's conduct.

Brandon also explains why he had not told anyone of Willoughby's treatment of Eliza Jr.: "'I would not have suffered myself to trouble you with this account of my family afflictions, with a recital which may seem to have been intended to raise myself at the expense of others'" (2:9). With the Colonel's permission, Elinor tells the story of the two Elizas to Marianne, who "felt the loss of Willoughby's character yet more heavily than she had felt the loss of his heart." Marianne, whose health continues to decline, still finds consolation in believing that Edward is true to Elinor, who is ever silent about her knowledge of his engagement to Lucy Steele.

Lucy, her elder sister Anne, and Edward arrive in London. Lucy visits Mrs. Jennings' home, and in a scene that uncomfortably places Lucy, Elinor, and Edward together in a room, Lucy reiterates to Elinor her ownership of Edward. Encounters with Edward's mother through the John Dashwoods' subsequent arrival in London (Fanny Dashwood, remember, is Edward's sister) make it clear that Mrs. Ferrars will not accept Elinor as a bride for Edward. She insults her in any way she can. Thin, small, and sour-faced, Mrs. Ferrars has her eye on the Honourable Miss Morton, daughter of Lord Morton. Although Miss Morton and Edward have never met, she could bring not only an aristocratic lineage, but also £30,000 to the marriage settlement.

Lucy's cunning flattery secures the moneyless Steele sisters an invitation to live with Mr. and Mrs. John Dashwood at their London house, where Mrs. Ferrars is also residing. Seeing how kind the John Dashwoods and Mrs. Ferrars are to Lucy and herself, the over-confident but naïve Anne Steele blurts out the secret of Lucy and Edward's engagement.

Hysteria ensues, with Mrs. Ferrars not only disinheriting, but also disowning Edward, casting him off forever when Edward says he will honor his engagement to Lucy. During these episodes, Marianne's health continues to decline. Consequently, it is decided that she and her sister should travel with Mrs. Jennings and Colonel Brandon to Cleveland. It is the estate of Mrs. Jennings' other son-in-law, Mr. Palmer, who is married to her younger daughter Charlotte. The Palmers are set to return home with their new baby boy. This move will bring the Dashwood sisters closer to their home at Barton.

At Cleveland, Marianne goes walking on the estate's long wet grass after a rainstorm; she comes in and neglects to change her stockings. With wet feet in wet stockings (a Regency medical diagnosis), she soon becomes so sick that the local apothecary utters the frightening word "infection." Growing increasingly feverish, Marianne is now in a condition that worries everyone at Cleveland. Fearful of infection spreading to their newborn child, the Palmers leave their own home for safety. The kindly, if gossipy Mrs.

Jennings insists on staying to help Elinor nurse Marianne. Colonel Brandon rides off to Barton Cottage to escort Marianne and Elinor's mother to Cleveland, for Marianne has been rambling in her fever about mama. Again, Brandon is helping a fallen woman—but this time, Marianne has fallen into a fever. The apothecary returns to try one more remedy and leaves hoping it will help her.

On another proverbial dark and stormy night, Elinor, the only person still awake at Cleveland, hears a carriage outside. Thinking it must be Colonel Brandon and her mother, she finds Willoughby at the door: again, she faces a surprise to her sensible thinking. Hearing in London from Sir John Middleton that Marianne "'was dying of a putrid fever at Cleveland,'" Willoughby rushed off to see her and insists on telling Elinor his story, in which he attempts to exonerate himself. He claims to picture Marianne "'dying—and dying too, believing me the greatest villain upon earth, scorning, hating me in her latest moments.'" With splendid dramatic irony, Willoughby foregrounds himself in Marianne's dying thoughts even as readers know that her feverish talk was of her mama.

In a rather showy oration, Willoughby, "in liquor," as Elinor realizes, emphasizes his misery. He admits to toying with Marianne's affections initially as an amusement to his vanity. But soon growing attached to her, he decides he will "'openly assure her of his affection.'" Before he has the opportunity, however, he is confronted by his elderly cousin Mrs. Smith, who had, as Willoughby says, "been informed by some distant relation, whose interest it was to deprive me of her favour" (not Colonel Brandon as many suppose, as Brandon is not related, even distantly, to Mrs. Smith), of his involvement with Eliza Jr. The tone of Willoughby's words conveys egocentric self-righteousness as if Mrs. Smith is a prudish goody-goody:

> "In the height of her morality, good woman! she offered to forgive the past, if I would marry Eliza. That could not be—and I was formally dismissed from her favour and her house."

The content of his words reminds us of his greed. He heads to London, where he marries Miss Grey, heiress to a £50,000 fortune (2:8), which gives her an annual income of £2,500 through the 5% investment in government bonds (Comparatively, Marianne has £1,000, giving her an income of £50 per annum.) Willoughby then admits that at the London party,

> "I had seen Marianne's sweet face as white as death.–*That* was the last, last look I ever had of her;–the last manner in which she appeared to me. It was a horrid sight!–yet when I thought of her to-day as really dying, it was a kind of comfort to me to imagine that I knew exactly how she would appear to those, who saw her last in this world."

These words suggest that Willoughby thinks Marianne is dying of unrequited love for him and finds it oddly comforting.

He even contemplates his wife's death, thus freeing him for Marianne, which Elinor discourages. He asks Elinor to "'Tell [Marianne] of my misery and my penitence–tell her that my heart was never inconstant to her, and if you will, that at this moment she is dearer to me than ever.'" His story is so effective that even Elinor winds up feeling sorry for Willoughby, who then leaves Cleveland.

With the arrival of Colonel Brandon and Mrs. Dashwood, Marianne apologizes to the Colonel for her thoughtless behavior towards him. She recovers and is able to return to Barton Cottage with her mother and sister, escorted by Brandon, who then leaves for Delaford.

With the four Dashwood ladies now all home at the cottage, their servant tells them that during an errand to Exeter, he saw Lucy Steele and her husband Mr. Ferrars in a carriage. Assuming that he speaks of Edward, Elinor silently acknowledges "in spite of herself, she had always admitted a hope, while Edward remained single, that something would occur to prevent his marrying Lucy" (3:12, another example of free indirect discourse). So Elinor and the others are, of course, shocked when Edward rides up to the cottage. He explains that the Mr. Ferrars married to Lucy is his brother Robert. Learning that Edward had been disinherited, Lucy set her sights on the newly deemed elder son and heir and succeeded in marrying him. Hearing this, Elinor runs out of the room and bursts into tears, reminding the reader of the painful self-control she has exercised over her feelings.

After Robert's elopement with Lucy, Mrs. Ferrars temporarily disinherited and disowned both her sons. As the narrator ironically observes:

> Her family had of late been exceedingly fluctuating. For many years of her life she had had two sons; but the crime and annihilation of Edward a few weeks ago, had robbed her of one; the similar annihilation of Robert had left her for a fortnight without any; and now, by the resuscitation of Edward, she had one again.

Relenting after a while, Mrs. Ferrars bestows £10,000 on Edward, just as she did for Fanny when she married John Dashwood. Edward and Elinor marry and settle happily at the Delaford Parsonage. Lucy's artful flattery of her mother-in-law eventually triumphs as it had with Edward, Robert, Lady Middleton and Fanny Dashwood: Lucy and Robert are admitted to Mrs. Ferrars' highest favor.

Colonel Brandon marries Marianne, who "could never love by halves"–something Willoughby hears "with a pang." For many years, Austen scholars expressed dissatisfaction with this marriage, especially as the narrator has Elinor thinking that Marianne is the Colonel's "reward," making it sound as if Marianne is a sacrificial object. I am pleased to note that since my 2005-article, "'The Amiable Prejudices of a Young [Writer's] Mind': The Problems of *Sense and Sensibility*," readers have acknowledged that Colonel Brandon is the balanced hero of the book–a soldier, a dueler, a rescuer of fallen women (damsels who truly are in distress), and a gentleman who demonstrates the desirable balance of sense and sensibility. He has the self-confidence not to cause a fuss when gossips like Mrs. Jennings talk about young Eliza as his "'little love-child.'" And he is a true man of feeling. Colonel Brandon is, in fact, the "hero of a favourite story" that Marianne had fantasized. (My article about the novel is accessible online at http://www.jasna.org/persuasions/on-line/vol26no1/ray.htm.) While Austen was proofreading *Sense and Sensibility* and staying at their brother Henry's home in London to be near her publisher, she wrote to her sister on 25 April 1811, "No, indeed, I am never too busy to think of S. and S. I can no more forget it, than a mother can forget her sucking child." She also mentions that Mrs. Knight, Edward's adopted mother, is anxious to read the novel.

Published at the end of October 1811, *Sense and Sensibility* was advertised several times in London's *Morning Chronicle* with small headlines reading "Extraordinary Novel" and "Interesting Novel." Both reviews, in *The Critical Review* (Feb. 1812) and *The British Critic* (May 1812), were lengthy (mostly plot summary) and favorable.

From Norland Park to Pemberley

With *Sense and Sensibility* in press in 1810, the following year was very busy for the novelist. Cassandra recalled that her sister began *Mansfield Park* "sometime around" February 1811 and finished it "soon after June 1813"; this was the first novel she completely conceived and composed at Chawton. According to Jane's April 1811 letter to her sister, in the spring she was in London at Henry's house correcting page proofs for her first published novel.

By the end of May, she was back in Chawton. And in fall/winter 1811, she started revising another manuscript from her early 20s, *First Impressions*, under its new title *Pride and Prejudice*. As observed in Chapter 1, Austen was at this time handling three novels at once—proofing *Sense and Sensibility* for its Oct. 1811 publication date, starting her revisions of *First Impressions* as *Pride and Prejudice*, and composing *Mansfield Park*.

Austen likely changed the title of her early Darcy/Elizabeth manuscript because of the publication in 1800 of *First Impressions*;

or, *The Portrait* by Margaret Holford. *The Critical Review* (June 1801) said of this novel, "there is nothing reprehensible in 'First Impressions' except its bulk." The cited "bulk" of Holford's novel is thought-provoking relative to Austen's revisions of her *First Impressions*. For if Jane's father was correct in saying in his letter of 1797 to the publisher Cadell that the *First Impressions* he was offering was "about the length of Miss Burney's *Evelina*," then Austen made extensive cuts in her revision that we read today. While still comprised of three volumes, as was *Evelina*, *Pride and Prejudice* is about one-third *Evelina*'s length. (Novels comprised of three volumes, such as *Pride and Prejudice* and *Emma*, were known as "triple-deckers," a popular form for publishing fiction through the 19th-century, and not to be confused with a trilogy. Publishing a single novel in three volumes was a commercial idea: a reader could borrow volume 1 from a circulating library, while another could borrow vols. 2 and 3, thus increasing readership.)

As with Austen's other completed novels, we have no manuscripts with which to compare the *Pride and Prejudice* that she sold in the autumn of 1812 to Egerton for £110. It was published as "by the author of *Sense and Sensibility*" on January 28, 1813. She changed it from the original epistolary format, but it is interesting to note that 20 letters conveying important information remain in the novel in its present form.

We read about some letters, but read others with the character-recipient. The most important letter that Austen handled the latter way is Darcy's lengthy letter to Elizabeth: this letter gets its own chapter, and we read it through as she reads it, without interruption from Elizabeth's reactions (2:12). This allows readers to reach their own conclusions about Darcy, whom we've been judging and misjudging through Elizabeth's perspective, which has been heavily shaded because he "mortified" her "pride" at the Meryton Assembly. She overheard Darcy telling Bingley that she was not pretty enough to be his dancing partner—an ironic admission from Elizabeth because she views him as the prideful one (1:5). Elizabeth's responses to the letter come only in Chapter 13.

Elizabeth Bennet is Jane Austen's most popular heroine for many reasons. She is lively, athletic, and witty, and she has a strong sense of self, which at first leads her into conflict with Darcy. She does not dance pirouettes of admiration around him in the style of Caroline Bingley. When Mr. Collins refuses to believe that she is rejecting his marriage proposal, she asks him to consider her "a rational creature" (1:19). This is the same phrasing as Mary Wollstonecraft used in Chapter 12 of her *Vindication of the Right of Woman* (1792)–"make women rational creatures." No wonder Darcy admires Elizabeth "'For the liveliness of [her] mind'" (3:18).

Sir Frank MacKinnon, an English lawyer and High Court Judge, had a great avocational interest in 18-century British literature. His book of entertaining essays, *On Circuit 1924-1937* (Cambridge Univ. Press, 1940), covering his legal career, cases, and travel around the circuit, includes a section on his visit to an area he determined was the original for the estate for *Mansfield Park*. A good friend of R.W. Chapman, long deemed the father of modern Jane Austen scholarship, MacKinnon also looked for a "dramatic date" for *Mansfield Park*. He studied the ascertainable dates given in that novel in terms of calendars and almanacs from the years around the time Austen was writing. Chapman, the first professional scholar to edit Austen's novels, accepted MacKinnon's method and applied it to *Pride and Prejudice*, noting her "punctilious observation of 1811 and 1812" calendars for plotting her revision. As Chapman states in the "Introductory Note" to his Oxford University Press (1923) edition of the novel, "[S]o intricate a chronological scheme cannot have been patched on to an existing work without extensive revision." While scholars have since queried MacKinnon and Chapman's methodology, *Simply Austen* is not the place for such debate. But it makes sense to me.

Receiving her copy of the novel on January 27, 1813, Austen wrote to Cassandra two days later, "I have got my own darling child from London." Recounting to her sister (who was at the Steventon Rectory with the James Austens) a visit from their friend Miss Benn that same day, Austen wrote that "in the evening we fairly set at it [the book], and read half the first vol. to her, prefacing that having intelligence from Henry that such a work would appear," they asked him to send a copy to Chawton. "It passed with her unsuspected," noted the coy novelist, who desired public anonymity. Miss Benn, she continued, "really does seem to admire Elizabeth. I must confess that I think her as delightful a creature as ever appeared in print."

The cleverest and second eldest of the five Bennet daughters, ranging in age from Jane (23) to Lydia (16), Elizabeth and her sisters face the typical problem of Regency gentlewomen: finding husbands to support them. The Bennet home, Longbourn, is entailed on male heirs, and so Mr. Bennet's distant cousin, the obtuse Rev. Mr. Collins, will succeed him. The brilliant first chapter, rendered nearly entirely through a conversation between Mr. and Mrs. Bennet, begins with one of the most famous opening lines in all of British literature, "It is a truth universally acknowledged, that a single man in possession of a good fortune must be in want of a wife." A knowing qualifier follows this axiom:

> However little known the feelings or views of such a man may be on his first entering a neighbourhood, this truth is so well fixed in the minds of the surrounding families, that he is considered as the rightful property of some one or other of their daughters.

Austen's use of the word "property" serves a twofold purpose: it reduces the single man to an object to be purchased (remember the marriage settlements from the "Introduction") by one of "the surrounding families" with marriageable daughters, and it reminds us that gentry families sought gentry husbands, men of property, for their daughters.

Appropriately, the first line of dialogue that follows is Mrs. Bennet's asking her husband if he is aware of what has finally occurred at a neighboring property, "'My dear Mr. Bennet . . . have you heard that Netherfield Park is let at last?'" Even better for Mrs. Bennet's purposes, she continues, "'Netherfield is taken by a young man of large fortune from the north of England.'" She is determined that this young man will become the property of one of her daughters, especially the eldest and most beautiful Jane or the youngest and liveliest Lydia. Why is the first line of dialogue appropriate for Mrs. Bennet? She has five daughters of marriageable age living on an estate that is entailed on Mr. Collins.

Mr. Benet wryly offers his "hearty consent" to Bingley's marrying any of his daughters, but adds, "'I must throw in a good word for my little Lizzy.'" Lizzy is his favorite because she "'has something more of quickness than her sisters.'" She is her mother's least favorite. The narrative voice ends the chapter:

> Mr. Bennet was so odd a mixture of quick parts, sarcastic humour, reserve, and caprice, that the experience of three and twenty years had been insufficient to make his wife understand his character. Her mind was less difficult to develope. She was a woman of mean understanding, little information, and uncertain temper. When she was discontented, she fancied herself nervous. The business of her life was to get her daughters married; its solace was visiting and news.

Here the reader, who is apt to agree with whatever Austen's affable narrative voice says, needs to use her own critical reading skills. In 3:8, the same narrator reports:

> When first Mr. Bennet had married, economy was held to be perfectly useless; for, of course, they were to have a son. This son was to join in cutting off the entail, as soon as he should be of age, and the widow and younger children would by that means be provided for. Five daughters successively entered the world, but yet the son was to come; and Mrs. Bennet, for many years after Lydia's birth, had been certain that he would. This event had at last been despaired of, but it was then too late to be saving. Mrs. Bennet had no turn for economy, and her husband's love of independence had alone prevented their exceeding their income.

With £5,000 settled on Mrs. Bennet and her daughters from the marriage settlement, each daughter would likely have just £1,000 upon marriage, just as Marianne Dashwood had. In a society where marriage had heavy financial considerations and with an entailed Longbourn, Mrs. Bennet's "business" of getting "her daughters married" is a serious one, indeed.

In the first volume of *Pride and Prejudice*, four single men arrive in the Bennets' village of Meryton: Fitzwilliam Darcy, Charles Bingley, George Wickham, and William Collins. All but one, Bingley, will come into direct conflict with Meryton's cleverest daughter, Elizabeth Bennet, and Darcy will have the greatest clash with her.

The Meryton neighborhood meets the new renter of Netherfield, the pleasant Mr. Bingley, when he and his companions arrive at the Meryton Assembly, a local evening of dance for which attendees buy tickets. Bingley is attracted to the most beautiful girl in the room, Jane Bennet, while his sisters make catty remarks about the country folk. But all attention soon focuses on Bingley's friend Mr. Darcy with "his fine, tall person, handsome features, noble mien; and the report, which was in general circulation within five minutes after his entrance, of his having ten thousand a year." Austen has not lost her talent for dropping the other shoe as she demonstrated early on in "Jack and Alice" when she wrote, "the remains of a very handsome face" at the end of a clause similar to "and the report which was in general circulation within five minutes after his entrance, of his having ten thousand a year."

Soon, however, the community turns against Darcy because he refuses to dance with any of the young ladies who are without partners. And when Bingley good-naturedly encourages his friend to dance, particularly with one of Jane Bennet's sisters, "'sitting down just behind you, who is very pretty, and I dare say very agreeable,'" Darcy utters the line that will sting Elizabeth and determine her hostile attitude towards its speaker for most of the novel:

"Which do you mean?" and turning round, he looked for a

moment at Elizabeth, till catching her eye, he withdrew his own and coldly said, "She is tolerable; but not handsome enough to tempt *me*; and I am in no humour at present to give consequence to young ladies who are slighted by other men."

Although Elizabeth jokes at the ball about Darcy's rejection of her, she admits to her best friend Charlotte, "'I could easily forgive his pride, if he had not mortified mine'" (1:5). The major conflict is established, and only an epiphany for both hero and heroine will resolve it.

While Bingley and Jane are attracted to each other and are perfect companions, his snobbish sisters do their best to discourage him because of her mother's family background: her father was a country attorney, and her brother, Mr. Gardiner, is in trade in London. Of course, the Bingley sisters, Caroline and the married Louisa Hurst, conveniently forget that their fortunes come from their father's business in the north of England, where the manufacturing cities were located, and that their northern accents have been corrected by their attendance at "one of the first private seminaries in town [London]" (1:4). The two women also think that their brother should marry Darcy's younger sister, Georgiana, which could lead to Darcy's marrying Caroline Bingley. Darcy also discourages Bingley's interest in Jane, simply because her calm and placid demeanor does not indicate her interest in him, a point that Charlotte Lucas will also note to her best friend, Elizabeth. As Darcy will later confess, he had often seen Bingley attracted to pretty young ladies.

But Darcy, in spite of his pride and his prejudice against her vulgar mother and youngest sister, Lydia—notice as you read this novel how pride and prejudice, both good and bad, affect both hero and heroine in different ways and that Austen is not giving us flat, one-dimensional characters—observes Elizabeth over a period of weeks and finds himself attracted to her beautiful eyes and lively intelligence. She is oblivious to this, thinking of Darcy only as the man who rejected her as not pretty enough for a dancing partner. The two have additional chances to interact when Jane, sent by her mother by horseback on a threatening day to a luncheon at Netherfield, becomes ill and must remain there ("'it seems likely to rain; and then you must stay all night'")–Mrs. Bennet certainly knows how to place her daughters in proposable situations. A day or two later, Elizabeth walks across the fields to see her sister–a walk "at a quick pace" that includes "jumping over stiles and springing over puddles with impatient activity" (1:7).

In the Netherfield drawing room, she amuses herself by observing how Caroline Bingley tries to arouse Darcy's attention by reading the second volume of the book of which he is reading the first and by praising his handwriting as he writes a letter. Watching Darcy watch Elizabeth, Caroline utters little insults about Elizabeth to him, thinking she will discourage any interest he has in her. In the evening conversations, Elizabeth maintains her stand and refuses to dance with Darcy when Caroline Bingley plays the pianoforte. Elizabeth has a sufficient sense of self-worth not to fall at Darcy's feet just because he is handsome and wealthy, but her hurt pride at his insult at Meryton causes her to play Miss Pert with him for two-thirds of the novel.

Her pride still chaffing from Darcy's refusal to dance with her, Elizabeth is flattered by the attentions of a new visitor to the village, the handsome Mr. Wickham, who soon joins the local militia. She notices that when Darcy and Wickham see each other in the village, "Both changed colour, one looked white, the other red" (1:15). Isn't that sentence delightfully ambiguous?

Wickham soon explains this curious incident at a party at the home of Elizabeth's aunt, Mrs. Phillips. There are many young ladies with vacant chairs next to them, but he chooses to sit next to and converse with Elizabeth. She finds this attention flattering. But she doesn't know Wickham's attention to her is deliberate because he saw her witness his odd meeting with Darcy in the village. A fluent and congenial speaker, Wickham explains that he knew Darcy when they were boys because his late father worked for Darcy's father as an estate steward at Pemberley. With a total lack of suspicion about Wickham and much prejudice against Darcy, Elizabeth listens to Wickham's story. He convincingly tells her about being raised with Darcy and being Darcy's father's favorite, which made Darcy jealous of him. He goes on to say that he received a pledge from the late Mr. Darcy to aid his career by giving him a church living, a pledge that the proud and temperamental Darcy broke upon his father's death, because he saw Wickham was extravagant, irresponsible, and imprudent. He also tells Elizabeth that Darcy exhibits, "brotherly pride" in his younger sister, Georgiana. When Elizabeth enquires about her, Wickham replies, shaking his head,

> "I wish I could call her amiable. It gives me pain to speak ill of a Darcy. But she is too much like her brother, —very, very proud. —As a child, she was affectionate and pleasing, and extremely fond of me; and I have devoted hours and hours to her amusement. But she is nothing to me now. She is a handsome girl, about fifteen or sixteen, and, I understand, highly accomplished." (1:16)

As Elizabeth listens, she wonders how a pleasant and congenial Bingley could befriend a proud and arrogant Darcy. (Actually, Darcy is not a total social snob as Bingley's father was in trade, while Darcy's ancestors were long-established gentry and on his mother's side, nobility: if Darcy were an elitist, he would not be in the company of the Bingleys.) By the time Wickham and Elizabeth part company, she is sympathetic toward him, while her animosity toward Darcy is heightened. When Elizabeth shares Wickham's story with Jane, her sister takes a more temperate view: "'It is, in short, impossible for us to conjecture the causes or circumstances which may have alienated them, without actual blame on either side. . . . One does not know what to think.'" (1:17). "'I beg your pardon; —one knows exactly what to think,'" replies the adamant Elizabeth, for Wickham's version reinforces her own perception of

Darcy, which is still colored by his insulting refusal to dance with her several weeks earlier at the Meryton Assembly.

A few evenings later, at Bingley's Netherfield Ball, Elizabeth looks for Wickham, hoping to dance with him. She is surprised that he is nowhere to be seen, even though he has been invited, and he had said to her with bravado at her Aunt Phillips' party, "'It is not for *me* to be driven away by Mr. Darcy. If *he* wishes to avoid seeing *me*, he must go.'" She is taken by even greater surprise when Darcy asks her to dance, and she accepts, but berates herself for, as she confides to Charlotte, dancing with a man she is determined to hate.

Standing opposite each other in their dancing positions, Elizabeth breaks the silence, "fancying that it would be the greater punishment to her partner to oblige him to talk." She observes that private balls (the Netherfield Ball) are more pleasant than public balls (the Meryton Assembly): she can't resist going back to the evening, a month earlier, when Darcy insulted her. She then tells him that they are very similar, each of "'an unsocial, taciturn disposition, unwilling to speak, unless we expect to say something that will amaze the whole room, and be handed down to posterity with all the éclat of a proverb.'"

Soon, "unable to resist the temptation, [she] added, 'When you met us [in Meryton] the other day, we had just been forming a new acquaintance.'" "The effect was immediate. A deeper shade of hauteur overspread his features, but he said not a word." But he soon replies, "in a constrained manner, 'Mr. Wickham is blessed with such happy manners as may ensure his *making* friends—whether he may be equally capable of *retaining* them, is less certain.'" As their dialogue continues, Elizabeth takes personal delight in taunting Darcy, paying him back for his insulting behavior at the Meryton Assembly. She claims to him that she "is trying to make" out his character, but Darcy is gaining a real understanding of hers. So when their dance ends, and they part company, they are "on each side dissatisfied, though not to an equal degree, for in Darcy's breast there was a tolerable powerful feeling towards her, which soon procured her pardon, and directed all his anger against another." He is far more generous than Elizabeth could ever believe.

With the Bingley party off to London, Jane feels that her relationship with Bingley is ending, though Elizabeth, prejudiced in Jane's favor, tries to assure her that while his sister Caroline is trying to break them up, Bingley is as much in love with Jane as he ever was.

The departure of the Bingley group opens the stage for the Christmas arrival from London of Mr. and Mrs. Gardiner, Mrs. Bennet's younger brother- and sister-in-law about whom the Bingley sisters snickered because they live "'somewhere near'" a business in a commercial district in London. The Gardiners are a charming couple with young children; films of the novel depict them in their late 40s or early 50s, but Mrs. Gardiner is likely in her early 30s, and her husband is a bit older. The narrator states that Mr. Gardiner was a:

> sensible, gentlemanlike man, greatly superior to his sister, as well by nature as education. The Netherfield ladies would have had difficulty in believing that a man who lived by trade, and within view of his own warehouses, could have been so well bred and agreeable. Mrs. Gardiner, who was several years younger than Mrs. Bennet and Mrs. Philips, was an amiable, intelligent, elegant woman, and a great favourite with all her Longbourn nieces. Between the two eldest and herself especially, there subsisted a very particular regard. They had frequently been staying with her in town.

A tradesman, as Mr. Bingley Sr. was, Mr. Gardiner lives in Cheapside, which, as we saw in the Introduction, was a fashionable shopping neighborhood.

When Darcy meets the Gardiners at Pemberley, Elizabeth thinks, "He takes them now for people of fashion" (3:1). Austen's treatment of the Gardiners reminds us that she was keenly aware of England's changing social strata through the effects of the early industrial revolution. The word "gentleman" was starting to extend in application from the gentry to polite, intelligent businessmen like Edward Gardiner. While the Bingley sisters desire to hide their Northern English trade roots and are ambitious for their brother to buy an estate to gentrify the family, the Gardiners are rightly confident in their personal worth.

About 10 years prior to her marriage to Edward Gardiner, Mrs. Gardiner lived for "a considerable time" in the town of Lambton, near Darcy's Derbyshire estate, Pemberley, which she has seen. She has also heard of Darcy's father, and after hearing Elizabeth's praise of Wickham, she observes him carefully and chats with him about Pemberley and the Darcy family. Before leaving for home, though, Mrs. Gardiner "punctually and kindly" cautions her favorite niece about being attracted to Wickham:

> "You are too sensible a girl, Lizzy, to fall in love merely because you are warned against it; and, therefore, I am not afraid of speaking openly. Seriously, I would have you be on your guard. Do not involve yourself, or endeavour to involve him in an affection which the want of fortune would make so very imprudent. I have nothing to say against *him*; he is a most interesting young man; and if he had the fortune he ought to have, I should think you could not do better. But as it is—you must not let your fancy run away with you. You have sense, and we all expect you to use it. Your father would depend on *your* resolution and good conduct, I am sure. You must not disappoint your father.

The narrator calls this "a wonderful instance of advice being given on such a point without being resented." A practical and sensible woman, Mrs. Gardiner knows the facts of economic life for ladies of their day.

Meanwhile, Mr. Collins has been busy. Earlier, acting on his promise to his patroness, Lady Catherine De Bourgh, to find himself a wife, he proposed to Elizabeth, but she rejected him. He sought comfort in Charlotte Lucas, who, at 27 and without family money, was anxious to marry. The couple settles in Kent at the Hunsford

Parsonage on the Rosings estate of Darcy's aunt, Lady Catherine De Bourgh. Escorted by Charlotte's father, Sir William Lucas, and younger sister Maria, Elizabeth visits Charlotte in her marital home. The new Mrs. Collins makes the best of her situation with her husband, encouraging him to stay outside and garden as it is good for his health; she also gives him the best room with a front window view for his study. Charlotte applies a similar tactic, physical separation from one's spouse, to Mr. Bennet, who retreats to his library to avoid encountering his mainly "silly" daughters, as he calls them, and his nervously chattering wife. So Charlotte is delighted to have Elizabeth's company.

The obsequious Collins is thrilled when he, Charlotte, and their visitors receive an invitation from Lady Catherine to dine at her estate, Rosings. Darcy's maternal aunt, Lady Catherine is the widow of Sir Lewis De Bourgh, a knight who built the modern Rosings mansion; they have a daughter Anne. (That Rosings is "modern" reminds readers that Catherine, the Earl's daughter, married a commoner who had the money to build an estate and join the gentry.) The daughter of an earl and thus entitled to call herself Lady, Lady Catherine is "a tall [like her nephew Darcy], large woman, with strongly-marked features, which might once have been handsome. [Here we hear an echo of Lady Williams from "Jack and Alice," a juvenile writing.] Her air was not conciliating, nor was her manner of receiving them such as to make her visitors forget their inferior rank" (2:16). She dominates conversations with an "authoritative" voice.

While Collins, Sir William Lucas, and Maria are awestruck by her, Charlotte and Elizabeth remain sensible and polite. This is more than can be said for Lady Catherine, who enquires nosily about Elizabeth's age, upbringing, and family situation with their property entailed on Collins: "'I see no occasion for entailing estates from the female line'" she announces. "'It was not thought necessary in Sir Lewis de Bourgh's family.'" Thus, Lady Catherine enjoys residing at Rosings after her husband's death, and their thin, small, sickly-looking, and unusually quiet daughter is next in line to inherit the

Rosings estate. Oblivious to her daughter's or nephew's desires, Lady Catherine proudly states that she and her sister, Lady Anne Darcy, planned that their children would marry, prompting a snide Elizabeth to think they deserve each other. With Sir William going home to Meryton, and Maria and Elizabeth left at the parsonage for over two weeks, another set of visitors arrives at Rosings: Lady Catherine's nephews Colonel Fitzwilliam and his cousin Fitzwilliam Darcy. The two gentlemen soon call on the parsonage with Colonel Fitzwilliam entering "into conversation directly with the readiness and ease of a well-bred man," while Darcy utters a polite remark or two but otherwise remains silent. With her nephews there, Lady Catherine does not need the Collinses' company.

But a week after Fitzwilliam and Darcy's arrival, Lady Catherine invites the Hunsford Parsonage group for the evening of Easter Day, which in 1812 was March 29. The Meryton Assembly occurred on October 18. But with her pride still bruised by Darcy's refusal to dance with her, Elizabeth raises the topic when he joins her at the pianoforte, Fitzwilliam sitting by her side. Promising to tell Fitzwilliam something "'very dreadful'" about his cousin Darcy, she relates how, at the Meryton Assembly several months earlier, Darcy "'danced only four dances! I am sorry to pain you–but so it was. . . . [A]nd, to my certain knowledge, more than one young lady was sitting down in want of a partner'"(2:8). The subsequent important repartee between hero and heroine deserves our full attention.

Unflustered, Darcy simply replies that he did not know anyone in Meryton other than the Bingley party. Taunting him with the reply that "'nobody can be introduced in a ball room,'" she turns back to Fitzwilliam and asks what she should next play. But Darcy persists in his attempts to help Elizabeth understand him, "'Perhaps,' said Darcy, 'I should have judged better, had I sought an introduction, but I am ill qualified to recommend myself to strangers.'" Elizabeth still won't let him off the hook: "'Shall we ask him why a man of sense and education, and who has lived in the world, is ill qualified to recommend himself to strangers?'" Fitzwilliam plays along with

Elizabeth, "'I can answer your question . . . without applying to him. It is because he will not give himself the trouble.'"

Again, Darcy explains himself, "'I certainly have not the talent which some people possess . . . of conversing easily with those I have never seen before. I cannot catch their tone of conversation, or appear interested in their concerns, as I often see done.'" Elizabeth, of course, has a response,

> "My fingers do not move over this instrument in the masterly manner which I see so many women's do. They have not the same force or rapidity, and do not produce the same expression. But then I have always supposed it to be my own fault—because I would not take the trouble of practising. It is not that I do not believe *my* fingers as capable as any other woman's of superior execution."

"Darcy smiled, and said, 'You are perfectly right. . . . No one admitted to the privilege of hearing you, can think any thing wanting. We neither of us perform to strangers.'" Their repartee is interrupted by Lady Catherine "who called out to know what they were talking of." I have reproduced much of the Darcy / Elizabeth conversation here because readers frequently question why Darcy has not "practiced" the gentlemanly behavior that Elizabeth raises. When Mrs. Gardiner recalled the Darcy family for Elizabeth during her Longbourn visit, she remembered that Darcy as a boy was said to be "'ill-tempered.'" If his mother, Lady Anne, was anything like her sister, Lady Catherine, young Darcy did not have an upbringing that emphasized "condescension" in its original meaning: "Voluntary abnegation for the nonce of the privileges of a superior; affability to one's inferiors, with courteous disregard of difference of rank or position" (OED, def. 1 a).

Of course, when the Gardiners and Elizabeth visit Pemberley in 3:1, Mrs. Reynolds, the long-time housekeeper, volunteers that as a boy, Darcy was "'sweet-tempered.'" It is likely that when they were growing up together at Pemberley, Wickham, fuelled by jealousy, criticized Darcy behind his back.

Darcy's behavior toward Elizabeth and everyone else will change after the important scene at the Hunsford Parsonage, which leads to Darcy's and Elizabeth's epiphanies (2:11). But consider, too, where Austen sets the current pianoforte conversation: in Lady Catherine's drawing room and within her hearing. This is not the place for Darcy to explain to Elizabeth his anger towards Wickham because it concerns the latter's foiled elopement with Darcy's sister, an incident about which Lady Catherine knows nothing.

Darcy's unexpected proposal to Elizabeth when they are alone at the parsonage—where the Collinses are rarely emotionally honest with each other—begins with his frank acknowledgment that he has struggled with his feelings for her in vain, but came to realize that he admires and loves her. This statement is both flattering and insulting to Elizabeth:

> In spite of her deeply-rooted dislike, she could not be insensible to the compliment of such a man's affection, and though her intentions did not vary for an instant, she was at first sorry for the pain he was to receive; till, roused to resentment by his subsequent language, she lost all compassion in anger.

She throws at him his interference in her sister's relationship with Bingley, as well as his cruel treatment of Wickham, causing him to respond that she would not be saying those words, "'had not your pride been hurt by my honest confession of the scruples that had long prevented my forming any serious design.'" (He is correct: Darcy "'mortified [her] pride,'" while Wickham played to it, stroking her ego.) Although Elizabeth's anger is growing, she nevertheless replies with forced composure, "'You are mistaken, Mr. Darcy, if you suppose that the mode of your declaration affected me in any other way, than as it spared me the concern which I might have felt in refusing you, had you behaved in a more gentleman-like manner.'"

The narrator's short description of Darcy's reaction is telling, "She saw him start at this, but he said nothing." He is utterly shocked: to "start" means "to flinch or recoil" in shock or surprise. As Darcy will explain after repeating her words about his failure to behave "'in a more gentleman-like manner'" following his second, successful proposal to Elizabeth (3:16), this accusation tortured him, "'though it was some time, I confess, before I was reasonable enough to allow their justice.'" The next day, in his letter, Darcy begins acknowledging the justice of her "words." We read the letter with Elizabeth: she and the reader learn his version of Wickham's character with an appeal to turn to Colonel Fitzwilliam for verification. He confides to her Wickham's attempted seduction of the innocent 15-year-old Georgiana Darcy the previous summer, and the reason for Darcy's discouraging Bingley's attraction to Jane. (The recent Georgiana event likely also accounts for his extremely guarded, albeit impolite, behavior at Meryton a month or so later, for he knows he has a lot at stake as the master of Pemberley.) Charlotte Lucas was, indeed, correct in observing that Jane's calm and ever-sweet demeanor was "'too guarded'" (1:6) to convey to any onlooker her love for Bingley. Darcy ends his letter, "God bless you" (2:12).

After reading and rereading the letter multiple times, Elizabeth moves from anger to incredulity to eventual belief in Darcy's words and his blamelessness. She recognizes that Wickham said nothing about Darcy until after he left for London; that it was inappropriate of Wickham to tell tales about Darcy and his family upon first meeting her; that while Wickham claimed he was not afraid of meeting Darcy, he failed to attend the Netherfield Ball; that Charlotte was right about Jane's need to express in her normally placid way her love for Bingley; and that even though she loves her family, she, too, has been embarrassed by their vulgarity, particularly her mother's, Lydia's, Mary's, and Mr. Collins'. At the Netherfield Ball, for instance, Mr. Collins went over to Darcy to introduce himself, a social *faux pas* that even Elizabeth tried to prevent. At the supper during the ball, Mrs. Bennet bragged about Jane and Bingley as if they were actually engaged, and Mary monopolized the piano, playing badly. Even Mr. Bennet called out to her to leave the keyboard and let other ladies play, thus publically embarrassing Mary. (The polite and correct action would have been for Mr. Bennet to go over to Mary and whisper to her. His behavior is corrected in some film versions of the novel, but Austen had a point in showing that even Mr. Bennet was guilty of poor social behavior.)

Walking around the park, contemplating the letter and her behavior, Elizabeth reaches an epiphany as strong as that of any hero in a Greek tragedy:

> She grew absolutely ashamed of herself. −Of neither Darcy nor Wickham could she think, without feeling that she had been blind, partial, prejudiced, absurd. "How despicably have I acted!" she cried.
> . . . . "Till this moment, I never knew myself" (2:13).

Darcy's honest letter shows his utter confidence in Elizabeth's discretion. When she finally returns to the parsonage, she learns that Darcy and his cousin stopped by to bid good-bye and then left.

Arriving home and thinking about Darcy's letter, Elizabeth tells Jane the Wickham story, but keeps Darcy's interference in the Jane-Bingley attraction to herself. The two sisters agree to keep the truth about Wickham to themselves because it involves Georgiana Darcy. With the militia preparing to head to Brighton to protect the coast against French invasion, Lydia begs to go there, too. (The militia protected the homeland, while the army normally fought abroad.) This reminds us that Austen was well aware of England's war with the French, which spanned almost all of her life.

Elizabeth tries to persuade her father to refuse Lydia permission because of her blatant flirtation with the militia officers. But her father thinks Lydia's flirting in Brighton is better than her flirting at home. Elizabeth also runs into Wickham and tells him about spending time at Rosings and being with Darcy and Colonel Fitzwilliam for several weeks. When Wickham enquires about Darcy, she replies, "'I think Mr. Darcy improves on acquaintance'"(2:18). An embarrassed Wickham regains his composure and attributes Darcy's behavior to his desire to please Lady Catherine, which doesn't fool Elizabeth for a minute. Elizabeth looks forward to traveling through the Lake District with her aunt and uncle Gardiner. But business requires Mr. Gardiner to take a shorter trip, and so they will travel to Mrs. Gardiner's former residence, Derbyshire.

While there, the Gardiners encourage a visit to Pemberley. Learning from a maid that no member of the Darcy family is currently in residence, Elizabeth joins her party on the beautiful drive to an estate and house where good taste reigns: "at that moment she felt that to be mistress of Pemberley might be something!" (3:1). She realizes what Darcy has at stake and what it meant for him to ask her to marry him and become the next mistress of this grand and important estate. Austen's heroines never marry for money, but they never marry without it because they are prudent.

Greeted at the house by the longtime housekeeper, the polite and welcoming Mrs. Reynolds, the three guests receive a guided tour of certain rooms. They see that a miniature of Wickham painted during the late Darcy senior's lifetime is still hanging with other family miniatures: Mrs. Reynolds says she has heard he became "'very wild.'" That Darcy allows it to remain on display testifies to his respect for his late father. As she guides her visitors, Mrs. Reynolds praises Darcy as a landlord, master, and brother, and also volunteers that as a child, Darcy was "'always the sweetest-tempered, most generous-hearted, boy in the world,'" and that "'good-natured'" children retain these character traits in adulthood. Elizabeth recognizes the praise of a longtime, intelligent family servant is trustworthy.

When they reach the art gallery, Elizabeth is taken by a portrait that presents "a striking resemblance of Mr. Darcy, with such a smile over the face as she remembered to have sometimes seen, when he looked at her." This portrait, too, was done in Darcy senior's lifetime. Her recollection of the way he smiled at her reminds us that Darcy in the novel is not the way he is usually depicted in the film versions: like a scowling Heathcliff who missed the stop for Wuthering Heights and got off the post-chaise in Meryton by mistake. The "novel" Darcy has been observing Elizabeth and smiling congenially and admiringly—amused and charmed by her.

Leaving the house, the visitors are left in the hands of the gardener, who proudly shows them the estate until they unexpectedly run into Darcy: both he and Elizabeth blush. After making polite enquiries, he departs but soon returns and asks her to introduce her friends, who he thinks are "people of fashion," as Elizabeth senses. He then invites Mr. Gardiner to fish in Pemberley's streams as frequently as he desires, also offering to supply him with equipment. The morning of Georgiana's arrival, Darcy escorts her to the Gardiners' hotel to introduce her to them and to Elizabeth: now 16, Georgiana shows no signs of pride and is sweet and polite, if a little shy. Bingley soon arrives, showing no romantic interest in Georgiana—his snobbish sisters were hoping to get the two together—and enjoys talking with the group in his usual congenial manner. Darcy invites everyone to dinner the night after next.

When Mrs. Gardiner and Elizabeth visit Georgina in the morning, Elizabeth sees that the girl is still shy. Miss Bingley is attempting to get Elizabeth to say something about Wickham—Miss Bingley knows nothing of the Wickham/Georgiana episode of the previous summer. Elizabeth remains composed, and Georgiana looks relieved at Elizabeth's behavior. After the visit, Darcy escorts Elizabeth and her aunt to their carriage. The jealous Miss Bingley begins openly criticizing Elizabeth, noting that her skin looks so brown that it is surprising anyone can recognize her. Georgiana doesn't bite. And Darcy simply says that her tan is not surprising, given that she has been traveling in an open carriage in the sun. Trying again to get Darcy to criticize Elizabeth, Miss Bingley continues to insult her looks and her eyes, saying she is amazed that Darcy once thought her pretty. Darcy, "who could contain himself no longer," closes her down by saying, "'Yes, but *that* was only when I first knew her, for it is many months since I have considered her as one of the handsomest women of my acquaintance'" (3:3).

The following morning Elizabeth receives two letters from Jane; the first one presents the terrible news that Lydia has eloped with

Wickham, possibly to Scotland, where couples could marry at Gretna Green without a license. But Jane's second letter states that the two have not gone to Scotland, leaving the reader to infer that they are living together without matrimony. In tears, Elizabeth runs to the door, expecting to see her aunt and uncle, only to find Darcy. She tells him everything. Listening to Elizabeth, Darcy remains silent, "walking up and down the room in earnest meditation; his brow contracted, his air gloomy." The words "brow contracted" and "air gloomy" prompt some scholars to suggest that Darcy is based on a Gothic villain, like Montoni from *Udolpho* or even Heathcliff from *Wuthering Heights*: contracted brows and gloomy airs mark the common physiognomy of Gothic villains.

But as we later learn, Darcy has been thinking about what he can do to help the Bennets: Gothic villains help no one but themselves. Furthermore, Darcy is the only person who has both the money to bribe Wickham–who is always short of money and readily bribe-able–and the knowledge of where Wickham would be in London. (Wickham was in cahoots with Georgiana's former lady companion who abetted his attempts to seduce the 15-year-old Miss Darcy.) Darcy leaves, and Elizabeth feels that with Lydia's shame now staining her family, all hope of Darcy's loving her is lost. The Gardiners return, learn what has happened, and the three immediately head for Longbourn.

Back at the Bennet house, Mrs. Bennet is hysterical; Jane is trying to hold things together, and Mr. Bennet has left for London in a futile search for Wickham and Lydia. Mrs. Bennet worries that her husband will fight a pistol duel with Wickham and die, leading the Collinses to take over Longbourn and eject the Bennet ladies. Mr. Gardiner promises to help, and he and his wife leave for their London home. Through a series of letters from London to Longbourn, Elizabeth learns that her uncle Gardiner has discovered that Wickham has gambling debts and is sending Mr. Bennet home to Longbourn, while he continues to search for the guilty parties. Mr. Bennet retreats, as usual, to his library with philosophical composure. A letter from Mr. Gardiner arrives for Mr. Bennet the next day: Lydia and Wickham have been found; they are unmarried, but if Mr. Bennet can supply Lydia with her share of the £5,000 marriage settlement plus £100 annually, he hopes Wickham will marry her. A relieved Mr. Bennet agrees, thinking Mr. Gardiner has paid off Wickham with a lot more money. When Mrs. Bennet hears the news, her hysteria turns to joy as she plans a fancy wedding for her beloved youngest daughter. Of course, Mr. Bennet refuses to add a penny to what Wickham demands, sorely disappointing his wife.

Elizabeth and Jane convince their father to allow Lydia and Wickham to come to Longbourn. When they do, Lydia can't stop gloating about being married and showing off her wedding ring, while Wickham appears blasé about the whole incident. He has left the militia and joined the regular army as an officer–a curious decision, since it cost money to secure an officer's rank in the army. Amidst her bragging about her wedding, Lydia lets it slip that Mr. Gardiner was late to escort her to church, but if necessary Mr. Darcy could have acted as a substitute. Her curiosity aroused at hearing Darcy's name, Elizabeth writes to her Aunt Gardiner, who replies with a long letter detailing Darcy's total involvement in making Lydia an honest woman.

As soon as he left Elizabeth in Lambton, he went to London and was able to locate Wickham and Lydia, correctly inferring that Wickham would be in touch with Georgiana's former female companion. Failing to convince Lydia to leave Wickham, who she thinks will eventually marry her, Darcy discovered that Wickham had no intention to do so: he planned to leave Lydia and go somewhere to find a wealthy wife. But Darcy paid off Wickham's gambling debts, bought his army commission, and bribed him to marry Lydia. According to Aunt Gardiner, Darcy demanded that the Bennets not be told of his role. Her aunt concludes the letter, coyly asking Elizabeth to invite her to Pemberley so she can see its park.

The Wickhams leave, and shortly thereafter both Bingley and Darcy return to Netherfield and visit Longbourn. Darcy seems disinterested and silent. Elizabeth wonders why he even came. A few days later, Darcy goes to London, and Bingley comes to Longbourn by himself. Showing her skills again at putting her daughters into proposable situations, Mrs. Bennet first lures Kitty out of the room and then Elizabeth. Soon Jane emerges happily to tell the family of her engagement to Bingley. From being deemed the unluckiest family in the Meryton area because of Lydia's behavior, the Bennets are now considered to be the most fortunate ones because of Jane's engagement to Bingley, who is worth £4,000 per annum.

Another unexpected visitor appears: Lady Catherine arrives and orders Elizabeth to accompany her on a walk. Demanding to know if Elizabeth is engaged to Darcy, Lady Catherine is relieved to hear her say that she is not. She insists that such an engagement is impossible because she and her late sister, Lady Anne, agreed years ago that Darcy would marry his cousin Anne de Bourgh. "'What is that to me?'" queries Elizabeth. She upsets Lady Catherine by continuing, "'If Mr. Darcy is neither by honour nor inclination confined to his cousin, why is not he to make another choice? And if I am that choice, why may not I accept him?'" Growing even angrier, Lady Catherine accuses Elizabeth of being obstinate, pretentious, and headstrong, and advises her, "'If you were sensible of your own good, you would not wish to quit the sphere in which you have been brought up.'" This gives Elizabeth the ammunition to fluster, at least monetarily, the determined Lady Catherine: "'In marrying your nephew, I should not consider myself as quitting that sphere. He is a gentleman; I am a gentleman's daughter; so far we are equal.'" "'True,'" admits her interrogator, but she reminds Elizabeth that her relatives were in trade, to which Elizabeth replies that if her relatives do not bother Mr. Darcy, they should be of no concern to his aunt either.

When Lady Catherine demands a promise that Elizabeth will not become engaged to Darcy, Elizabeth replies, "'I will make no promise of the kind.'" Dismissing Lady Catherine with "'You have insulted me in every possible method. I must beg to return to the house,'" Elizabeth rises to leave. Lady Catherine cannot stop herself from firing more demands and insults at Elizabeth, who resists them completely and walks home. One wonders who is more ladylike in this encounter: Lady Catherine or the young lady she berates.

Soon Mr. Bennet receives a letter from Mr. Collins, first congratulating Mr. Bennet on the impending nuptials of Jane and Bingley and then on the impending engagement of Elizabeth to one of the "most illustrious personages in this land." Teasing his daughter, Mr. Bennet says the idea of Elizabeth's engagement to Darcy, of all persons, is delightfully "absurd." Collins says he told Lady Catherine about the match the other evening, and she, of course, totally disapproved of it. Thus, Collins, continues, he is writing to forewarn his cousin Elizabeth and Darcy of Lady Catherine's position, so they do not run headstrong into a marriage unsanctioned by Darcy's aunt–not that they need her approval as both are of age. Although Mr. Bennet finds the whole idea of a Darcy-Elizabeth match amusing and absurd, Elizabeth hides her true feelings. Collins' letter ends, expressing relief that Lydia's relationship with Wickham prior to their marriage has been "hushed up" and advising the Bennets to forgive their daughter, as Christians should, but to banish her from their home and lives. "'*That* is his notion of Christian forgiveness!'" Mr. Bennet exclaims sarcastically. Here Austen delivers another slash at the patronage system in the Anglican Church, where inappropriate persons secured church livings.

A few days after Lady Catherine's visit, Darcy and Bingley return to Longbourn, and Bingley proposes walking. He and Jane go off together, and Elizabeth winds up with Darcy. She opens the conversation by expressing gratitude for his help with Lydia and Wickham. At first annoyed that his trust in Mrs. Gardiner was misplaced, Elizabeth quickly corrects him and reports that Lydia was the source. Gallantly, Darcy says, "'Your family owe me nothing. Much as I respect them, I believe I thought only of you.'" Now it is the embarrassed Elizabeth who is silent, and Darcy takes advantage of it by continuing, "'If your feelings are still what they were last April, tell me so at once. My affections and wishes are unchanged, but one word from you will silence me on this subject for ever.'" Reassuring him that her feelings have undergone a material change, Elizabeth listens as Darcy says he gained hope after Lady Catherine told him that during her visit to Longbourn, Elizabeth refused to promise not to accept Darcy's proposal. They walk for miles and talk about his letter and her reaction to it, with each confessing to terrible behavior in the past—he to pride and she to impertinence. That night, Elizabeth tells Jane about Darcy's proposal and her acceptance, which Jane at first cannot believe, given her sister's much-professed hatred of Darcy. Jane asks when she first started to love Darcy, and Elizabeth jokes, "'It has been coming on so gradually, that I hardly know when it began. But I believe I must date it from my first seeing his beautiful grounds at Pemberley.'" Begging her sister to be serious, Jane is soon convinced by everything her sister says that she truly loves Darcy: Elizabeth is not the material girl as some readers have thought when reading this conversation between the sisters.

In fact, a close reading of the novel shows that Elizabeth gained a gradual acceptance of Darcy. First, after reading and thinking about his letter, she feels gratitude and respect for him (2:14). When she visits Pemberley and studies his smiling portrait, she feels "a gentle sensation" toward him (3:1). After running into Darcy at Pemberley, she wonders "whether, in defiance of everything, she was still dear to him" (3:1). The next day, she realizes not only that she does not hate him, but also that she is actually ashamed of ever having hated him (3:2). Feeling good will toward him, she realizes that the change he has shown at Pemberley in cordially greeting her and the Gardiners must be attributed to his "ardent love" for her (3:2). After telling him about the contents of Jane's letters regarding Lydia's running off with Wickham, Elizabeth "honestly felt that she could have loved him . . . when all love must be in vain" (3:4). She is still misjudging Darcy here, assuming he would never marry the woman whose sister ran off with a man like Wickham. Finally, when Lydia is set to marry Wickham, Elizabeth thinks Darcy would never ally himself with a family in which his brother-in-law was a man "whom he so justly scorned" (3:8). Believing he is lost to her, she is convinced "she could have been happy with him" and that "he was exactly the man, who, in disposition and talents, would most suit her" (3:8). She realizes her love for Darcy *before* she learns of his role in finding Lydia and Wickham and getting them married and financially solvent.

When Darcy goes to see Mr. Bennet to ask for Elizabeth's hand, Mr. Bennet is so shocked that he calls Elizabeth to his library to question her about her true feelings for Darcy. In doing so, Mr. Bennet admits the problem with his own marriage:

> "I know your disposition, Lizzy. I know that you could be neither happy nor respectable, unless you truly esteemed your husband; unless you looked up to him as a superior. Your lively talents would place you in the greatest danger in an unequal marriage. You could scarcely escape discredit and misery. My child, let me not have the grief of seeing *you* unable to respect your partner in life. You know not what you are about."

Earlier (2:19) we read about the Bennets' marriage:

> Her father, captivated by youth and beauty, and that appearance of good humour which youth and beauty generally give, had married a woman whose weak understanding and illiberal mind had, very early in their marriage, put an end to all real affection for her.

But Elizabeth is able to reassure her father, who responds, "'I could not have parted with you, my Lizzy, to any one less worthy.'" She then tells him of Darcy's actions on Lydia and Wickham's behalf.

When Darcy and Elizabeth go out to walk again, they talk about their relationship in the typical mode of young lovers. Replying to her question about why he first came to admire and love her, he says that "the liveliness" of her mind attracted him the most. Mr. Bennet writes to Collins, wryly advising him to side with Darcy who has "more to give." Elizabeth and Darcy marry and live at Pemberley, where she is an excellent mentor to Georgiana. And of course, Mr. and Mrs. Darcy are great friends with the Gardiners.

The reviews for the second novel were laudatory: "Written with Great Spirit As Well as Vigour" praised *The British Critic* (Feb 1813); "Very Superior" enthused *The Critical Review* (March 1813); "the Author's talents" were acclaimed in *The New Review* (April 1813). Lady Byron (poet Lord Byron's wife) thought it "a very superior work" and called it "the *most probable* fiction I have ever read" (Letter to her mother, May 1, 1813). The flattered Austen joked in a letter to Cassandra that "The work is rather too light, and bright, and sparkling" (Feb 4, 1813). The novel's luster has endured to this day. With *Pride and Prejudice*, Jane Austen was on the literary map—although her name, as you can see from the title page of the first edition, remained a secret from the reading public at large.

While working on *Simply Austen*, I saw in the NY *Times* (Feb 15, 2017, C) Kimiko de Freytas-Tamura's article, "Mr. Darcy, You're No Colin Firth," reporting on a widely publicized "Darcy"-study by British Professors John Sutherland and Amanda Vickery. In an effort to learn what Darcy may have looked like—given that Austen gives little physical description of her hero—they examined portraits of eighteenth-century noblemen. But Mr. Darcy is not a nobleman. They looked at a portrait of the youthful Austen's erstwhile romantic interest, Thomas Lefroy, a miniature painted in 1798, in which he is shown possibly with powdered hair (other images show his hair as light blond): but why assume Darcy would powder his hair like this young law student at Lincoln's Inn, one of London's four Inns of Court? According to the NY *Times* article, they did not look at Austen's text.

Let's read how Austen, albeit minimally, describes Darcy in her novel. The son of an Earl's daughter, Lady Anne Darcy, Austen's Darcy was sired by a member of the landed gentry, whose home, Pemberley, boasts a library that "has been the work of many generations" (PP 2:8). The Darcy family, therefore, has a long heritage as landed gentry, but they are not nobility on the paternal side. When Elizabeth Bennet visits Rosings and first encounters Darcy's maternal aunt, Lady Catherine De Bourgh, she sees "a tall, large woman, with strongly-marked features, which might once have been handsome . . . in whose countenance and deportment she soon found some resemblance to Mr. Darcy" (2:6).

When Darcy entered the Meryton Assembly, he "soon drew the attention of the room by his fine, tall person, handsome features, noble mien . . . . The gentlemen pronounced him to be a fine figure of a man . . . ." (1:3). While he has a noble mien, Elizabeth observed on seeing Lady Catherine that he also has her "strongly-marked features," which do not suggest the sedate oval face, pointy-chin, and long nose of the Sutherland / Vickery nobleman. That the gentlemen at the Assembly deem Darcy "a fine figure of a man" suggests that his physique is an improvement over the typical slim shouldered noblemen studied by Sutherland and Vickery. Mrs. Bennet later sighs over her future son-in-law, "'so handsome, so tall'" (3:17), implying that Darcy is taller than your average Regency gentleman. Finally, Darcy's sister, Georgiana, was "tall, and on a larger scale than Elizabeth [who is little]; and, though little more than sixteen, her figure was formed, and her appearance womanly and graceful" (3:2).

The two Darcy siblings are tall and well-formed—Georgiana notably so for her age. Darcy and his sister are wealthy members of the gentry class, as is Elizabeth Bennet, who asserts correctly to Lady Catherine (who never forgets that she is an Earl's daughter, but ignores that she holds the title "Lady" as a courtesy title, which will not be inherited by her daughter!): "'He is a gentleman; I am a gentleman's daughter; so far we are equal'" (3:14).

As a fictional character, Darcy looks like what we readers imagine by paying attention to Austen's text. He does not look like the screen's Colin Firth, Matthew Macfadyen, or Laurence Olivier, but neither is he the powdered-haired nobleman that Professors Sutherland and Vickery propose.

6. Austen's Three Chawton Novels

A usten's final three completed novels were all products of her Chawton life, not revisions of manuscripts conceived in her 20s while living at the Steventon Rectory. For years critics and biographers called *Mansfield Park*, *Emma*, and *Persuasion* her "mature" novels. But that was because they thought she had not vigorously revised the two manuscripts begun at the Steventon Rectory–"Elinor and Marianne" and "First Impressions." So *Simply Austen* refers to her last three novels as her "Chawton Novels."

Mansfield Park is Austen's first published novel that was conceived in its entirety during her Chawton years, although she may have also written parts of it while visiting friends and family at Steventon, in London, and elsewhere. Presented by a published, well-received novelist now in her mid-30s, the novel emanates real confidence in presenting a heroine, Fanny Price, who, as frequently noted, succeeds by doing nothing: "'I cannot act,'" she protests. We first observe her and her interior life when she is 10 and leave her at the novel's end when she is about 20 and happily married with a child on the way. By the time she is 16, we witness her emotional life through Austen's use of free indirect discourse; these feelings are marked by envy, moral piety, and even sexual jealousy. Fanny's sad childhood forms the adult heroine, who has been as critically browbeaten as she is emotionally and even physically browbeaten at Mansfield Park.

Consider Fanny's childhood:

1. At 10 she is removed from her poor, large birth family in Portsmouth, where, as the eldest girl, her role in the household is that of a caregiver to her younger siblings, and she had a wonderful, trusted, loving friend in her brother William, one year her elder.

2. She is sent to Mansfield Park, the distant estate of her baronet

uncle, Sir Thomas Bertram. She is overwhelmed by the mansion's magnificence and size.

3. She is ignored or belittled by her mother's officious eldest sister, Aunt Norris, who wields power at the Park.

4. She is humiliated by her cousins Maria, age 13, and Julia, 12, daughters of her other aunt (and Sir Thomas' wife, Lady [Maria] Bertram). The two girls make fun of Fanny with the cruelty that only children can inflict on other children.

5. She is relegated to the bedroom, "reckoned too small for anybody's comfort," in "the little white attic" in the servant's quarters, where she "cannot have a fire," even in the cold of winter. This sounds like Austen's version of Cinderella.

Even at 16, and into her young womanhood:

6. She is belittled by Aunt Norris who reminds her she will always be "'lowest and last'" and orders the servants not to light the fireplace in the old school room that becomes Fanny's personal refuge.

7. She is treated as a cypher by her tranquil and passive Aunt Lady Bertram: when Sir Thomas announces that Fanny should move to Aunt Norris' cottage, Lady Bertram blithely agrees, saying to Fanny "'It can make very little difference to you, whether you are in one house or the other.'" Lady Bertram is oblivious to Fanny's having any feelings of her own.

8. She is forced to walk "beyond her strength at the instigation of" Aunt Norris, who assigns her over-taxing physical tasks.

9. She is left out of social occasions such as local balls and dinner parties, while her female cousins enjoy them.

10. She is shy, nervous, and physically weak, compared to her robust cousins who enjoyed a childhood of exercise and good nourishment.

As you can see, Fanny Price has 10 strikes against her in terms of what we expect in a heroine, especially after the self-confident, strong, witty, and assertive Elizabeth Bennet of Austen's previous novel. Scholars deemed *Mansfield Park* Austen's "dark" novel, her authorial response to calling *Pride and Prejudice* "too light & bright

& sparkling–it wants shade" (Letter, Feb 4, 1813): but it is possible to read her comment as Austen's jokingly speaking of her great pleasure in her novel. Many see *Mansfield Park* as Austen's single artistic failure. Writing about it, critic and novelist Kingsley Amis famously asked, "What Became of Jane Austen?" (*The Spectator*, 4 October 1957). He bemoaned Fanny Price's abhorrent "complacency" and "pride," and called Edmund Bertram and Fanny "morally detestable," and snidely added that inviting them "round for the evening" would ensure a dull time. Other critics, writing as late as the early 21st century, agreed. In his highly influential *Jane Austen: Irony as Defense and Discovery*, the late Marvin Mudrick noted the absence of irony in the novel on the first page of his book (Princeton UP, 1952; rpt. U Cal, 1968). But irony runs throughout this novel and begins in its first sentence.

The novel opens with sharp Juvenalian satire about the economic forces that determined marriage in the gentry:

> About thirty years ago Miss Maria Ward, of Huntingdon, with only seven thousand pounds, had the good luck to captivate Sir Thomas Bertram, of Mansfield Park, in the county of Northampton, and to be thereby raised to the rank of a baronet's lady, with all the comforts and consequences of an handsome house and large income. All Huntingdon exclaimed on the greatness of the match, and her uncle, the lawyer, himself, allowed her to be at least three thousand pounds short of any equitable claim to it.

Maria is the middle among the Ward daughters. Her elder sister, who is never given a first name in the novel, must finally settle for marriage to Sir Thomas' friend, the Rev. Mr. Norris, who has little fortune and is dependent on the baronet for his church living at Mansfield Park. This enables Mrs. Norris to mooch everything she can from the great house. She also grabs control wherever she sees an opening for it; she manipulates her sister and brother-in-law; she harmfully indulges her Bertram nieces, allowing them to develop their egos to a dangerous degree; and she seethes with anger at her younger sister Frances, Fanny's mother. Readers know Mrs. Norris as Aunt Norris, and it is no coincidence that J. K. Rowling named the busybody, tattle-tale pet cat of Argus Filch, Hogwarts' School's caretaker, "Mrs. Norris."

Frances insults her entire family by daring to marry the rough and not very ready Marine Lieutenant Price, "without education, fortune, or connexions," leading to a long-lasting breach with her sisters. But unable to care for a family of nine children and a husband now on disability half-pay who likes his grog, Frances swallows her pride and writes to her baronet brother-in-law, explaining that her eldest child, the "fine spirited," 10-year-old William, would love to see the world. She suggests Woolwich, the home of the Royal Military Academy, for her son—recall that Francis and Charles Austen went to the Royal Naval Academy at age 12. She also asks if William might be of use to Sir Thomas, who owns an estate in Antigua, at his "West Indian property?"

Fiction built on facts

Those words, "West Indian property," would have immediately alerted Austen's contemporary readers to think about the novel's title, Mansfield Park. "Mansfield" strongly resonated in Austen's day as the name of the Lord Chief Justice, William Murray, 1st Earl of Mansfield. In the history-making 1772 case of Somerset (a slave) vs. Stewart (his British master), Lord Mansfield ruled that no slaves could be held on English soil. He stated that slavery "is so odious, that nothing can be suffered to support it, but positive law. . . . I cannot say this case is allowed or approved by the law of England; and therefore the black must be discharged." The Mansfield ruling was one of the most important in the campaign for abolition. Austen was certainly aware of this movement as abolition continued to appear in the news.

The slavery issue is also reflected in Austen's naming the cruel aunt, Norris. Her surname is likely derived from Liverpool-born slave-ship captain, the infamous Robert Norris (1700?- 1791), who was descended from a family of slave traders. Arriving in Africa in 1722 and spending the three decades between the 1750s and 1780s at sea as a slave ship captain, he retired to Liverpool as slave-trading merchant and lobbyist in Parliament for the interests of Liverpool's slave owners. When Norris appeared before the House of Commons in June 1788, he stressed the "delightful" conditions on the ships: the slaves, he said, had nourishing food, plenty of fresh air, enjoyed music and dancing on the ship's deck, and roomy, clean accommodations. We hear Robert Norris's ideas reflected in Aunt Norris who, as Sir Thomas recalls, is an "'advocate, and very judiciously, for young people's being brought up without unnecessary indulgences,'" such as Fanny's having no fire in her bedroom (in "the little white attic") or the East Room (formerly, the Bertram sisters' school room), which Fanny uses as her personal retreat after several years at Mansfield.

Robert Norris delivered written pro-slavery propaganda, too. His *Memoirs of the Reign of Bossa Ahádee: King of Dahomy, an Inland Country of Guiney* (London: 1789) stresses the brutality, violence, and chaos in Africa, thus supporting the common pro-slavery argument that slavery in the New World saved the Africans from a worse fate in their native countries. As David Shane Wallace writes, "Sir Thomas views his niece Fanny as little more than a perpetual servant to whom he has extended his benevolence in taking her from her poor parents and providing for her" ("The White Female as Effigy and the Black Female as Surrogate in Janet Schaw's *Journal of a Lady of Quality* and Jane Austen's *Mansfield Park*," *Studies in the Literary Imagination* [2014]:127.) If Sir Thomas considers Fanny a servant, Aunt Norris treats her as a slave, sending her to pick and deliver flowers on a blistering hot day and demeaning her as "'lowest and last.'"

Even in her youth, Jane Austen would have heard about slavery at home. James-Langford Nibbs of Antigua was the godfather of her eldest brother, James: Nibbs knew Rev. George Austen from their days together at St. John's College, Oxford. Mr. Nibbs's son George was a student at Rev. Austen's school at the Steventon Rectory between 1781 and 1783. Rev. Austen also became a trustee for the Nibbs plantation. But the Nibbs family was not the only way Austen knew about slavery as she grew up.

Mrs. Austen's brother James Leigh was married to an heiress to plantations in Barbados. Rev. Tom Fowle, Cassandra's fiancé, died of yellow fever on a naval ship in the British West Indies, where a slave rebellion erupted in 1791 in St. Domingo. So Austen was quite familiar with the slavery issue, and it appears in this novel. While scholars and readers complained in the past about her ignoring the major political and social issues of her day, modern scholarship corrects that opinion.

The plot thickens

Aunt Norris convinces Sir Thomas and Lady Bertram to take in their sister's eldest daughter, Fanny, who is nine. At first, Sir Thomas questions the advisability of bringing a girl into his family with its two teenage strapping sons. Always ready to cry out an answer, Aunt Norris insists that to the Bertram boys Fanny will "'never be more to either than a sister'" because they will grow up with her. Romance between cousins in such circumstances, reiterates Aunt Norris, "'is morally impossible.'" Ironically, the end of the novel will morally require Fanny's marriage to one of the Bertram sons.

Inviting the eldest Price daughter rather than the son to the estate is a curious choice prompted by Aunt Norris. The "fine spirited" William would not be as easy for her to humiliate, boss, and abuse. Named Frances after her mother, young Fanny is a substitute for Aunt Norris to punish her sister's cavalier disobedience of her family with her unsuitable marriage choice. From the time of the timid Fanny's arrival at the estate, Aunt Norris pits her against her Bertram nieces, Maria and Julia. This is very easy to do as her sister,

Lady Bertram, the mistress of Mansfield Park, spends her days on the sofa, making useless fringe, totally oblivious to what is going on in her home. And Sir Thomas, while well-meaning, is not only strangely immune to Aunt Norris's officious interference, but also physically separated from his family; for most of the year, he lives in London to see to his Parliamentary duties.

Arriving at Mansfield Park, far away from her home in Portsmouth, Fanny is overwhelmed by persons talking at her. As the narrator states, "Nobody meant to be unkind, but nobody put themselves out of their way to secure her comfort." The exception is 15-year-old Edmund, the younger of the two Bertram brothers. When he finds Fanny crying on the stairs after being at Mansfield Park for a week, he speaks kindly to her and learns that she misses her brother William, to whom she wishes to write a letter. Edmund helps her with the letter and even encloses half a guinea. He also advises Fanny how to play with Maria and Julia so they will be nicer to her. With Edmund's advice and help, Fanny becomes less frightened and overwhelmed by the mansion and its inhabitants.

By the second chapter, when Fanny is about 15, Mr. Norris dies, and Aunt Norris consoles herself "by considering that she could do very well without him." Additionally, she will save money and be able to spend more time at the great house.

To compensate for the heavy debts accrued by his elder son Tom's gambling, Sir Thomas must sell the church living, originally intended for Edmund, to the Rev. Dr. Grant. Sir Thomas tells his wastrel of a son about how this sale will drastically cut Edmund's future income, as he will now have to take a lesser living. But Tom is simply bored by his father's moralizing. Sir Thomas must also leave England to resolve issues at his plantation in Antigua. He takes Tom with him in the hope that the experience will give his son some sense of responsibility and maturity. At the time Austen was writing this novel, slave uprisings plagued the British colonies in the Caribbean. With the arrival of the Grants to the Mansfield parsonage, Austen introduces new characters who will be the catalysts for adding the major complications to the novel.

Knowing that Aunt Norris has vacated the parsonage, Sir Thomas proposes that she take Fanny into her new home. Aunt Norris protests that she must always have "'a room for a friend'" (what friend?) at her little cottage, and so to Fanny's relief, she is able to remain at Mansfield Park. As Sir Thomas departs for Antigua, his last words to Fanny sting her sharply. Hoping that she might be able to see her beloved elder brother William, who is now in the Navy, Fanny is mortified when Sir Thomas says, "'I fear, he must find his sister at sixteen in some respects too much like his sister at ten'": "She cried bitterly over this reflection when her uncle was gone; and her [female] cousins, on seeing her with red eyes, set her down as a hypocrite." Maria and Julia, far from teary-eyed, feel great relief in their father's departure.

With his father and elder brother abroad, Edmund, now about 23, becomes the surrogate master of the house, although Sir Thomas is reassured knowing that Aunt Norris will be in charge, a duty she had already assumed herself, anyway. One of the first things Edmund sees is that Fanny needs exercise, especially after the death of her dear old grey pony, which has deprived her of riding. Of course, Maria and Julia never think of lending their horses to Fanny for exercise. Much against Aunt Norris's vehement protests, Edmund arranges for Fanny to have a horse. Initially frightened of the large animal, she eventually learns to ride for exercise.

Although she is now past 16, the age of coming out, Fanny never attends social events like dinner parties and balls. But her Bertram female cousins are now out in society as the "belles of the neighborhood." With Aunt Norris as their chaperone—Lady Bertram can't bear to leave her sofa—Maria, a tall, fair beauty, attracts the eye of a young gentleman, James Rushworth, the new master of Sotherton Court; he has an income of £12,00 per annum. Maria is at an age where she thinks marriage is her duty, and marriage with Mr. Rushworth will give her exactly what she desires: a larger income than her father's and a house in London. So much for her childhood and adolescent education under the guidance of Aunt Norris, who stressed learning facts by rote but totally neglected "the less common acquirements of self-knowledge, generosity, and humility. In everything but disposition [the Bertram girls] were admirably taught."

Aunt Norris zealously promotes the couple, and the two become engaged at the appropriate time—though properly they will wait until Sir Thomas officially gives his consent. Only Edmund sees a problem with the match: "If this man had not twelve thousand a year, he would be a very stupid fellow," thinks Edmund (1:4).

By the time Fanny reaches the age of 18, two visitors arrive at the Grant parsonage, bringing with them the novel's major complications. Mrs. Grant, who is about 30, is a pleasant woman with a beloved orphaned half-brother and half-sister, Henry and Mary Crawford. They have been living in London since their childhood with their uncle and aunt, Admiral and Mrs. Crawford. Both Henry and Mary enjoy wealth: Henry, at 23, owns a fine estate in Norfolk, and Mary has £20,000. While Mrs. Crawford was still alive, Mary enjoyed a good home with her aunt and uncle. But a few months after his wife's death, the widowed Admiral, "a man of vicious conduct," moved his mistress into the house. The childless Mrs. Grant welcomes her half-sister to the Mansfield parsonage. City-bred and sophisticated, Mary fears that living in the country may be dull, and Mrs. Grant fears the same for Mary. But Mary is pleased with her sister, her respectable if over-eating brother-in-law, and their home. And she is very pleased to have a baronet's family with sons and daughters around her and her brother's ages right in the neighborhood.

Mary's brother, Henry, is less concerned about living in the area because, even with his own estate, he has an aversion to settling down; he must be on the move. The Bertram sisters have no trouble welcoming Mary to their circle. She is petite and pretty with dark eyes and dark complexion, and therefore she is no competition to Julia and Maria Bertram, who are "tall, full-formed, and fair." At first, the Bertram sisters do not find Henry Crawford at all attractive; dark like his sister, he is not tall, and they regard him as "plain." But he is congenial, witty, and articulate, and by the next meeting, the sisters notice his good white teeth and well-formed body; they also notice his expressive face. By the third meeting, the Bertram sisters regard him as the "most agreeable man they had ever met." Maria excuses her attraction to him as harmless: he knows she is engaged, and so Henry must look out for himself, she rationalizes. With matchmaking foremost in her mind, Mrs. Grant decides that Mary should marry the elder Bertram son, Tom, thus eventually becoming a baronet's wife, and that Henry should marry Julia. Henry teases his elder half-sister, promising to "'like Julia best,'" but also observing that while the beautiful Maria is engaged, he sees that she "'does not care three straws'" for Rushworth and adds,

> "An engaged woman is always more agreeable than a disengaged. She is satisfied with herself. Her cares are over, and she feels that she may exert all her powers of pleasing without suspicion. All is safe with a lady engaged: no harm can be done."

Readers foresee that Henry's specious logic will do a great deal of harm.

With the Crawfords' sights set on Maria Bertram and Tom, who has returned from Antigua, Fanny remains off stage, dutifully disentangling Lady Bertram's fringe. Neighborliness grows between the mansion and the parsonage. But Tom's decision to go off to meet friends at the races delays any courtship that might occur between him and Mary.

With Edmund again at the head of the table doing the carving duties and regularly visiting the Grant parsonage, Fanny observes his many kindnesses to Mary. While he and Fanny privately share their moral concerns about Mary's often-thoughtless remarks about her uncle, the Admiral, he also finds himself exonerating her the next moment, attributing her flippancy to Mary's "'lively mind.'" He lends Mary the horse he acquired for Fanny's exercise and even guides her riding as Fanny watches from above. Austen's free indirect discourse takes us into Fanny's thoughts:

Edmund was close to her; he was speaking to her; he was evidently directing her management of the bridle; he had hold of her hand; she saw it, or the imagination supplied what the eye could not reach. (1:7)

The readers' "access" to Fanny's mind encourages commentary about her immaturity and priggishness. But isn't Austen showing the normal reaction of a shy, 18-year-old girl who, inexperienced in any kind of mature love, feels the first pangs of sexual jealousy when she witnesses the young man she initially loved as a brotherly friend displaying his romantic attraction to another young woman?

Edmund is increasingly, albeit subconsciously, drawn by Mary Crawford's sexual allure. When her harp arrives from London, Edmund visits the parsonage daily "to be indulged with his favourite instrument" (1:7). Although not one to give in to symbolism, Austen alludes to the beautiful but dangerous mythological sirens that lured and enchanted sailors to their deaths by playing music on a variety of instruments, especially harps. As Austen suggestively writes:

A young woman, pretty, lively, with a harp as elegant as herself, and both placed near a window, cut down to the ground, and opening on a little lawn, surrounded by shrubs in the rich foliage of summer, was enough to catch any man's heart. (1:7)

The Bertrams host a dinner for the Crawfords and Mr. Rushworth. The latter has just returned from a visit to his friend Smith whose estate, Compton, has been "improved." As explained in Chapter 1 of this book, improving one's estate was very much *au courant* in Austen's time, and the most famous improver was Humphry Repton (1752-1818), who refashioned landscapes at over 400 properties in England. In Chapter 6 of *Mansfield Park*, Repton's name is repeated six times; he was responsible for the work at Smith's Compton estate, which he improved so much that Rushworth tellingly utters,

"'I never saw a place so altered in my life. I told Smith I did not know where I was'" (1:6).

Repton sought to create a more natural, picturesque effect. As Rushworth says, "'two or three fine old trees [were] cut down . . . and it opens up the prospect amazingly.'" The group plans to visit Rushworth's 700-acre Sotherton and inspect it for improvement.

HUMPHRY REPTON, ESQ.

Samuel Shelley's drawing of Humphry Repton, the leading landscape architect of Austen's day, is the frontispiece to John C. Loudon, The Landscape Gardening and Landscape Architecture of the Late Humphry Repton, Esq. (London: Longman, 1840). Repton did the landscaping improvement for property visited by the Austen ladies in 1806.

The visit to Sotherton will be the first of what I call two "gathering" scenes that Austen created for this novel. The second such scene appears a little later in volume one, when most of the characters decide to put on a play at Mansfield Park. The two "gathering scenes" enabled Austen to collect her many characters at one event for interaction and increase the narrative momentum that complicates the action.

Of course, Aunt Norris sees no reason for Fanny to join the Sotherton party, but Edmund intervenes on her behalf. Mrs. Grant ultimately rescues the girl by volunteering to sit with Lady Bertram in Fanny's place and help her with her fringe. Preparing to leave for the drive to Sotherton, friction occurs between Maria and Julia based on who will sit next to Henry when he drives his barouche. The passenger side of the driver's box is the "envied seat," and while Maria desires it, Julia secures it.

Barouche
With Ackerman's Patent Movable Axles

Henry Crawford drives a barouche, a four-wheeled carriage with a convertible top. Carrying four persons on two seats facing each other inside the coach, the barouche has a driver's box seating two. Because four horses draw it, a barouche was expensive to own and carried a lot of cachet. No wonder in *Sense and Sensibility*, the socially ambitious Fanny Dashwood wishes her brother Edmund would drive a barouche (photo by Deb Barnum from Ralph Straus, *Carriages and Coaches Their History and Their Evolution*. Philadelphia: Lippincott, 1912: facing 232.) In the image's caption, note that Straus misspelled Ackermann with one n.

Chafing at Julia's happily sitting next to Henry, Maria finds her spirits uplifted as they enter the Rushworth estate, with its extensive land, woods, tenant farmers' houses (run-down), and roads (that improve the closer they come to the great house). She is proud that "Mr. Rushworth's consequence was hers."

The visitors first tour the old mansion, dating back to Elizabeth I. Rushworth's mother is the tour guide, parroting what she has learned from her housekeeper. When the group arrives at the chapel, Fanny is disappointed to hear that it is no longer used and that the household staff is not required to attend religious services. Here Austen is satirizing the decline of the wealthy gentry. "'Every generation has its improvements,'" snidely remarks Mary, shocking the piety of both Fanny and Edmund. But when Maria and Rushworth stand together near the altar, Julia teases that if Edmund were ordained, he could marry them on the spot. Now it is Mary Crawford's turn to be shocked. With Tom Bertram off on an extended trip to the races, she has become increasingly attracted to Edmund. He is kind, attentive, and intelligent. And near the end of the novel, we also learn that Edmund is quite the hunk. Writing to Fanny about Edmund's appearance at a London dinner party hosted by her friend Mrs. Fraser, "no bad judge" of men's looks, Mary reports Mrs. Fraser's saying "she knows but three men in town who have so good a person, height, and air; and I must confess, when he dined here the other day, there were none to compare with him, and we were a party of sixteen" (3:12). So the captivating Mary finds herself being captivated by Edmund, but for one issue. To Mary, "'A clergyman is nothing.'"

After their meal, the visitors and their hosts split into three groups to explore the estate for future improvement: Fanny, Mary, and Edmund; Maria, Henry, and Rushworth, and lagging behind, Julia, Aunt Norris, and Mrs. Rushworth. Readers first follow the Fanny-Edmund-Mary group. As they walk, Fanny feels weak, and he takes her arm, inviting the small and sturdy Mary to take his other arm as they follow "'a very serpentine course'" toward the wilderness. This Biblical and Miltonic reference anticipates Edmund's increasing sexual and moral turmoil over his attraction to Mary.

While Mary uses every argument she can muster to dissuade Edmund from his chosen clerical vocation, he "'wishes [he] could convince Miss Crawford'" of its worth and the sincerity of his clerical ambition. Fanny's tiredness prompts Edmund to locate a bench with a view of the woods across a ha-ha. An iron gate blocks entrance to the park seen at a distance.

A *ha-ha*, here seen on the grounds of the Chawton House Library in Hampshire, is a concealed vertical trench that prevents livestock from getting across it, while not blocking the view as a fence would. The term "ha-ha" reflects the amusing but unexpected discovery when, upon reaching the *ha-ha*, its unseen vertical drop suddenly surprises the walker: "Ha-ha!" (photo by Joan Ray). For full information with illustrations about what an estate's wilderness and shrubbery gardens were like, see Robert Clark, "Wilderness and Shrubbery in Austen's Works," accessible at *Persuasions On-Line*. 36 (Winter 2015).

Mary announces, "'resting fatigues me'" and desires to walk onward to find an alternate path beyond the ha-ha and the gated fence. Fanny indicates she has rested enough to continue. But Edmund, fooling himself but not the reader, earnestly warns her about over-taxing herself, and promising to return in a few minutes, goes off with Mary. Twenty minutes elapse, and Fanny's solitude is broken by the arrival of the second group, Henry-Maria-Rushworth.

With an iron gate blocking their entry to the park, Maria says they will gain better ideas about improvement if they can get past the gate, the ha-ha, and beyond, where Henry sees a distant knoll that would perfectly suit their purposes of estate improvement.

Bemoaning that he left the key to the gate back at the great house, Rushworth lumbers back to fetch it, leaving Henry, Maria, and Fanny. Flirtatious talk between Henry and Maria ensues, and Maria says as she walks toward the gate, "'that iron gate, that ha-ha, give me a feeling of restraint and hardship. 'I cannot get out, as the starling said,'" referring to the caged starling in Laurence Sterne's novel of sensibility, *A Sentimental Journey*. "'Mr. Rushworth is so long fetching this key!'" she complains. Following her to the gate, Henry tempts Maria:

> "And for the world you would not get out without the key and without Mr. Rushworth's authority and protection, or I think you might with little difficulty pass round the edge of the gate, here, with my assistance; I think it might be done, if you really wished to be more at large, and could allow yourself to think it not prohibited."

Showing her independent mind and spirit, Maria avails herself of Henry's aid, ignoring Fanny's apposite warning, figuratively predicting what will happen to Maria with Henry, "'You will hurt yourself, Miss Bertram, . . . you will certainly hurt yourself against those spikes; you will tear your gown; you will be in danger of slipping into the ha-ha. You had better not go'" (1:10). But off go Maria and Henry as Fanny sits and waits, next encountering a huffing Rushworth who has returned with the gate key. Angry that Henry and Maria have left, he walks off, and Fanny decides, with an hour now passed, to go in search of her former companions. But she soon hears Mary's voice. Mary and Edmund plead ignorance of their time away, saying they had found a lovely tree under which they sat and talked. Reading Fanny's reaction to their explanation again leads many readers into thinking Fanny is too self-indulgent. Yet isn't our young and inexperienced heroine having a normal reaction to being forgotten by Edmund? Here are her thoughts:

> Fanny's best consolation was in being assured that Edmund had wished for her very much, and that he should certainly

have come back for her, had she not been tired already; but this was not quite sufficient to do away with the pain of having been left a whole hour, when he had talked of only a few minutes, nor to banish the sort of curiosity she felt to know what they had been conversing about all that time; and the result of the whole was to her disappointment and depression. . . .

With Julia stuck with her Aunt Norris and Rushworth's mother, and Rushworth annoyed about his futile key fetching, the party that went to Sotherton to work on landscape improvement return to Mansfield Park with no ideas for Repton and worsening feelings about their personal situations. Julia sees that Henry prefers her sister, who is caught between her desire for Rushworth's income and Henry's sexual and personal attraction. Mary is disappointed at Edmund's planned clerical career. Edmund is distressed that Mary will not accept his clerical plans. Fanny deals with what today we'd call sexual jealousy over Edmund's increasing attraction to Mary.

Edmund, growing more enamored of Mary, continues to discuss with her their contrary views of clerical careers, when Tom Bertram arrives home from his six-week horseracing holiday at Weymouth. Mary finds herself indifferent to his absence and his return as she is attracted to Edmund, except for his clerical plans. It is now late August, and at the beginning of September Henry departs for his Everingham estate in Norfolk. A letter home announces that Sir Thomas plans to return from Antigua in November. With only Rushworth to bore her, Maria awaits Henry's return to the Grant parsonage, while Julia, "distrusting his attentions" and intentions, wishes he'd stay away.

With Henry gone, another newcomer arrives: the Honorable John Yates, Tom's "intimate friend" made at Weymouth during a mere ten days' acquaintance. At an impromptu ball at Mansfield Park, which is Fanny's first ball, albeit informal and danced to the music of a single fiddler, Fanny quietly observes Maria's indifference toward her fiancé, even as Mrs. Rushworth and Aunt Norris confidently discuss their upcoming marriage. Fanny has her first dance–with Tom Bertram, who only wants to avoid being drawn to Aunt Norris's whist table.

Yates, the wealthy and effete younger son of a lord, has come to Mansfield Park by way of Ecclesford, the estate of Lord Ravenshaw in Cornwall. There they had planned to produce a private theatrical, performing Elizabeth Inchbald's translation of August von Kotzebue's *Lovers Vows*. But three days before the opening night, word of the Dowager Duchess's death arrives at Ecclesford, and the Duke cancels the production–much to the disappointment of Yates who tellingly complains that the deceased was "'only a grandmother.'"

Theatricals and tensions

Putting on a play at Mansfield Park becomes Austen's second big "gathering scene," involving all her characters in a tense scenario. Tom immediately suggests that they, too, do a play, much to Edmund and Fanny's disapproval, both indicating that they will not act. Quibbles soon arise about the planned performance–should it be a comedy or a tragedy? Also, there are too many parts in one play and not enough in another. But after flipping through many drama anthologies, the actors decide to use Eccleford's choice: *Lovers' Vows*. Austen had likely seen this play in Winchester during August 1809.

Playbill from the Hampshire Chronicle *collection, 1809 (3A00W/E14)*

The playbill announces a production of Lovers' Vows in August 1809 at the theatre in Winchester, the nearest city to Chawton. While Austen's letters for 1809 end with July 26th, she, her sister, and mother were now settled at Chawton and may have traveled to Winchester to see the play (playbill at Hampshire Record Office, photo by Isobel Snowden, Jane Austen House Museum).

Soon disagreements arise over the parts. Who will play Agatha, the female lead? Both Julia and Maria want the role of this outcast woman who many years ago bore a bastard in its primary meaning—a child born out of wedlock. Henry has the role of Frederick, Agatha's long-lost bastard son, but also—in terms of Henry's actions—a bastard in its secondary meaning of scoundrel or cad. Henry attempts to cajole Julia not to try for the role, but she gets the message non-too-happily. Why is Henry anxious to cast Maria as his long-lost mother, and why are the sisters in conflict over who will act the part?

A review of the stage directions for the play shows that in Act I, when Agatha, now a beggar and an outcast, and her adult son Frederick are reunited after many years, they embrace and engage in other physical contact. Agatha "leans her head upon his breast"; Frederick "takes her hand, and puts it to his heart." Mother and son again "embrace." As a grateful mother, she "presses him to her breast." Maria and Henry, cast as mother and son, not only play roles foreshadowing their futures (fallen woman and cad), but also follow stage directions allowing them to indulge in the physical contact they desire. But only Fanny notices that they need to rehearse Act I repeatedly.

Hearing of the decision to perform *Lovers' Vows*, Edmund can't believe the choice. He insists that a play dealing with adultery and a child born out of wedlock is morally questionable for a performance at home. He argues that for Maria, "'whose situation'" as a soon-to-be-married young lady, "'is a very delicate one, considering everything, extremely delicate,'" and taking on the part of the adulterous Agatha is dangerously immodest. He also feels it is inappropriate to put on a play while Sir Thomas is across the Atlantic Ocean, facing a potentially dangerous crossing home. To make matters worse, staging requirements mean taking liberties with the absent Sir Thomas's home in creating a stage and using his study.

Mary is cast as the flirtatious young female character Amelia, but with no one to play the part of Anhalt, her young clergyman tutor, Mary suggestively asks, "'What gentleman among you am I to have the pleasure of making love to?'" She feels Edmund can be persuaded to take the role: "'If *any* part could tempt *you* to act, I suppose it would be Anhalt,' observed the lady archly, after a short pause; 'for he is a clergyman, you know'" (1:15). Edmund, however, refuses to act and insists that they choose another play.

Tom, oblivious to squabbles, and instead focused on getting all the parts cast and the show up and running, calls out to Fanny one evening when all are gathered. He tells her that her services are needed to play a small role of the Cottager's Wife. A frightened Fanny repeats, "'I cannot act,'" to all the arguments they use to try to persuade, cajole, and humor her into taking the part. Commentators have long seen that phrase, "I cannot act," as a sign of Fanny's passivity; however, more recent sympathetic views of her character take that phrase to mean that she will not betray her personal moral code.

She even resists Aunt Norris's using guilt and humiliation to pressure her into acting, "'I am quite ashamed of you, Fanny, to make such a difficulty of obliging your cousins in a trifle of this sort—so kind as they are to you!'" The hitherto silent Edmund rises to Fanny's defense, "'Do not urge her, madam. . . . Let her chuse for herself, as well as the rest of us. . . . Do not urge her any more.'" But Aunt Norris is not one to relent:

> "I am not going to urge her," replied Mrs. Norris sharply; "but I shall think her a very obstinate, ungrateful girl, if she does not do what her aunt and cousins wish her—very ungrateful, indeed, considering who and what she is." (1:15)

An "astonished" Mary, seeing Fanny's tearful eyes, immediately says "with some keenness":

> "I do not like my situation: this *place* is too hot for me," and moved away her chair to the opposite side of the table, close to Fanny, saying to her, in a kind, low whisper, as she placed herself, "Never mind, my dear Miss Price, this is a

cross evening: everybody is cross and teasing, but do not let us mind them"; and with pointed attention continued to talk to her and endeavour to raise her spirits, in spite of being out of spirits herself.

Here the author skillfully complicates the character of Mary, who, despite her flippancy, displays "the really good feelings by which she was almost purely governed." Because of her intelligence, wit, humor, physical energy, and beauty, Mary could be a heroine, but for the qualifier "almost." She handles Aunt Norris's infliction of pain and humiliation on Fanny with the same tact as Elizabeth uses at Pemberley when, unaware of Georgiana's involvement with Wickham the previous summer, Caroline Bingley attempts to humiliate Elizabeth by asking about the militia and Wickham. Elizabeth replies in "a disengaged tone," allowing Georgiana time to recover her composure (3:3).

Still, without an Anhalt, Tom suggests asking a neighboring gentleman to participate. Edmund protests on the grounds that the production should be kept within the confines of the Mansfield circle. Claiming his consideration for Mary's feelings in having to play Amelia with a stranger, Edmund asks Fanny whether to relent and take the role of Anhalt himself.

The scene between Edmund and Fanny in the East Room that is now Fanny's retreat is reminiscent of Chapter 2 of *Sense and Sensibility*, where Fanny Dashwood convinces John to convince himself to give his half-sisters nothing. Selfish and egocentric to begin with, John easily yields to his wife's prodding. Selfish and egocentric to begin with, John merely needs to be reminded of the arguments against helping the Dashwood ladies that he is perfectly willing to accept from his wife. Similarly, Edmund, intent on acting opposite Mary, is armed with all the reasons for taking the part of Anhalt when he arrives at Fanny's door, supposedly in need of her approval. To Fanny's every hesitating doubt, Edmund is ready with an answer—which includes evoking Mary's kindness to Fanny when Aunt Norris humiliated her. What can Fanny say as he goes off to tell the news of his willingness to take Anhalt's role to Mary and the other actors? She is left to think and suffer in her cold little room, where Aunt Norris forbade the lighting of a fire. And although Edmund warns Fanny not to stay in her room for too long because it is cold, his mind is so filled with Mary that he neglects to ensure that there is a fire in the East Room in the future. When Edmund reports his new decision to Tom and Maria, who had been adamant in support of the play, the two privately "congratulated each other" on triumphing over "the jealous weakness to which they attributed the change, with all the glee of feelings gratified in every way" (1:17).

Free from pressure to act in the play, Fanny tries to help Rushworth with the hopeless task of learning his lines and cues. But she must also endure the emotional pain of listening to Edmund rehearse Anhalt's speech to Mary's character: "When *two* sympathetic *hearts* meet in the marriage state, matrimony may be called a happy life" (*Lovers' Vows*, Act 3). Unlike Fanny, who helps the players with their lines, an angry Julia has no part in the play and ignores the actors; she is on the periphery of the acting group as she was during the visit to Sotherton.

But on the night of the dress rehearsal, Julia has the most central part of all the Mansfield Park players. With Fanny asked again merely to read the lines of the cottager's wife because Mrs. Grant, who is playing the part, is compelled to remain home, Julia makes a dramatic entrance into the "theatre": "The door of the room was thrown open, and Julia, appearing at it, with a face all aghast, exclaimed, 'My father is come! He is in the hall at this moment.'" Austen certainly knew how to create a wonderful curtain-dropper to Volume I.

"Playing" on her own experience

That may have been because she was familiar with amateur theatricals from her youth. When Jane's eldest brother James was home from Oxford, he put on plays at the Steventon Rectory, with brothers, cousins (including the glamorous Eliza de Feuillide, later Mrs. Henry Austen), and boarding students acting. Commentators on this novel have asserted that Fanny and Edmund's criticism of acting at home echoes Jane Austen's criticism of acting at home. Critics who long viewed Fanny and Edmund's finding a home theatrical morally irresponsible mistook their criticism of amateur performances as Austen's personal criticism of them. But familiar from her youth with home theatricals, obviously approved by her parents, Austen cleverly used *Lovers' Vows* to heighten the sexual tensions between Mary and Edmund, as well as Maria and Henry.

"How is the consternation of the party to be described?" asks our ironical narrator when the acting suddenly ceased. The actors' collective disappointment reflects Yates's at Ecclesford. Fanny is the only one who is relieved that she does not have to act or read the cottager wife's lines; she is also relieved, far more than his selfish daughters, that Sir Thomas is safely home. Henry continues to press Maria's hand to his heart, as the stage directions suggest. But soon the Crawfords, sensitive to the Mansfield household's ways, leave for the parsonage, inviting Yates to join them there. Totally inattentive to "parental claims," however, Yates insists that Sir Thomas's return will be just a temporary interruption of their theatrics and decides to stay and greet him, causing the Crawfords to shake their heads in disbelief. Rushworth, after considerable shillyshallying, decides to join the Bertram siblings who have gone to join their father.

After the Crawfords and Rushworth leave the room, a trembling Fanny recalls Sir Thomas's forbidding manner and his final words to her before leaving for Antigua: when, speaking of her elder brother William, he told her "'I fear, he must find his sister at sixteen in some respects too much like his sister at ten.'" She hesitatingly moves toward the drawing room and remains at the far edge of the gathering when she hears Sir Thomas ask, "'But where is Fanny? Why do not I see my little Fanny?'" At this moment she sees him moving towards her "with a kindness which astonished and penetrated her, calling her his dear Fanny, kissing her affectionately, and observing with decided pleasure how much she was grown!" His attention and tenderness make Fanny blush.

An extremely happy Lady Bertram blithely announces to her husband that their children have been amusing themselves with putting on a play. An embarrassed Tom tries to cover up his mother's innocent slip of the tongue by announcing how protective he and Edmund have been of Sir Thomas's game, "'We respect your pheasants, sir, I assure you, as much as you could desire.'" But Sir Thomas is anxious to see "his own dear room," which, of course, has been turned into part of the dreaded theater. Austen writes a wonderful scene where, as Sir Thomas enters to find his bookcases moved, he hears a voice ranting from the billiards room; she creates a narrative moment that deserves to be recalled. Yates is on stage, performing the role of Baron Wildenheim, which he had longed to play with all its ranting—an early 18th-century declamatory style of acting, made famous by actor and playwright Colley Cibber (1671-1757). This style also included the "start," wherein the actor wore a highly dramatic facial expression and extended his arms forward:

> Some one was talking there in a very loud accent; he did not know the voice—more than talking—almost hallooing. He stepped to the door, rejoicing at that moment in having the means of immediate communication, and, opening it, found himself on the stage of a theatre, and opposed to a ranting young man, who appeared likely to knock him down backwards. At the very moment of Yates perceiving Sir Thomas, and giving perhaps the very best start he had ever given in the whole course of his rehearsals, Tom Bertram entered at the other end of the room; and never had he found greater difficulty in keeping his countenance. His father's looks of solemnity and amazement on this his first appearance on any stage, and the gradual metamorphosis of the impassioned Baron Wildenheim into the well-bred and

easy Mr. Yates, making his bow and apology to Sir Thomas Bertram, was such an exhibition, such a piece of true acting, as he would not have lost upon any account. It would be the last–in all probability–the last scene on that stage; but house would close with the greatest éclat. (2:1)

With all copies of the play destroyed, Sir Thomas's "dear room" is restored to its proper form and Mansfield Park returns to order. Aunt Norris secretly takes the green baize curtain home, figuring she can use the material for something. Yates senses how life at the Park operates under Sir Thomas and leaves. But Fanny enjoys hearing her uncle's evening tales of the West Indies, and even enquires about the slave trade–only to find her query met with dead silence.

Henry Crawford departs, sending neither message nor letter after three or four days. The angrily disappointed Maria's thoughts are rendered in biting free indirect discourse:

Henry Crawford had destroyed her happiness, but he should not know that he had done it; he should not destroy her credit, her appearance, her prosperity, too. He should not have to think of her as pining in the retirement of Mansfield for *him*, rejecting Sotherton and London, independence and splendour, for *his* sake. (2:3)

Sir Thomas sees Rushworth's inferiority in overall intelligence and business sense and even perceives Maria's indifference, if not coldness, toward her fiancé. However, the groom's wealth and societal position are too tempting to Sir Thomas to disapprove of the match when Maria is determined to go through with it. After an appropriately tasteful wedding, the new Mr. and Mrs. Rushworth head off on their honeymoon. Maria is happy to have Julia join them as far as Brighton: "Some other companion than Mr. Rushworth was of the first consequence to his lady." Clearly, this does not bode well for the newlyweds. The ne'er-do-well Tom goes off to join "friends" at the races.

From shadows to limelight

With the Mansfield circle diminished in size, Fanny soon moves from the periphery of the action as observer toward the center as actor. Mary befriends her, and Henry returns to the parsonage, where Edmund and Fanny are invited to dine–though Aunt Norris says everything she can to belittle Fanny's invitation there.

Seeing the well-dressed, pretty, Fanny with her "soft light eyes" and without her tall and striking female cousins around as comparisons, Henry alters his plans to return to London, blithely announcing to Mary how he will spend the next two weeks, "'[M]y plan is to make Fanny Price in love with me. . . . I cannot be satisfied without Fanny Price, without making a small hole in Fanny Price's heart.'" While Mary warns her brother not to hurt Fanny, the cavalier Henry rationalizes that he really cannot hurt her in two weeks' time. Surprisingly to Henry, his intentions to toy with Fanny will change.

Henry is particularly enchanted by Fanny's warm-hearted response when "her dearly loved brother" William, now a midshipman, is invited to Mansfield Park. Seeing "the glow of Fanny's cheek, the brightness of her eye, the deep interest, the absorbed attention" as she listens to her brother recount his naval adventures, Henry is soon strongly attracted to "the sensibility" that "beautified her complexion":

> He was no longer in doubt of the capabilities of her heart. She had feeling, genuine feeling. It would be something to be loved by such a girl, to excite the first ardours of her young unsophisticated mind! She interested him more than he had foreseen. A fortnight was not enough. His stay became indefinite. (2:6)

Listening to William's seagoing tales of shipwrecks, travels, and wartime dangers, Henry eagerly wishes he could have had such adventures. This rather transient desire reminds readers of Henry's announcement when acting is first suggested at Mansfield Park,

"I really believe, . . . I could be fool enough at this moment to undertake any character that ever was written, from Shylock or Richard III down to the singing hero of a farce in his scarlet coat and cocked hat. I feel as if I could be anything or everything; as if I could rant and storm, or sigh or cut capers, in any tragedy or comedy in the English language." (1:13)

In spite of her refusal to act, Fanny enjoyed watching the rehearsals and deemed Henry "the best actor" of the entire Mansfield troupe. Likewise, his flirting with Julia and his even more egregious flirting with Maria involved acting. As he attests to growing sincerely attracted to Fanny, the ultimate test will be if he can fulfill in life, rather than merely act the part, of being genuinely in love with and true to Fanny.

William's visit ends much too soon for Fanny. But upon his asking how Fanny dances, Sir Thomas, realizing that he has never seen her dance, decides to host a ball at Mansfield Park in honor of his niece. In preparation for her first ball, Fanny seeks Mary's advice about the propriety of wearing her only ornament, an amber cross that William brought her from Sicily, on a ribbon around her neck. The amber cross is Austen's novelistic acknowledgment to her brother, 2nd Lieutenant Charles, for the topaz crosses he had purchased as gifts for his sisters with prize money: money distributed to the crew of a ship when it captures an enemy vessel.

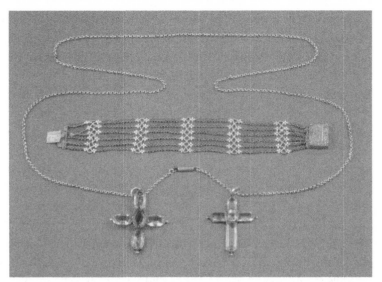

Charles Austen purchased topaz crosses with chains for his sisters; Jane's is on the left. As the author wryly wrote to her sister on 26-27 May 1801, "He has been buying Gold chains & Topaze Crosses for us;—he must be well scolded. . . . We shall be unbearably fine." The display at the Jane Austen House Museum also shows a bracelet that once belonged to the novelist (photo by Joan Ray).

Mary approves of Fanny wearing the lovely dress that Sir Thomas purchased for her to wear at Maria's wedding and asks her about the amber cross. Embarrassed at not having a chain for it (William could not afford one), Fanny sees a trinket box in Mary's hand; she encourages the very hesitant Fanny to choose a necklace or chain from the box for her cross. Afraid of appearing ungrateful, Fanny seeks the least expensive one, but also sees that Mary seems to be calling her attention to a fancy gold necklace, which leads Fanny to believe it is the one she least values. Although Fanny desires a plain gold chain, she accepts the necklace, but is shocked when Mary confesses that Henry gave it to her as a gift. Mary requests that Fanny think of both Crawford siblings when she wears the necklace. The troubled Fanny, who has noticed that Henry's manners have improved, and that he has been increasingly "gallant" and attentive to her, yields to Mary's pressure to take the necklace, but distrusts Mary "as a woman and a friend." She also distrusts the seemingly kinder Henry, thinking that he is treating her the way he did Julia and Maria and suspecting him of trying "to cheat her of her tranquility as he had cheated them" (2:8).

Returning to the Park, Fanny finds that the Crawford necklace ignites a chain reaction–pun intended. Coming upon Edmund who was just writing a note to her, she sees that he has purchased a plain gold chain, far more appropriate in style for the cross. Edmund admires Mary and Henry for the gift and encourages Fanny to wear the Crawford necklace. But dressing for the ball, Fanny finds their necklace too big for the ring of the cross. Wearing the cross from William on the chain from Edmund, Fanny is touched to be using gifts from the two most beloved persons in her life.

While Fanny is excited about the ball that evening, she meets a troubled Edmund, returning from the parsonage, where he went to engage Mary for the first two dances. Accepting the dances, Mary also said it would be the last time she would dance with him: the day after the ball, Edmund will go to Peterborough to be ordained, and Mary declares she has never before and will never again dance with a clergyman. Edmund and Fanny again moralize over "'the effect of [Mary's] education,'" the result of her living at the Admiral's home in London, which, as Edmund believes, has negatively affected Mary's "'finest mind.'" Again, scenes like this one have led readers to comment about the cousins as a priggish duo. In 1:7, Edmund asks Fanny if she thinks, as he does, that Mary's little joke about Admirals and seeing "Vices" and "Rears" at her uncle's house–referring to the buggery that occurred in the British navy and about which the author could have easily learned from her naval brothers –is improper. She concurs about its impropriety. Here the narrator adds, "Having formed her mind and gained her affections, he had a good chance of her thinking like him." And with no one else ever asking her opinion, Fanny's agreement with Edmund is to be expected.

Dancing the opening two dances with Henry, Fanny meets Sir

Thomas's approval in terms of both her looks and dancing partner. When Edmund asks Fanny to dance, they proceed in silence, as he is worn out by "'civility'" and disappointed by Mary's gaiety. Fanny feels a little guilty seeing Edmund suffer the apparent loss of Mary, as she, too, loves Edmund. But the cousins' appearance on the ballroom floor shows no sign of romantic attraction between them.

The following morning, Edmund heads to Peterborough. Henry, having offered William a place in his coach to London, where he claims to have business, also invites the young midshipman to have dinner with his uncle, the Admiral. Sir Thomas approves of Henry's invitation to William. Edmund is away longer than Mary anticipated, and she asks Fanny about the sisters of his friend, Mr. Owens, with whom he is staying; despite his ordination, Mary is still thinking about Edmund and worried about possible competition from the Owens sisters.

When Henry returns from London, he confides to Mary that his intentions toward Fanny are "'fixed'" and serious. Arriving at Mansfield Park early the next morning, Henry proudly and happily announces to Fanny that William was promoted from the rank of midshipman to "Second Lieutenant of H.M. Sloop *Thrush*." Henry explains to a shocked and thrilled Fanny "very particularly what he had done" in prevailing upon his uncle, the Admiral. Seeing how grateful Fanny is on William's behalf, Henry decides it is a propitious moment to strike: he proposes to Fanny.

In utter disbelief, Fanny protests, "'I know it is all nothing'" and flees to her retreat in the East Room. Unlike Darcy, who desired to keep his helping Lydia and Wickham a secret from Elizabeth, Henry uses his favor to William to influence Fanny's decision, just as he had used Mary's necklace "to buy" her goodwill.

When Henry returns to Mansfield Park for dinner, the meal is an anxious and nerve-wracking event for Fanny. The evening becomes even more stressful when, after the meal, he hovers over her as she tries to respond to a letter from Mary, which congratulates her on William's promotion and on Henry's proposal, encouraging Fanny to accept. Making his case to Sir Thomas for marrying Fanny, Henry is confident of success. But as the narrator says, "He knew not that he had a pre-engaged heart to attack" (3:2). Sir Thomas, who had knowingly given Maria's hand to Rushworth, approves Henry's request for Fanny's hand.

The next day Sir Thomas seeks Fanny in the East Room. The first thing he notices is that despite the cold, the fire is not lit. When she stumblingly explains about Aunt Norris's decision to deprive her of the fire, he mentions Aunt Norris's belief that young people should not be indulged—an ironic comment insofar as she has indulged Julia and Maria right under his nose. But soon the room heats up with Sir Thomas's anger at Fanny's refusal of Henry. Reminding her of the favor Henry did for William, Sir Thomas turns into something of an Aunt Norris, scolding Fanny, "'You think only of yourself.'" Accusing her of folly and selfishness, he continues, "'Gladly would I have bestowed either of my own daughters on him'"—unaware of the way Henry toyed with both Julia and Maria, a fact that Fanny will not disclose because of her loyalty to them, a loyalty they did little to deserve. He leaves her crying, her mind in total disorder. But the next time she is in the East Room, she sees that a fire is now lit in the fireplace.

Fanny hopes that her courteous but cold treatment of Henry the previous day has discouraged him. But the self-confident Henry is back at Mansfield Park and invited to dinner. Edmund, now ordained, also returns, and is surprised and disappointed that Mary is still at the parsonage. While Edmund and his father remain in the dining room so that Sir Thomas can explain to his son Henry's proposal to Fanny and Fanny's refusal, Henry finds Fanny reading *Henry VIII* to Lady Bertram in the drawing room. Requesting the Shakespeare volume from her, Henry begins reading, moving from speech to speech and character to character with alacrity. Although Fanny concentrates on her work (sewing), her interest is soon aroused by Henry's splendid reading, displaying "a variety of excellence beyond what she had ever met with" (3:3). "'You have a great turn for acting, I am sure, Mr. Crawford,' said her ladyship"

(3:3). Henry is delighted, thinking that if his reading moves the normally passive Lady Bertram, then her niece must be moved, too. Edmund and Sir Thomas now join the others, and the conversation turns to public reading. Edmund comments that even in the clerical profession, much attention has lately been paid to better reading and speaking from the pulpit. Henry replies that he has often been in church thinking of how well he could read the lessons and prayers. He even speculates that as a priest, he would prefer to preach only to the educated and not every Sunday: "'It would not do for a constancy.'" Fanny shakes her head slightly at this remark. Henry immediately pounces, querying Fanny about this gesture, firing questions at her, trying to get her to speak. She finally responds that when he said he would not serve his church "'for a constancy,'" he finally knew himself. Henry takes it as an opening to continue, professing the steadiness of his intentions towards her and insisting that he deserves her: "'My conduct shall speak for me,'" Henry proclaims. And it will.

Edmund tries to encourage Fanny to accept the proposal, dismissing her concerns about Henry's flirtatious behavior toward Julia and Maria, and pleased to hear that Mary has also urged her to accept her bother. He even belittles Fanny's protest that she and Henry are of totally different temperaments. Outlining all of Henry's perceived good points, Edmund misunderstands Fanny when she says, ""I think it ought not to be set down as certain, that a man must be acceptable to every woman he may happen to like himself'" (3:4). He replies that he now understands that Henry must not expect to succeed immediately with Fanny, and that he must exercise persistence. Henry does, indeed, persist.

The Crawford siblings leave for London, but not before Henry returns to the Park to sit with Fanny and try again to convince her to marry him. Sir Thomas sees Henry's departure as yet another way to encourage Fanny's attraction to him and to the way of life he can provide for her. Under the guise of wanting Fanny to see William before he ships out on the *Thrush*, Sir Thomas arranges for her to go home to Portsmouth.

Expecting a warm and loving welcome from her mother and father, Fanny finds "home" to be busy, filled with children, dirty, and noisy, with little, if any, attention given to her. Within a short time, when Fanny remembers the orderliness and cleanliness of Mansfield Park, she thinks of it as her home. However, she finds friendship and possibilities with her younger sister Susan, who sees how squalid the Price home is and does her best to improve it. A diamond in the rough, Susan needs some mentorship, which Fanny provides. She also takes action and joins a circulating library; just as Edmund did with Fanny, she helps Susan with reading. Fanny also acts by buying a penknife to stop the squabbling between Susan and their little sister Betsey: their deceased sister Mary left her knife to Susan, but little Betsey keeps taking it. Through Fanny's action, Betsey now has her own penknife. Into this environment of noise, dirty dishes, greasy food, and two penknives, Henry Crawford arrives.

He is on his best behavior and acts with consideration towards Fanny and her family, who clean up well, at least on Sundays. When Mrs. Price asks Henry to join their Sunday meal, he says he has another dinner invitation, relieving Fanny of potentially huge embarrassment over the greasy soup and forks. Seeing so much improvement in Henry, she wonders, "so very feeling as he now expressed himself, and really seemed, might not it be fairly supposed that he would not much longer persevere in a suit so distressing to her?" (3:11).

Austen proceeds quickly to the denouement through a series of letters that characters write to Fanny, who is still at Portsmouth.

She receives a letter from Mary detailing the social success of Maria Rushworth's first party in London, how Edmund's very good looks impressed the society ladies, and how Henry is returning to his estate to make improvements. Back at Mansfield Park, Edmund writes to say how much the family misses her and to bemoan Mary's London friends, saying they have changed Mary's ways; she now values money and societal position above all. He is disappointed at this as, he claims, "She is the only woman in the world whom I could ever think of as a wife." Edmund also reports seeing Henry and Maria at a London party, where she behaved in a coolly indifferent way toward Crawford. Sir Thomas is so busy that he cannot send for Fanny for another two months.

Lady Bertram also writes, reporting that Tom has fallen gravely ill at Newmarket, where his erstwhile friends have left him. Edmund has gone to retrieve his brother and bring him home. Fanny wonders why Maria and Julia, about whom she hears nothing more, do not go home to see their ailing brother and comfort their worried parents.

At Portsmouth for three months, Fanny receives another letter from Mary, querying about Tom's illness. She also tastelessly jokes that should events turn so that Edmund becomes the new baronet-in-waiting, Mansfield would have a very fine "Sir" in him. Mary offers Henry's services to come to Portsmouth and escort Fanny home to Mansfield Park. Fanny declines, saying she must wait for Sir Thomas's permission to return. Another letter, this one cryptic, arrives from Mary, who tells Fanny not to believe the rumors she may hear and that Henry is innocent. A confused Fanny does not know what to think when her father announces an article in the newspaper:

> it was with infinite concern the newspaper had to announce
> to the world a matrimonial *fracas* in the family of Mr. R.
> of Wimpole Street; the beautiful Mrs. R., whose name had
> not long been enrolled in the lists of Hymen, and who had
> promised to become so brilliant a leader in the fashionable
> world, having quitted her husband's roof in company with
> the well-known and captivating Mr. C., the intimate friend
> and associate of Mr. R., and it was not known even to the
> editor of the newspaper whither they were gone. (3:10)

Although she cannot believe it at first, Fanny quickly understands that the newspaper article explains the cryptic references in Mary's letter.

After a few days, Edmund writes to report more bad news: Julia has eloped with Yates, but at least they are married. Sir Thomas asks Fanny to return with Susan, and a depressed Edmund arrives to escort the sisters to Mansfield Park. He calls Fanny, "'My Fanny, my only sister; my only comfort now!'" (3:10).

When Fanny enters Mansfield Park, Lady Bertram "came from the drawing room . . . with no indolent step," to embrace Fanny, saying, "'Dear Fanny, now I shall be comfortable.'"

At the Park, a humiliated and angry Aunt Norris blames Fanny's refusal of Henry's proposal for Henry and Maria's adultery. It turns out that Rushworth left Maria with loose-living friends in Twickenham to fetch his mother home from Bath. Maria used this opportunity to go off with Henry. As with the key episode at Sotherton, Rushworth's going off to fetch something or someone gives Maria and Henry amorous opportunities. Meanwhile, Julia, seeing that Maria and Henry were getting together in Rushworth's absence, left for the home of other relatives, who happened to live near Yates.

During one evening at the Park, Edmund recounts to Fanny his final encounter with Mary in London. He is shocked at Mary's attempt to cover over Henry and Maria's "'folly'" as she calls it. Edmund continues:

> "She spoke of you with high praise and warm affection; yet, even here, there was alloy, a dash of evil; for in the midst of it she could exclaim, 'Why would not she have him? It is all her fault. Simple girl! I shall never forgive her. Had she accepted him as she ought, they might now have been on the point of marriage, and Henry would have been too happy and too busy to want any other object. He would have taken no pains to be on terms with Mrs. Rushworth again. It would have all ended in a regular standing flirtation, in yearly meetings at Sotherton and Everingham.' Could you have believed it possible? But the charm is broken. My eyes are opened." (3:11)

Mary, he continues, advised that now they must convince Henry to marry Maria, and after a few large dinners and parties and acceptance by certain friends, the new Mr. and Mrs. Crawford will be able to enter at least some social circles. Mary is astonished at Edmund's protest of this plan in the name of decency. Blushing, she soon recovers her composure and facetiously asks him if his oration on morality was part of his last sermon. As he leaves the room, she calls "'Mr. Bertram,'" doing so "'with a smile . . . . a saucy playful smile, seeming to invite in order to subdue me; at least it appeared so to me. I resisted; it was the impulse of the moment to resist'" (3:11). Mary's smile is, of course, seductive. But Edmund doesn't fall for it. He blames Mary's faults on those who raised her.

Austen begins the final chapter with an overt authorial statement of intention:

> Let other pens dwell on guilt and misery. I quit such odious subjects as soon as I can, impatient to restore everybody, not greatly in fault themselves, to tolerable comfort, and to have done with all the rest. My Fanny, indeed, at this very time, I have the satisfaction of knowing, must have been happy in spite of everything.

Fanny is happy in her knowledge that she is free of Henry's persistence, that Edmund's spirits are improving, and that Sir Thomas and Lady Bertram welcome her as the daughter they require, desire, and love. Sir Thomas banishes Maria, whom Henry deserts and whom Rushworth divorces, sending her and Aunt Norris to a different "country," which means not a different nation, but a different county or borough. There Aunt Norris and Maria will live together as each other's torment. Tom recovers, and from his illness experiences the conventional improvement "by sickness" in sense and behavior, showing that he will be a worthwhile successor to his father. The Bertrams forgive Julia and Yates, who has more money than they thought. Henry regrets his affair with Maria because it deprives him forever of Fanny. Susan, taking Fanny's place at Mansfield Park, becomes a great help to Lady Bertram. Rev. Dr. Grant secures a better church living in London, but soon dies. Edmund realizes that he can love another woman besides Mary and that Fanny is the right woman to be his wife. Sir Thomas and Lady Bertram approve their marriage. With Rev. Dr. Grant's death, the Mansfield living becomes available just when Rev. and Mrs. Edmund Bertram, who had been living at the Bertrams' lesser, smaller church living of Thornton Lacey, "had been married long enough to begin to want an increase of income, and feel their distance from the paternal abode an inconvenience." This is Austen's euphemistic way of saying that a new little Bertram is on the way.

Austen ends this book with total poetic justice, irritating some readers that everyone who did ill by Fanny is punished. The heroine, Fanny Price, continues to inspire debates about whether she is a heroine or not.

MANSFIELD PARK:

A NOVEL.

IN THREE VOLUMES.

———◆———

BY THE

AUTHOR OF "SENSE AND SENSIBILITY,"
AND " PRIDE AND PREJUDICE."

———◆———

VOL. I.

———————

London:

PRINTED FOR T. EGERTON,
MILITARY LIBRARY, WHITEHALL.

1814.

The title-page of the first edition of Mansfield Park *disguises, as did the title pages of her two earlier published novels, the identity of the author (photo by Isobel Snowden, Courtesy Jane Austen House Museum).*

From Fanny to Emma

Ironically, after writing affectionately in the final chapter of *Mansfield Park* about "My Fanny," a heroine who has long had a hard time with critics and readers, Jane Austen deemed her next female protagonist, "a heroine whom no one but myself will much like." *Emma* is the final novel Austen lived to see in print. Emma Woodhouse casts a spell on readers in spite of her flaws, just as she does on Mr. Knightley, who sees her as "this sweetest and best of all creatures, faultless in spite of all her faults" (3:13). How did Austen do this?

In his classic book *The Rhetoric of Fiction*, Wayne Booth calls *Emma* a "triumph in the control of distance," which leads readers to sympathize with and even love Austen's "self-revealing protagonist," Emma Woodhouse, in spite of her flaws, errors, and other shortcomings, based on her "disposition to think a little too well of herself" (E 1:1). Austen accomplishes this, says Booth, "by showing most of the story through Emma's eyes." He is speaking about the free indirect discourse we now recognize as Austen's great contribution to the novel. Booth also discusses how Austen uses in *Emma* direct discourse (speech) and dialogue, as well as a narrator presented as "friend and guide," as correctives for the reader's interpretation of Emma's character (*The Rhetoric of Fiction*, 2nd ed. Chicago: University of Chicago Press, 1983: 240, 264). For this, critics laud this novel as Austen's masterpiece, written with the energy and assuredness of a successful author: she wrote *Emma* in a little over 14 creative months, between January 21, 1814 and March 29, 1815.

Emma is also the work of a confident novelist in another way: she changed publishers, from Thomas Egerton to John Murray II, whose clients included the most famous writers of the day—Lord Byron and Sir Walter Scott. A reason for her leaving Egerton may have been that when the novelist and her brother Henry went to London on November 30, 1814, to meet with Egerton about doing a second edition of *Mansfield Park*, he refused. Austen then made the big leap from Egerton to the very prominent John Murray. When he sent the manuscript of *Emma* for review to his trusted friend, the editor William Gifford, Gifford wrote back, "Of 'Emma' I have nothing but good to say."

After a series of letters between Henry Austen and John Murray, the publisher met with Jane at Henry's London home in November 1815. He offered £450 for *Emma*, along with the copyrights for *Sense and Sensibility* and *Mansfield Park*. The final agreement was that the author would retain the copyright and pay for the publication of *Emma* with a 10 percent commission going to Murray. In February 1816, Murray would publish Austen's desired second edition of *Mansfield Park*.

JOHN MURRAY
1788–1843

An engraving of John Murray II by Edward Francis Finden provides the frontispiece to Samuel Smiles, A Publisher and His Friends: Memoir and Correspondence of the Late John Murray, Volume 2. London: John Murray: 1891 (photo by Crystal Dussart). Founded in 1768, John Murray is England's oldest publishing house.

Austen's extant letters are silent about her progress on the novel. Having sent to press *Mansfield Park* with its heroine predominantly on the periphery of the action, she was now producing a novel with a female character at the center of her world, with every action in the novel either initiated by or reverberating on Emma.

Critics have long repeated—to the extent of its becoming a cliché—Austen's compliment written in a letter (September 9-18, 1814) to her niece Anna (James's elder daughter by his first wife) about Anna's novel-in-progress, which in an earlier letter (August 10-18) Jane identified as called either "Which is the Heroine?" or her preferred title "Enthusiasm": "You are now collecting your People delightfully, getting them exactly into such a spot as is the delight of my life;—3 or 4 Families in a Country Village is the very thing to work on." Many persons still think this is what Austen did in her novels. But *Emma* is the only novel in which Austen actually did this. Emma Woodhouse is a stay-at-home heroine who dutifully and lovingly looks after her father, "having been a valetudinarian all his life." No wonder she is bored and starts meddling in other persons' lives.

A "modern" heroine

Emma is Austen's one novel where the complications and situations are as true today as they were when she wrote it. Think about Austen's other works. Catherine Morland is so entranced by a Gothic horror book when she visits an Abbey that she foolishly thinks it harbors the owner's dying or murdered wife; would she be that silly today and would General Tilney have even gotten away with murdering his wife, thus leaving previously overlooked clues for Catherine to discover? The Dashwood sisters must marry because, having been disinherited from Norland Park, they have no career paths open and no legal rights, thus compelling them to wed to survive financially. Today the sisters would have careers open to them. Elizabeth Bennet, great interlocutor that she is, today would be a self-supporting lawyer and likely have no need for Darcy and his £10,000 annual income. Fanny Price would not be sent to Mansfield Park, and even if she were, social services would come, arrest Aunt Norris for child abuse, and place Fanny in a foster home. Once grown, the clever and intelligent teenage Fanny would likely earn a scholarship for college. And Anne Elliot, whom we will meet in *Persuasion*, would not have to wait for Captain Wentworth because she would text him on her cell phone to propose to him. And she might not even have to do that because, as an intelligent and "elegant" woman, she would not have had to refuse his first proposal out of duty to her family, duty to him, and duty to herself as the Anne Elliot of 1806 does.

But there will always be young women who want to run others' lives, and there will always be class and status-conscious cliques as we saw in Amy Heckerling's brilliant 1995 film adaptation of *Emma*, *Clueless*. Heckerling placed her version of Emma—a teenager named Cher—in a Beverly Hills high school. The little community of a high school, like the little community of Highbury, is from Austen's one novel that actually takes place among "Three or four families in a country village."

The novel opens with a clear focus on its heroine who, unlike Austen's other heroines, does not need to marry for financial reasons because she has a fortune of £30,000:

> Emma Woodhouse, handsome, clever, and rich, with a comfortable home and happy disposition, seemed to unite some of the best blessings of existence; and had lived nearly twenty-one years in the world with very little to distress or vex her.

That little word "seemed" alerts readers that even with her looks, intelligence, and wealth, Emma will have issues to confront. And the reason for these issues is clarified in the fourth paragraph of the first page:

> The real evils, indeed, of Emma's situation were the power of having rather too much her own way, and a disposition to think a little too well of herself; these were the disadvantages which threatened alloy to her many

enjoyments. The danger, however, was at present so unperceived, that they did not by any means rank as misfortunes with her.

Austen will apply what Booth called her "triumph in the control of distance" and what is now normally termed free indirect discourse (FID) to give us Emma's perspective on persons and events. Of all Austen's characters, Emma has the most FID. Through Emma's FID, readers learn her opinions about everyone and everything.

The novel opens just after Miss Taylor, who had been Emma's governess since her mother died 16 years previously, and more recently become her best friend, marries the congenial, widowed Captain Weston, who has saved enough money to buy a small estate, Randalls, near the Woodhouse estate, Hartfield. With Miss Taylor now Mrs. Weston, Hartfield is a lonely place for Emma, though she credits herself for the Miss Taylor-Captain Weston connection.

"'I made the match myself,'" she assuredly tells their evening visitor, the bluff, gentlemanly Mr. Knightley of neighboring Donwell Abbey, who has just come home from London. He has been visiting his younger brother John and his wife, Isabella, who is Emma's elder sister. His arrival is a welcome one "to cheer a long evening" she faces with her beloved father, who has already fallen asleep in his chair. To Emma's matchmaking claim, "Mr. Knightley shook his head at her." A "sensible man about seven or eight and thirty," Mr. Knightley "was one of the few people who could see faults in Emma Woodhouse, and the only one who ever told her of them . . . though this was not particularly agreeable to Emma herself."

With no one in the "populous village of Highbury" to replace Miss Taylor as a friend, the lonely Emma seeks a possibility for at least a companion when her father's friend, Mrs. Goddard, who runs a village school, asks if she might invite a young lady from the school to join them. As a member of what the class-conscious Emma deems "the second set" in Highbury, Mrs. Goddard can always be counted on to play cards or dine with Emma's father. She introduces to Hartfield a young lady from her school, Miss Harriet Smith, for an evening get-together. Emma watches Harriet, "the natural daughter of somebody," who had placed Harriet at the school as a student and recently raised her to the status of "parlour-boarder," and while not particularly clever, Harriet

> was a very pretty girl, and her beauty happened to be of a sort which Emma particularly admired. She was short, plump, and fair, with a fine bloom, blue eyes, light hair, regular features, and a look of great sweetness and, before the end of the evening, Emma was as much pleased with her manners as her person, and quite determined to continue the acquaintance. (1:3)

Yes, some commentators say that Emma is displaying latent lesbian tendencies here. But I prefer to think of this passage about Harriet's appearance as descriptive of a doll, with whom Emma will play and assign feelings in the way 12-year-old girls used to play with their dolls, and maybe some still do. With utter feelings of goodwill, Emma now has something and someone to occupy her empty time. She is a case of arrested development, and like the 16-year-old Cher in "Clueless," a matchmaker in high school, Emma now has a project,—"a Harriet Smith" for whom, as she generously thinks, she "can do everything."

As Emma listens to Harriet chatter happily about the time she spent with the Martins at Abbey Mill Farm, and in particular with Robert Martin, who turns out to be the young farmer whom Harriet admires and who appears to admire her, Emma reflects (FID):

> The acquaintance she had already formed were unworthy of her. The friends from whom she had just parted, though very good sort of people, must be doing her harm. They were a family of the name of Martin, whom Emma well knew by character, as renting a large farm of Mr. Knightley, and residing in the parish of Donwell—very creditably, she believed—she knew Mr. Knightley thought highly of them—but they must be coarse and unpolished, and very

unfit to be the intimates of a girl who wanted only a little more knowledge and elegance to be quite perfect. She would notice her; she would improve her; she would detach her from her bad acquaintance, and introduce her into good society; she would form her opinions and her manners. It would be an interesting, and certainly a very kind undertaking; highly becoming her own situation in life, her leisure, and powers. (1:3)

Undoubtedly, Emma strikes readers as a snob here. And she is because no other female in Highbury has Emma's wealth and status. She chiefly ignored Miss Taylor's advice; Mr. Woodhouse thinks his daughter is perfect; and so she has no one to correct her, except Mr. Knightley, whose advice she ignores.

Matchmaking and confusion

She creates a courtship for Harriet with the handsome local vicar, Mr. Elton, convincing Harriet,–who, despite rejecting Robert Martin, has strong feelings for him–that the young farmer is not fine enough for her.

Emma and Mr. Knightley argue politely but firmly over the Harriet-Robert Martin subject. While Mr. Knightley agrees that Emma has cured Harriet of her "'school-girl giggle,'" he is shocked that Emma persuaded Harriet to refuse Robert's proposal, especially after he approved, albeit hesitatingly, Robert's request for advice before proposing. Mr. Knightley hesitated only because he felt Robert was "'her superior in sense as in situation,'" and that Emma, infatuated with Harriet, has caused her to miss a wonderful opportunity to marry a steady, highly respectable farmer with a loving family of sisters. He continues:

"Miss Harriet Smith may not find offers of marriage flow in so fast, though she is a very pretty girl. Men of sense, whatever you may chuse to say, do not want silly wives. Men of family would not be very fond of connecting themselves with a girl of such obscurity—and most prudent men would be afraid of the inconvenience and disgrace they might be involved in, when the mystery of her parentage came to be revealed." (1:8)

Countering his reason with her own opinion that Mr. Elton is the man for Harriet, Emma insists that her young protégé is obviously a gentleman's daughter and with her looks and sweetness will be the perfect wife for Mr. Elton. But Mr. Knightley knows Elton, saying, he is

"not at all likely to make an imprudent match. He knows the value of a good income as well as any body. Elton may talk sentimentally, but he will act rationally. He is as well acquainted with his own claims, as you can be with Harriet's. He knows that he is a very handsome young man, and a great favourite wherever he goes; and from his general way of talking in unreserved moments, when there are only men present, I am convinced that he does not mean to throw himself away. I have heard him speak with great animation of a large family of young ladies that his sisters are intimate with, who have all twenty thousand pounds apiece."

Emma interprets every event for Harriet in terms of Mr. Elton's being her serious admirer. In so doing, Emma misreads every cue:

1. Mr. Elton praises Emma's painting of Harriet, whom the artist makes a little taller and with better features, but he is complimenting the artist, not the subject. Emma sees the reverse.

2. Mr. Elton rides off to London to have the portrait framed as a favor to Emma. But Emma tells Harriet that he is showing her picture to his admiring family, telling them of his love for her.

3. Mr. Elton writes a riddle for Harriet's riddle book, and the answer to it is "courtship," with its object praised for her "ready wit." While Emma is surprised that Elton could think of Harriet as having

"ready wit," she shrugs it off, thinking, "'A man must be very much in love, indeed, to describe her so.'" But Mr. Elton intended the riddle to be for Emma.

4. Mr. Elton runs into Emma on Christmas Eve as she is returning from a visit to Harriet, who is in bed with a sore throat. Hearing this, he replies, "'A sore-throat!–I hope not infectious. I hope not of a putrid infectious sort. Has Perry seen her? Indeed you should take care of yourself as well as of your friend. Let me entreat you to run no risks.'" Emma takes this as his apprehension about Harriet's health, and advises him to take no risks, as he will be sick for the Christmas church services. Elton is really voicing concern about Emma's catching the infection.

Even Mr. John Knightley, who is visiting Hartfield for Christmas with Isabella and their young children, suspects that Elton is interested in Emma. But Emma again dismisses his ideas.

Utterly convinced that she is correct and making a successful match between Harriet and the vicar, Emma is shocked when Mr. Elton, who "had been drinking too much of Mr. Weston's good wine," and is alone in a carriage with Emma as they return home from Christmas Eve dinner at Randalls, grabs her hand, declares his ardent love for her, and swears he will die without her. Taken aback, she replies that she will deliver any message to Harriet he wishes. Equally shocked, he persists with what Emma takes as a "boastful pretense of amazement": "'Miss Smith!–message to Miss Smith!–What could she possibly mean!'" Reprimanding him for his inconstancy to Harriet, she insists that he has shown his love for Harriet in every manner. Countering that he never once thought of Harriet Smith as anything other than Emma's friend, he claims that he believes himself well above Miss Smith's level and that he has come to Hartfield only to see Emma, who, in his mind, encouraged him. Each angry with the other, they finish the short ride in silence: "their straightforward emotions left no room for the little zigzags of embarrassment."

Back home and safe from Mr. Elton, Emma is alone in her room: "The hair was curled, and the maid sent away, and Emma sat down to think and be miserable." Feeling truly sad for Harriet, the now ashamed Emma wonders how her matchmaking could have been so mistaken. She feels guilt over persuading Harriet into thinking she was in love with Mr. Elton and vice versa.

Recalling Mr. Knightley's saying that the vicar wanted a wife with money, she deplores Mr. Elton's only desiring to aggrandize himself through marriage, "and if Miss Woodhouse of Hartfield, the heiress of thirty thousand pounds, were not quite so easily obtained as he had fancied, he would soon try for Miss Somebody else with twenty, or with ten," thinks Emma (1:16). Worried about her poor protégée, Emma momentarily thinks of another possible match for her, but then reigns herself in, only to berate herself for matchmaking. She is relieved when she awakens on Christmas morning and sees it is too snowy to attend church and thus face the vicar. Mr. Elton will soon leave for a holiday in Bath, which is a relief. But she guiltily ponders the "evil hanging over her in the hour of explanation with Harriet, as made it impossible for Emma to be ever perfectly at ease" (1:16)

Emma, more tranquil with a new day that she spends with her father and the visiting John Knightleys, turns her thoughts to Frank Churchill, Mr. Weston's son by his late first wife. Losing his mother as a little child and having a father who was busy working, Frank went to live up north with his childless uncle and aunt, who took care of him as their own and bestowed on him their surname Churchill as their heir. The Westons were expecting Frank to visit on their marriage, but Frank excused himself, explaining in a letter that Mrs. Churchill was in poor health, and he couldn't leave her side. The Westons were deeply disappointed by his absence. Frank has written various letters excusing his absence, which have been devoured by the Highbury community as epistolary marvels. Volume one ends with Mr. Knightley and Emma arguing over's Frank's failure to come to Randalls.

Mr. Knightley believes it is the young man's duty to visit his father on his remarriage and an insult to Mrs. Weston that he has not come to pay her his respect. Frank's eloquent letters of excuse to Mrs. Weston "'disgust'" Mr. Knightley.

While he faults the Churchills, he also blames Frank, observing that he has visited various watering places, such as Weymouth, but cannot find the time to come to Randalls. A man of "'three or four-and-twenty,'" insists Mr. Knightley, has the means to come. A man of "'three-or-four-and-twenty,'" he repeats, has the money and the freedom to visit the Westons and should declare frankly to the Churchills that it is his duty to do so on his widowed father's remarriage. Emma, while in some ways silently agreeing with her opponent, argues in Frank's favor, noting that he is dependent on the Churchills' goodwill.

She pictures Frank as a most amiable gentleman, one who can adapt his conversation to the person and situation, and who is charming and articulate. His irritation with Frank increasing, Mr. Knightley replies, "'If he turns out any thing like it, he will be the most insufferable fellow breathing! What! at three-and-twenty to be the king of his company—the great man—the practised politician.'" Seeing his irritation, Emma admits they will never agree, and Mr. Knightley dismisses Frank as someone whom he never thinks about, in spite of his being anxiously expected by the Westons and the rest of Highbury. Mr. Knightley's strong reaction to Frank puzzles Emma; after he leaves, she thinks his prejudice against Frank is not consonant with "'the real liberality of mind'" with which she had always credited him. Emma has not noticed, though the reader has, that Mr. Knightley has repeated several times Frank's young age. What could be on Mr. Knightley's mind?

With better weather and a healthier Harriet, Emma and her companion walk around Highbury, and Emma decides to call on Miss Bates and her elderly mother. The late Rev. Mr. Bates was Highbury's longtime vicar, and now, like the Austen ladies who had to tighten their financial belts on the death of Rev. Mr. Austen, the widow and daughter live in the village "in a small way" in rooms over a store (1:3).

Mrs. and Miss Bates are, to Emma's perception, among Highbury's second set; like Mrs. Goddard, they are happy when summoned to Hartfield to keep Mr. Woodhouse company. Miss Bates is one of

Austen's great creations, "a great talker upon little matters," whose constant chatter flows in *non sequiturs*. Austen describes Miss Bates with a wonderful, if semi-reversed, echo of her first sentence description of Emma: Miss Bates "enjoyed a most uncommon degree of popularity for a woman neither young, handsome, rich, nor married." Her popularity is based on her universal good will and overall happiness, deeming everyone wonderful. However, the narrator also tells us that she "stood in the very worst predicament in the world": "she had no intellectual superiority to make atonement to herself, or frighten those who might hate her into outward respect." The middle-aged Miss Bates represents another gentlewoman who has fallen on hard times, similar to Elizabeth Watson who cares for her elderly father, a retired clergyman, in *The Watsons*.

Arriving at the Bateses, Emma finds, much to her surprise and disappointment, that a letter from Miss Bates's niece Jane Fairfax has just come, and not at the normal time when Jane usually writes—an occasion Emma tries to avoid! Orphaned as a child (her father was a military officer and her mother Miss Bates' s younger sister, also named Jane), the 20-year-old Jane has lived in London from the age of nine with Colonel Campbell, his wife, and daughter, who is Jane's age. Colonel Campbell, who had been Lieutenant Fairfax's commandant, had such a high opinion of his young officer that when the lieutenant died, he and Mrs. Campbell took in Jane to raise with their own daughter. Brought up as gentlewomen, Jane and Miss Campbell were educated by "first-rate masters," and the two girls became very close friends. Although Jane is far prettier, a much better pianist, and more clever and elegant than Miss Campbell, the latter has one thing Jane does not: family money that will contribute to an attractive marriage settlement. Thus, Colonel Campbell has been raising Jane to assume the only occupation for an accomplished gentlewoman—that of a governess. But the Campbells so love Jane that they are all delaying the "evil day" when Jane must leave them to find a position.

The "evil day" appears to be coming closer when Miss Campbell marries Mr. Dixon, who owns Baly-craig, an estate in Ireland. The Campbells and the Dixons, as well as Jane, have been enjoying a holiday in Weymouth before Colonel Campbell and his wife join their daughter and new son-in-law on their journey to Ireland. Now alone, Jane will visit her grandmother and aunt in Highbury, which is announced in her letter. "Emma was sorry;—to have to pay civilities to a person she did not like through three long months!—to be always doing more than she wished, and less than she ought!" Mr. Knightley attributes Emma's dislike of Jane to envy:

> she saw in her the really accomplished young woman, which she wanted to be thought herself; and though the accusation had been eagerly refuted at the time, there were moments of self-examination in which her conscience could not quite acquit her. (2:2)

But in spite of her guilty conscience, Emma then thinks how everyone thought the two young ladies should be intimate and "so fond of each other," because they were of the same age. How could they be intimate, thinks Emma in self-defense: Jane Fairfax is always so cold and reserved.

Jane's letter also relates that during her stay with the Campbells and Dixons in Weymouth, they were out on a boat. As Miss Bates recounts the event, Jane,

> "by the sudden whirling round of something or other among the sails, would have been dashed into the sea at once, and actually was all but gone, if he [Mr. Dixon] had not, with the greatest presence of mind, caught hold of her habit."

Hearing about this incident, and also learning that while Miss Campbell and Mr. Dixon were courting, Jane accompanied the couple on their walks and listened with interest to his tales of Ireland, which he also illustrated with beautiful drawings, Emma senses "an ingenious and animating suspicion entering [her] brain with regard to Jane Fairfax, this charming Mr. Dixon, and the not going to Ireland." She imagines that Jane and Mr. Dixon are romantically involved, although he married Miss Campbell. So Jane, Emma suspects, is coming to Highbury, rather than going to Ireland, to remove herself from his company.

This is the third time Emma's matchmaking imagination has been spinning: she takes credit for the Miss Taylor/Mr. Weston marriage; she imagines a match between Harriet and Mr. Elton; and now she suspects an illicit love between Jane and Mr. Dixon. Ironically, though, when Harriet asks her, "'I do so wonder, Miss Woodhouse, that you should not be married, or going to be married! so charming as you are,'" Emma laughingly denies her own marriageability, "'I . . . have very little intention of ever marrying at all'" (1:10). Emma continues, "'If I know myself, Harriet, mine is an active, busy mind, with a great many independent resources.'" Observing that she can have no more important place than in her father's house, Hartfield, she enumerates all the activities she can do to use her time well: paint and draw (she rarely finishes a drawing or painting), read (she has made excellent booklists but not read the books on them), music (she practices the pianoforte very little), or carpet work (a most painstaking sewing project requiring great patience). Alluding to Miss Bates, Emma continues, "'It is poverty only which makes celibacy contemptible to a generous public.'"

"'If I know myself,'" asserted Emma rather confidently to Harriet. But Emma's problem is that she does not know herself. In fantasizing about others' courtships, she is working out her own sexual maturity. Both Robert Martin and Rev. Elton are obviously not the right men for her. However, now Frank Churchill is supposed to arrive, and Emma has always had an interest in him, though she has never met or even seen him. He is the right class for her—the Churchills' heir and the stepson of Miss Taylor, who is now Mrs. Weston. Even the Westons think of Frank and Emma as a couple, so along with the rest of Highbury, Emma awaits Frank's arrival.

But the week after Emma learns about Jane Fairfax's letter, Jane, herself, arrives, and Emma is soon sitting across from her at Hartfield. Both young ladies play the pianoforte, but even Emma realizes that Jane is the far superior musician, playing with both taste and execution. Emma is ready with questions about Frank Churchill. She recalls that Frank had been in Weymouth, as had the Dixons, and that Jane has just come from there as part of the Campbell party. But to every question that Emma poses on these topics, Jane is, to Emma's mind, "disgustingly" and "suspiciously reserved." To every question about Frank, Jane gives the most general of answers. "Emma could not forgive her." Jane does have a guilty secret about which she must be quiet, but it is about her and Frank, not her and Mr. Dixon, as Emma suspects.

Highbury's attention is soon taken by the return of Rev. Mr. Elton, announcing that he is engaged. But soon–arriving a day earlier than anticipated–Frank Churchill, himself, appears in the Hartfield drawing room, along with his father. Emma's reaction is highly positive, as she is predisposed to think well of Frank, who

> is a very good looking young man; height, air, address, all were unexceptionable, and his countenance had a great deal of the spirit and liveliness of his father's; he looked quick and sensible. She felt immediately that she should like him; and there was a well-bred ease of manner, and a readiness to talk, which convinced her that he came intending to be acquainted with her, and that acquainted they soon must be. (2:5)

Before leaving, he asks about a local family named Fairfax–"'I should rather say Barnes, or Bates. Do you know any family of that name?'" Saying that, as a courtesy, he should call on them, Frank makes the first of many excuses to visit the Bates home. Emma, of course, is oblivious to the real reason for his wanting to go there: to see Jane Fairfax, to whom he is secretly engaged. Acting as if Jane were a mere acquaintance, Frank concurs with Emma about the odd way Jane has fixed her hair and other flaws that Emma mentions. Throughout the remainder of the novel, Frank finds many reasons to go to the Bates home or to extend his visit there, so he can be near Jane: he must return scissors he borrowed from Miss Bates;

he is having trouble mending the rivet in Mrs. Bates's spectacles, requiring more time at the Bates residence than he anticipated. At the Crown Inn Ball, he hurries off with an umbrella, he says, to protect Miss Bates, but of course, he wants to protect Jane from the rain; while at the ball, he is quick to get Jane's shawl and place it on her shoulders before the group goes to supper.

At various events that include Jane, Emma, and Frank, Emma shares with Frank her suspicions about Jane and Mr. Dixon, particularly when a Broadwood (still a distinguished manufacturer of pianos with a Royal Warrant since King George II) pianoforte arrives anonymously at the Bates home—and just after Frank returns from a day trip to London, supposedly to have his haircut, causing Emma to believe he is foppish. Emma tells Frank she suspects Mr. Dixon sent the instrument, and he embroiders the tale by telling her of Jane's singing Irish ballads that Dixon enjoyed: Irish ballads are also, suspiciously, included with the sheet music that accompanies the pianoforte. But at the Coleses' dinner party, Frank and Jane sing together beautifully, with no suspicion on Emma's part that there is anything between them. He pays a lot of attention to Emma and shares with her continued suspicions about Jane and Mr. Dixon. Frank's attentiveness to her persuades Emma that he is falling in love with her. But his attention to Emma and the confidences they share are, of course, painful to Jane, even if his behavior is all a ploy to throw off any suspicions about Frank and Jane's secret relationship.

The arrival in Highbury of the new Mrs. Elton, the former Augusta Hawkins of Bristol, adds more troubles for Jane Fairfax. The vulgar and brash Mrs. Elton, with her £10,000 fortune, has taken Jane on as a project—the way Emma did Harriet—and insists on finding a suitable governess's post for her. Augusta Elton is a caricature of Emma, revealing our heroine's characteristics in a brassy way: Emma's attention to social rank is parodied with Mrs. Elton's constantly talking about her brother-in-law, Mr. Suckling, and his new estate, Maple Grove; everything she sees at Hartfield prompts her to compare it with Maple Grove. Like Emma with Harriet and

Mr. Elton, Augusta wastes no time in trying to get Jane connected with the Sucklings or their dear friends the Bragges, both *nouveaux riche* families with loaded names and new estates near Bristol: their surnames are, of course, Austen's jokes about their newly acquired money—a suckling is an unweaned pig, and Bragge is self-evident. A port city, Bristol was important in the Atlantic Triangle of the slave trade: British ships carried African slaves to the New World to pick cotton and tobacco, and then went to Bristol and other port cities in England to unload the same cotton and tobacco. From there, the empty ships returned to Africa for more slaves to repeat the pattern of travel. Austen likens slavery to the governess's position in Jane's response to Mrs. Elton, who is officiously contacting her friends Mrs. Bragge and Mrs. Partridge (another highly symbolic name, the partridge hatches young who will never follow it, which according to St. Jerome signifies an impious man who possesses wealth) about securing this post for Jane as soon as possible and simultaneously attacking Jane to get this job for herself. The exasperated Jane says she wishes to wait to apply for a job until the Campbells return from Ireland:

> "Excuse me, ma'am, but this is by no means my intention; I make no inquiry myself, and should be sorry to have any made by my friends. When I am quite determined as to the time, I am not at all afraid of being long unemployed. There are places in town, offices, where inquiry would soon produce something—Offices for the sale—not quite of human flesh—but of human intellect."
>
> "Oh! my dear, human flesh! [replies Mrs. Elton] You quite shock me; if you mean a fling at the slave-trade, I assure you Mr. Suckling was always rather a friend to the abolition." "I did not mean, I was not thinking of the slave-trade," replied Jane; "governess-trade, I assure you, was all that I had in view; widely different certainly as to the guilt of those who carry it on; but as to the greater misery of the victims, I do not know where it lies." (2:17).

Of course, Jane is really waiting for Frank to secure Mr. and Mrs. Churchill's permission for his engagement, so she is unburdened of her secret.

On the evening of the Crown Inn Ball, Mr. Weston invites Emma to come early to give her opinion on the décor; this flatters Emma's ego. But when she arrives, she is soon followed by Mr. Weston's varied cousins and old friends, all summoned to come early for their opinions. Emma ponders this:

> Emma perceived that her taste was not the only taste on which Mr. Weston depended, and felt, that to be the favourite and intimate of a man who had so many intimates and confidantes, was not the very first distinction in the scale of vanity. She liked his open manners, but a little less of open-heartedness would have made him a higher character.—General benevolence, but not general friendship, made a man what he ought to be.—She could fancy such a man. (3:2)

While Emma and Frank dance at the ball, her attention is not on her partner, but on Mr. Knightley, who is not dancing, but

> standing where he ought not to be; he ought to be dancing,—not classing himself with the husbands, and fathers, and whist-players, who were pretending to feel an interest in the dance till their rubbers were made up—so young as he looked!—He could not have appeared to greater advantage perhaps anywhere, than where he had placed himself. His tall, firm, upright figure, among the bulky forms and stooping shoulders of the elderly men, was such as Emma felt must draw every body's eyes; and, excepting her own partner, there was not one among the whole row of young men who could be compared with him.—He moved a few steps nearer, and those few steps were enough to prove in how gentlemanlike a manner, with what natural grace, he must have danced, would he but take the trouble. (3:2)

Mr. Knightley is observing Emma with a troubled look, which she notices. But she also feels guiltless because she and Frank are not flirting; in fact, their behavior together looks "more like cheerful, easy friends, than lovers." Emma sees that Harriet is the only young lady without a partner. The pregnant Mrs. Weston asks Mr. Elton, who is not dancing, to dance with Harriet, but he protests that he is too old to dance, and then goes off to talk to Mr. Knightley, "while smiles of high glee passed between him and his wife." Emma is mortified for Harriet, when suddenly Mr. Knightley leaves Elton and escorts a now jubilant Harriet to the dance floor, where they dance perfectly.

Before the final dance, Emma thanks Mr. Knightley for rescuing Harriet, and he replies, complimenting Harriet and criticizing the Eltons for their nasty treatment of the young woman. As the music begins, Mr. Knightley asks Emma to dance, and she agrees, saying,

> "Indeed I will. You have shewn that you can dance, and you know we are not really so much brother and sister as to make it at all improper."
> "Brother and sister! no, indeed." (3:2)

This is an important moment for Emma. She now sees Frank as a friend, rather than a potential mate. Earlier in the evening, when she realized that Mr. Weston had invited many persons to give their opinions on the décor, she considered what she would or would not "fancy" in a man. Observing Mr. Knightley's virility and youthful appearance while she was dancing with Frank, Emma is subconsciously experiencing sexual attraction to Mr. Knightley, who just before dancing with her discounted their previous sibling-like relationship.

But she must still make more mistakes in order to mature, both emotionally and sexually, to be worthy of Mr. Knightley, who is subconsciously the man she fancies. Austen locates the site of the next major step in Emma's emotional growth at Box Hill, a 735-ft. summit in the downs of Surrey that is still known today for its panoramic views. Ironically, while the views from Box Hill are far and wide, Emma will be at her most egocentric and self-involved here, unable to see her most egregious error until Mr. Knightley rightly shames her about it.

Unknown to all, the day prior to the Box Hill excursion, Jane and Frank had an altercation when she left on her own the Donwell Abbey strawberry-picking party. Consequently, at the picnic at Box Hill, Austen shows a lack of unity among the group. As in her gathering scenes in *Mansfield Park*, Austen uses the Box Hill picnic to show the discord among her many characters: all separate into groups at a picnic, which is usually considered a communal meal.

Frank flatters Emma with lots of open attention, and she reacts with equal flirtatiousness. Mr. Knightley watches the two disapprovingly, while Jane is a captive of the Eltons, with Mrs. Elton pressuring her to take a governess position that she has been busily arranging. Frank, as the self-appointed ringmaster, proposes a game that again flatters Emma:

> "Ladies and gentlemen—I am ordered by Miss Woodhouse to say, that she waives her right of knowing exactly what you may all be thinking of, and only requires something very entertaining from each of you, in a general way . . . and she only demands from each of you either one thing very clever, be it prose or verse, original or repeated—or two things moderately clever—or three things very dull indeed."
>
> "Oh! very well," exclaimed Miss Bates, "then I need not be uneasy. 'Three things very dull indeed.' That will just do for me, you know. I shall be sure to say three dull things as soon as ever I open my mouth, shan't I? (looking round with the most good-humoured dependence on every body's assent)—Do not you all think I shall?"

Austen then writes a sentence that stops the action: "Emma could not resist." At this moment readers can see why Austen called Emma "a heroine whom no one but myself will much like."

The usually courteous Emma cannot "resist" a mean-spirited joke at the older woman's expense:

"'Ah! ma'am, but there may be a difficulty. Pardon me—but you will be limited as to number—only three at once.'" (3:7)

Of course, the gentle and harmless Miss Bates makes the best of being humiliated. But Emma's behavior has violated the social decorum of the Highbury community to an extremely high degree. Even Frank Churchill earlier said of Miss Bates, "'She is a woman that one may, that one *must* laugh at; but that one would not wish to slight, '" even though when he stopped at the Bateses' home supposedly to pay his respects to Miss Bates, he was really intending to see Jane (2:12). Emma's flippancy towards a woman who had, as Mr. Knightley reminds her, "'seen [you] grow up from a period when her notice was an honour,'" and who has now fallen on hard times, was thoughtless conduct. "'It was badly done, indeed!'" emphasizes Mr. Knightley. This moment is an emotional epiphany for Emma, who recognizes the truthfulness of Mr. Knightley's words. Austen has her heroine tearfully think about herself, "Never had she felt so agitated, mortified, grieved, at any circumstance in her life. . . . How could she have been so brutal, so cruel to Miss Bates!"

The next day Emma pays a visit of atonement to the Bateses, where Miss Bates is her usual humble and welcoming self. She worries about poor, ailing Jane, who has accepted a governess position at the home of Mrs. Smallridge in the Maple Grove neighborhood: Mrs. Elton "'would not take a denial. She would not let Jane say, "'No'" (3:8). Leaving the Bateses' home, Emma "really" feels guilty and small about all her suspicions about Jane and Mr. Dixon, about all "her fanciful and unfair conjectures" about Jane, and about her maltreatment of Miss Bates.

The denouement flows rapidly from here on in. With Mr. Knightley off to London to visit the John Knightleys, news arrives that Mrs. Churchill, long complaining of illness, has actually died. Soon Emma learns from her erstwhile protégé Harriet that Jane Fairfax and Frank are engaged. But a still bigger shock awaits Emma: Harriet is in love with Mr. Knightley and sincerely believes he returns her feelings. Harriet even reminds the incredulous Emma that it was she who encouraged her to seek a gentleman as a husband: to think of Mr. Elton and then of Frank Churchill. All that Emma can do now is blame herself for bringing Harriet forward and for filling her head with ideas about marrying a gentleman so she could "elevate her position" (3:11).

Listening in disbelief to Harriet explain how she came to love Mr. Knightley and why she feels he returns her love, Emma experiences her sexual epiphany: "It darted through her, with the speed of an arrow, that Mr. Knightley must marry no one but herself!" Emma becomes aware of her true feelings for him, recognizing that she had only realized how much her happiness depended on Mr. Knightley now that she is threatened with its loss.

The next day's cloudy, rainy weather reflects Emma's personal melancholic mood. Thinking of Mr. Knightley, she is surprised that he appears in the garden where she has been wandering. He has ridden his horse through the rain from London (16 miles away) to comfort Emma upon learning of the Jane-Frank engagement, thinking that Emma is heartbroken over Frank's duplicity with her. Assuring him that she does not love Frank Churchill, she is, however, worried that he is about to tell her of his feelings for Harriet. Speaking at cross purposes, Emma, who has asked him to remain silent—thinking she will hear about his love for Harriet—is about to leave him, but then turns back and allows him to speak as he wishes. Mr. Knightley proposes to her, and Emma, overpowered by happiness and relief, responds in the affirmative, saying, "Just what she ought, of course. A lady always does"(3:13).

Some readers complain that Austen robs us of Emma's reply. But Austen is concerned with courtship, with the way hero and heroine get together, and not with what comes afterward. This is why her novels are called "courtship novels."

Thus, the novel ends rapidly with all the correct couples together: Frank and Jane (though most characters and readers agree that she is better than he is because Frank is never frank) with the Churchill estate still set on him to inherit; Harriet marries Robert Martin, and it turns out that her father is a tradesman, not the aristocratic gentleman Emma imagined; and Emma and Mr. Knightley marry, with the approval of Mr. Woodhouse, who has always disliked marriages as agents of change, but who desires Mr. Knightley's protection of Hartfield when he learns of chicken thieves in the area.

Appropriately, Mrs. Elton gets the last words of direct speech in the novel, as she demeans the Woodhouse -Knightley wedding: "'Very little white satin, very few lace veils; a most pitiful business!—Selina [Suckling] would stare when she heard of it.'" Austen continues her satire on a poor example of a clergyman, the social-climbing Mr. Elton, who would not dance with Harriet when she was the only wallflower at the Crown Inn Ball, and who will never forgive either Emma or Harriet. Mrs. Elton, we read, was not at the wedding: she had "the particulars detailed by her husband," the officiant who, while he was supposed to be celebrating a sacrament of the Church in performing a marriage ceremony, had been observing Emma's clothing (3:19) in order to gossip later with his wife. "But, in spite of these deficiencies," says our wise, knowing, and realistic narrator, "the wishes, the hopes, the confidence, the predictions of the small band of true friends who witnessed the ceremony, were fully answered in the perfect happiness of the union," even though Mr. and Mrs. Knightley's "perfect happiness" will still have to deal with the vulgar Eltons of the community. This is a subtle reminder that Austen is a satirist and realist who does not write tales with "happily ever after" endings. Most lives have Mr. or Mrs. Eltons in them.

EMMA:

A NOVEL.

IN THREE VOLUMES.

———◆———

BY THE
AUTHOR OF "PRIDE AND PREJUDICE,"
&c. &c.

———◆———

VOL. I.

LONDON:
PRINTED FOR JOHN MURRAY.
1816.

Although the title-page of the first edition of Emma *is dated 1816, the book was released on December 23, 1815 (photo by Isobel Snowden, courtesy Jane Austen House Museum).*

Critical acclaim

Sir Walter Scott's laudatory review of *Emma* (1816) is discussed in Chapter 1 of *Simply Austen*; it is the first published discussion of the novel. Since then, *Emma* continues to be praised by scholars and general readers: it is the "Book of Books" in terms of its technical skill (Reginald Farrar, *The Quarterly Review*, 1917), "revolutionary in its form and technique" (John Mullan, *The Guardian*, 12/5/2015), Austen's "masterpiece" (Robert McCrum, *The Guardian*, 11/4/2013), and "a truly modern novel fifty years in advance of its time" (Fay Weldon, *Letters to Alice on First Reading Jane Austen's Fiction*, 1985).

Persuasion, The Novel of Second Chances

Jane Austen died before her last completed novel was published. Finishing *Emma* on March 29, she began *Persuasion* at Chawton on August 8, 1815, and finished the first draft on July 16, 1816. However, two days later she returned to *Persuasion* and revised the ending to the version readers know, completing it on August 6.

On Sunday, March 23, 1817, an ailing Austen, who was not well enough to attend church, wrote to her beloved niece Fanny Knight that she had "another [work] ready for publication": "You may *perhaps* like the Heroine, as she is almost too good for me." When the novel opens, Anne Elliot, described later by the narrator as an "elegant little woman," is 27, the age when ladies were very much at the end of their marriageability. But Anne regains her bloom when all hope was thought to be lost.

Eight years before the novel begins—and Austen is careful to state in Chapter 1, "this present time (the summer of 1814)"—Anne, "an extremely pretty girl, with gentleness, modesty, taste, and feeling," fell, back in 1806, "rapidly and deeply in love" with a visiting naval officer, Frederick Wentworth, "a remarkably fine young man, with a great deal of intelligence, spirit, and brilliancy," and he with her (1:4). He was living near Anne because his clergyman brother resided in the neighborhood. Despite her deep love for Wentworth, Anne yielded to the persuasion of her godmother, Lady Russell, who believed that "Anne Elliot, with all her claims of birth, beauty, and mind" would be "throw[ing] herself away at nineteen . . . in an engagement with a young man, who had nothing but himself to recommend him, and no hopes of attaining affluence." Anne's father, the effete and thoughtless Sir Walter, reacted with passive negativity.

But even more than Lady Russell's persuasion, Anne persuaded herself with great strength of character that in refusing Wentworth she was "consulting his good, even more than her own . . . The belief of being prudent, and self-denying, principally for his advantage, was her chief consolation . . . ." She felt she was doing her duty to him. Wentworth, however, "feeling himself ill used by so forced a relinquishment," angrily left Anne; seething with hurt pride, he dropped all contact with her and headed back to sea. This is a novel in which the hero must mature emotionally, while the heroine, already mature and sensitive, "had been forced into prudence in her youth, she learned romance as she grew older: the natural sequel of an unnatural beginning" (1:4).

Anne will have "the bloom and freshness of youth restored" (1:12), and her romance with Frederick rekindled and satisfied. While Austen writes about second chances in her other novels—Darcy has to propose a second time to Elizabeth; Marianne and Brandon are each other's second loves; Edmund, over the seductive lures of Mary Crawford, finds love with Fanny; and Emma, thinking herself matched perfectly with Frank, realizes that Mr. Knightley is the man for her—no character enjoys a physical and romantic renaissance like Anne Elliot. This happens to "only Anne."

Anne is also Austen's only heroine who has nothing to learn in terms of character growth. (Even Fanny Price needed to learn her own worth and when to act.) Ignored by her snobbish and vain father, the cash-poor baronet Sir Walter Elliot, and his favorite daughter, Anne's elder sister, the equally snobbish and vain Elizabeth (Miss Elliot), Anne is nothing to them: she is "only Anne." She lives mostly with her godmother Lady Russell, her late mother's best friend, at Kellynch Lodge. Lady Russell truly loves and appreciates Anne. But as we've seen, she discouraged Anne from the Wentworth romance eight years earlier on the grounds that at age 19, the pretty, sweet Anne had better opportunities awaiting her in a society where property played a key role in marriage choices: "Wentworth had no fortune" (1:4).

An argument can be made that Lady Russell saw in the teenage Anne what she perceived many years earlier in her "very intimate friend," Elizabeth Stevenson. In 1784, at the same age as Anne was in 1806, Elizabeth, prompted by "youthful infatuation" and "attach[ed]" by a young man's "good looks" and rank had married "the remarkably handsome," 24-year-old Sir Walter Elliot (1:1). With ironic understatement, Austen observes that her marriage did not make her the "very happiest being in the world." Yet Lady Elliot requested no "indulgence." She spent the next 17 years dealing sensibly with her husband's flaws and finding solace and activity in her children, friends, and duties. Lady Russell saw during the Anne-Wentworth romance what appeared to her to be obvious indications that her goddaughter was acting like the young woman who 22 years earlier had foolishly married Sir Walter Elliot. In 1806 Frederick Wentworth had no money, connections for advancement in the navy, or high rank. For the daughter of a baronet, this marriage would have been imprudent. (Interested readers can consult my full argument online at the following site: http://www.jasna.org/persuasions/printed/number15/ray.htm.)

The first page of the novel shows Sir Walter Elliot's reading with great satisfaction his name in *The Baronetage*–a volume that lists the ancestors and descendants of a baronet's family. Of course, Sir Walter has done nothing to earn this entry: his name in the book is merely the luck of his birth. And Sir Walter does nothing but spend money and admire his good looks in the many mirrors in his dressing room.

As an irresponsible estate owner, Sir Walter is forced to lease his Kellynch estate to a now wealthy naval Admiral, whose wife, Sophia, is Frederick Wentworth's elder sister. Sir Walter moves to Bath with his eldest, favorite daughter, who is most like him (true parental narcissism), and they live at Camden Crescent. There they can still enjoy some luxury, but on a much smaller scale than at the estate.

While Camden Place, now called Camden Crescent, as it looks today, boasts elegant Georgian homes, the Elliots' leased Bath residence is nothing like Kellynch Hall on the Elliot estate (photo by Joan Ray).

Anne, whose company is unwanted in Bath, goes to nearby Upper Cross Cottage, where her younger sister, Mary Musgrove, a complaining hypochondriac, claims she needs Anne's help. Before leaving Kellynch, Anne is the only Elliot who takes inventory of the library, arranges with the gardener about the plants, and takes leave of the tenants—only Anne knows what needs to be done and does it properly and efficiently. Some years after the Wentworth-Anne episode of 1806, Charles Musgrove, now Mary's husband, had first proposed to Anne; by that time, Anne was encouraged to accept the proposal from this non-titled gentry neighbor as no other prospects seemed available. But Anne rejected his proposal, though they remain on good terms. Anne was, of course, still true to Wentworth, though all hope seemed gone.

The plot that draws on actual events

The Navy is back on land in the summer of 1814 because the defeated Napoleon had been exiled to the island of Elba on April 20, 1814. The Royal Navy, from sailors to admirals, are enjoying their "prize money," which they received from the sale of a captured ship and its cargo, and distributed among the captors. Austen's naval brothers, Frank and Charles, also collected prize money in their careers at sea. Admirals and other officers earned thousands of pounds in prize money; low-ranking sailors earned a few shillings, but that was often more than their weekly or monthly pay. Thus, Admiral Croft can easily afford to lease a baronet's estate. When Frederick Wentworth, now a Captain, returns to Kellynch to visit his sister- and brother-in-law, he has £25,000 in prize money.

Wentworth's and Croft's names are printed in the *Navy Lists*, another book mentioned in this novel. Austen implies the difference between *The Baronetage* and *The Navy List*: the former lists names of those who have inherited rank; the latter lists names of those who have earned and worked for their rank.

The patriarch of Upper Cross, Mr. Musgrove Senior, has paid a courtesy call on the Crofts when Wentworth was with them, and he invites the strapping Captain to dinner at the Upper Cross Great House. Soon Captain Wentworth regularly finds himself in the Musgroves' neighborhood to hunt with Charles Musgrove and flirt with the two elder Musgrove daughters, Henrietta and Louisa, who are thrilled to have a bachelor naval captain in their midst. But after seeing Anne for the first time in eight years, Wentworth tells Henrietta, who knows merely that Anne met him some time ago, that Anne was "'so altered he should not have known [her] again'" (1:7):

> The aggrieved Wentworth had used such words, or something like them, but without an idea that they would be carried round to her. He had thought her wretchedly altered, and in the first moment of appeal, had spoken as he felt. He had not forgiven Anne Elliot. She had used him ill, deserted and disappointed him; and worse, she had shewn a feebleness of character in doing so, which his own decided, confident temper could not endure. She had given him up to oblige others. It had been the effect of over-persuasion. It had been weakness and timidity. (1:7)

Wentworth is indulging himself in hurt feelings that have festered since 1806. Consequently, his behavior to Anne is coldly polite, even as he is lively, charming, and as he later discovers, flirtatious with the Musgrove sisters. It appears as if his love for Anne of eight years earlier cannot be rekindled. Yet when he seriously thinks about the kind of woman he'd like to marry, "Anne Elliot was not out of his thoughts." He desires a woman "'with a strong mind, with sweetness of manner'" (1:7). The hero of this book must learn how to discern between a strong mind that is obstinate and a strong mind that can practice gracious endurance and moral fortitude.

When Wentworth, the Charles Musgroves, Louisa and Henrietta, and Anne visit Lyme Regis, where Wentworth's Navy friends the Harvilles, live, the fresh sea air helps to revive Anne's looks—so much so that a gentleman who stands at the head of a staircase, allowing our party to pass, looks admiringly at only one woman, only Anne, a phrase that has changed in meaning from the diminutive, *merely* Anne to the superlative, *uniquely* Anne: the one and only Anne. Whereas Anne had to watch Wentworth's flirting with Louisa and Henrietta back at Upper Cross, he now sees Anne admired by the gentlemanly stranger. The stranger turns out to be the heir presumptive to the Kellynch estate, Mr. William Elliot, a recent widower, who years earlier had insulted Sir Walter and Elizabeth by not jumping at their bait to marry Elizabeth Elliot.

With Anne's bloom restored, the group continues another day at Lyme. During a walk from Uppercross to Winthrop a few days before the visit to Lyme, Anne, sitting on the other side of a high hedge, overheard Wentworth's semi-humorous oration to Louisa about the importance of having "a character of decision and firmness" (1:10). His adoring student takes his little lecture indiscriminately.

Louisa enjoys being "jumped" by Wentworth–"In all their walks, he had had to jump her from the stiles [i.e., steps built by a wall, fence, or hedge, allowing persons, but not animals to move from one meadow to another]; the sensation was delightful to her" (1:12). It is likely "delightful" for both of them because his hands are around her waist as he jumps her. Remember, this novel is set in a period when unengaged couples danced wearing gloves so their bare hands would not touch. Thus, Louisa's jumping with Wentworth's help provides quite a bit of bodily contact for them. Now at Lyme Regis, and in spite of Wentworth's cautioning her about the heavy winds, Louisa, proudly displaying her "firmness" of mind, insists on being "jumped" a second time from the steep steps of the Cobbe, the harbor wall that leads down to the beach. Missing Wentworth's hands "by half a second," she falls, hurting her head. As with little Charles Musgrove's fall from a tree back at the Cottage, everyone here loses his or head while Anne–only Anne–keeps hers and offers help and advice. Wentworth recognizes Anne's capabilities in this situation as she responsibly takes charge, but he is still nurturing the hurt pride of eight years earlier.

As Louisa slowly convalesces, Wentworth is "startled" to learn from the Harvilles that, on witnessing his behavior with Louisa, they believe he is planning to marry her. However, his conduct towards Louisa, the effect of his "angry pride" aroused eight years earlier by Anne's refusal, does not reflect his real feelings about her. He was only trying to hurt Anne. As a man who does his duty, Wentworth recognizes that he must be Louisa's "in honour if she wished it." (Whether he recalls that Anne yielded to duty eight years earlier is questionable.)

Needing time to think about the entanglement into which he has woven himself, Wentworth leaves Lyme for six weeks, which he spends with his recently married clergyman brother. Meanwhile, Anne is now in Bath with her father, sister, and Mr. Elliot, who is charming Sir Walter and Elizabeth Elliot, and behaving towards Anne as if he is anticipating their marriage.

Upon learning that Louisa is now engaged to Captain Benwick, who had been reading poetry to her as she recuperated at the Harvilles' home, Wentworth hurries to Bath, where he knows Anne is now living. Here he experiences what Anne did during his flirting with Louisa: he sees Mr. Elliot's active attentions toward Anne. At a concert scene at the Octagon Room, Anne graciously steps forward in the lobby to greet Wentworth. But when Mr. Elliot appears, Wentworth abruptly leaves. At the concert, Anne makes room for Wentworth at the end of her bench, but in his momentary hesitancy to sit down, Mr. Elliot taps Anne on the shoulder from his seat behind hers to ask her to translate the Italian lyrics of the song to be performed next. Wentworth, again in angry jealousy, abruptly leaves. Anne is left with the problem, "How was the truth to reach him? How, in all the peculiar disadvantages of their respective situations, would he ever learn of her real sentiments?" (2:8).

In a culture where a lady must be modest, the "elegant" Anne faces this problem, "How was the truth to reach him," as does the author. Supplying the resolution to this question will lead Austen to revise her final chapters of the novel.

Although momentarily bewitched by the idea of being what her beloved mother had been—Lady Elliot, the mistress of Kellynch Hall—Anne has been silently questioning Mr. Elliot's constancy and his morality. When her old school friend, the now crippled Mrs. Smith, reveals that years ago Mr. Elliot had been her husband's unscrupulous business partner and unkind to his first wife, whom he married simply for her money, Anne is relieved that she knows the truth about him, thus verifying her suspicions.

The final three chapters of the novel show Austen's way of providing the answer for Anne in having the truth of her feelings reach the jealous and emotionally wounded Wentworth. Altering a month later the original July conclusion of her novel, Austen revised her original chapter 10; wrote a completely new chapter 11; and rewrote old chapter 11 into a new chapter 12. Her biographer nephew James Edward Austen-Leigh called the original ending "too tame and flat." He recalls in his *Memoir*, "This weighed upon her mind, the more so probably on account of her weak state of health," which had started to fail in April. Ailing or not, Austen could see that her original ending failed to suit the subtlety of the rest of the story. Her first ending reads like something out of a screwball comedy, which is the wrong tone for this mature, thoughtful novel.

The so-called "cancelled" chapters written in Austen's hand are in the collection of the British Library. Interested readers can view them online at http://www.bl.uk/collection-items/manuscript-of-chapters-10-and-11-from-jane-austens-persuasion. Also at this time, some scholars say, she changed the title of her novel from *The Elliots* to *Persuasion*—though others believe that Henry suggested the latter title when he oversaw its posthumous publication.

For the dénouement of the novel, the Crofts have come to Bath because of the Admiral's gout. Bath was the home of a spring that supposedly had curative waters. Some persons bathed in the hot mineral springs in special pools. Drinking the water from hard flint glasses in the Pump Room was also said to have beneficial medicinal effects as a colonic irrigation. So it is reasonable for the Crofts to come to Bath, seeking relief for the Admiral's gout.

In the first version of the ending, Anne, returning home from

Mrs. Smith's, meets Admiral Croft on the street. He jokes with Anne, saying, "'Why, Miss Elliot, we begin to hear strange things of you,'" and then invites her to visit his wife, who, he says, is at home with her mantua-maker. He escorts Anne to a room to wait for Mrs. Croft, excusing himself for a trip to the post office. She sees Captain Wentworth sitting in the room, and he is as much discomforted as Anne. The Admiral returns, intending to give the two a subject for a "tête-à-tête," and calls Frederick out of the room for a minute. Through the closed door, Anne can hear the words "lease," "Kellynch," and her own name.

Wentworth returns to the room and stumblingly tells Anne that Admiral Croft has learned that everything is settled for Anne's marriage to Mr. Elliot and that if it is wished, Admiral and Mrs. Croft are willing to give up their lease, so the new Mr. and Mrs. William Elliot can live at Kellynch. When Anne denies such reports, Wentworth steps closer to her and with her "hand taken and pressed," the words "'Anne, my own dear Anne!'-[came] bursting forth in the fullness of exquisite feeling." By doing noisy things around the house, the Crofts give the couple plenty of time to rehash their past, and the events at Lyme and the Octagon Room concert.

With the Crofts in the roles of comical matchmakers operating under a misunderstanding about Anne and Mr. Elliot, the tone of the novel changes from serious and heartfelt to semi-comical. But with the new Chapter 11 containing Anne's lengthy and impassioned conversation with Captain Harville about which gender loves the longest and fullest, the "truth" reaches Wentworth far more subtly. He is writing a letter to Captain Benwick, but really listening to Anne and Harville: this is similar to the scene of Wentworth's firmness speech to Louisa that Anne overheard in Volume 1. Anne and Harville continue their lengthy discussion, each upholding his or her own sex as the stronger in love. In a momentary silence, the only sound is Wentworth's pen dropping. Picking it up, he then resumes writing–not his business letter to Benwick, but the passionate, desperate outpouring of his heart to Anne, which we read in the 2:11:

> I can listen no longer in silence. I must speak to you by such means as are within my reach. You pierce my soul. I am half agony, half hope. Tell me not that I am too late, that such precious feelings are gone for ever. I offer myself to you again with a heart even more your own than when you almost broke it, eight years and a half ago. Dare not say that man forgets sooner than woman, that his love has an earlier death. I have loved none but you. Unjust I may have been, weak and resentful I have been, but never inconstant. You alone have brought me to Bath. For you alone, I think and plan. Have you not seen this? Can you fail to have understood my wishes? I had not waited even these ten days, could I have read your feelings, as I think you must have penetrated mine. I can hardly write. I am every instant hearing something which overpowers me. You sink your voice, but I can distinguish the tones of that voice when they would be lost on others. Too good, too excellent creature! You do us justice, indeed. You do believe that there is true attachment and constancy among men. Believe it to be most fervent, most undeviating, in F.W.

Anne and Frederick get together in a way that is most in character for all involved. After reading the letter, which Wentworth pushes towards her after returning to the desk on the pretense of having left his gloves there, a thrilled and trembling Anne says she needs to go home. Mrs. Musgrove kindly asks her son Charles to escort her on her walk. The two run into Wentworth, who has been loitering outside. Charles, ever the avid huntsman, asks Wentworth if he is able to escort Anne to Camden Place as he wants to keep an appointment at a gunsmith's to see a splendid rifle before it is packed and sent to its buyer: this is a totally characteristic request from Charles Musgrove, who loves to hunt. Thus, Anne and

Wentworth, now alone, can make up for eight years of no communication.

As Frederick and Anne walk and talk, he asks, "'Tell me if, when I returned to England in the year eight, with a few thousand pounds, and was posted into the *Laconia*, if I had then written to you, would you have answered my letter? Would you, in short, have renewed the engagement then?'" "'Would I!' was all her answer; but the accent was decisive enough." He admits his angry pride had kept him from contacting her. The decorum of the period required that the gentleman initiate the contact, not the lady. Thus, our hero and passionate letter writer had been too jealous, angry, and immature to return to Kellynch in 1808, with his newly earned money and new naval post: with such improved circumstances, Wentworth would have succeeded with Anne Elliot.

Only Anne has such a renewed romance, as well as a renewed bloom. But Anne is unique in another way: she is the only heroine on whose marital happiness Austen places a tax. Anne is married to a Captain in the Royal Navy, and in setting the beginning of this novel in summer 1814, Austen, writing it in 1816, knew with historical hindsight that Napoleon would escape from Elba on February 26, 1815–likely just weeks after Frederick and Anne are reunited according to the novel's chronology. Wentworth will be called back to service. Hence, Austen's final sentence in the novel: "She gloried in being a sailor's wife, but she must pay the tax of quick alarm for belonging to that profession which is, if possible, more distinguished in its domestic virtues than in its national importance."

Why is Anne burdened by "the tax of quick alarm"? Could it be because she is the most mature and the most practical of all the heroines, and shows the greatest "strength of mind and sweetness of manner"? Only Anne possesses both.

7. A Wry Send-up of Health Spas by a Dying Novelist

J ane Austen began what was called in her day "a slow decline" in health, beginning in April 1816, suffering backaches, headaches, fevers, mottled skin, and a general malaise. Yet despite poor health, she returned to her writing desk when she could. On January 27, 1817, Austen began writing *Sanditon* and worked intermittently on it through February; she must have been feeling better during this period. On January 24 of the same year, she wrote to Alethea Bigg, "I have certainly gained strength through the Winter & am not far from being well. . . . I am more and more convinced that *Bile* is at the bottom of all I have suffered." But she was experiencing peaks and valleys.

Parts of her manuscript, including revisions here and there, are in pencil—presumably because she was too weak to use a quill pen. The handwriting varies from a strong, clear hand to the nearly illegible hand of a frail person, reflecting the vagaries of her illness, which forced her to lay down her pencil on March 18th (dated in her hand on the manuscript). She had written 24,804 words on paper bound in three sewn booklets, stopping in the middle of Chapter 12. The longest manuscript we have in the novelist's hand, *Sanditon* is interesting in two ways, one being the actual manuscript, the other being the written fiction.

In its penmanship and revisions made during the writing process, the manuscript, itself, is the sad but provocative tale of an ailing author. The fiction is a satirical tale of the craze for beach resorts and health spas, with a plot as shifting as the sand on which the town of Sanditon is built. The original manuscript is at King's College, Cambridge. A copy of the manuscript, transcribed and owned by the novelist's sister, is at the Jane Austen House Museum. Austen called her text "The Brothers," referring to the Parker brothers, the main male characters in the piece. Her family re-titled it *Sanditon.*

The novel begins with a gentleman and a lady "overturned" in their coach. The plot (if there is one) and characterizations in this fragment overturn expectations readers have of Jane Austen—whom I would not guess to be the author of this fragment if its writer were not identified for me. For as the story spins along, we meet an array of odd, mainly "flat" (one-dimensional) characters, Dickensian in nature. They are presented in a series of episodes that spin along like the "wheels within wheels" about which the manic-hypochondriac, would-be organizer Miss Diana Parker speaks.

Austen's six completed novels are all plotted around courtships. But up to the point where the novelist stopped writing, *Sanditon* has no discernible plot and no established courtship. We might infer that the observant, sensible, and lovely Charlotte Heywood (age 22), who travels with Mr. and Mrs. Parker to the seaside town and health spa, Sanditon, as their summer guest, will end up in a courtship with Mr. Parker's younger brother, Sidney (age 27). Charlotte finds him handsome and witty when he arrives near the end of the manuscript, leading readers to believe that they might emerge as the courting couple. The work ends with Charlotte and Mrs. Mary Parker's visit to Sanditon House. There, Charlotte spots the elegant, tall, beautiful, and intelligent Clara Brereton (being poor and dependent, she is a Jane Fairfax–like character), as well as the handsome but silly Sir Edward Denham sitting together in the garden having a tête-à-tête, suggesting that something is going on between them, though Edward's pompous silliness (he thinks of himself as a dashing roué) is not likely to fool the sharp Clara. Both Clara and Sir Edward are dependents of the "Great Lady" of Sanditon, the pompous Lady Denham. But what is going to happen is anybody's guess.

At the beginning of the fragment, Charlotte's father, Mr. Heywood, a farmer working with his haymakers in the village of Willingden, witnesses Tom and Mary Parker's coach accident and offers to help. Having sprained his ankle, Tom Parker insists on seeing a surgeon, but Heywood tells him there is no surgeon nearby, even though Parker has a newspaper ad stating that a surgeon and an assistant surgeon are in the village. Heywood points out that the Parkers are in the wrong location–Willingden, rather than East Willingden or Willingden Abbots, for "'There are two Willingdens in this Country [i.e. county].'" Parker is looking to hire a surgeon to work in Sanditon, an up-and-coming spa town in which he is investing. He describes the place with great optimism and enthusiasm during his two-week convalescence at the Heywoods' home, while the coach is being repaired. His investment partner is the twice-widowed, rich, and money-conscious Lady Denham, the "great lady" of Sanditon because, as our wry narrator quips, "Every neighborhood should have a great lady."

With 14 children, the Heywoods travel little (except for trips to London to collect dividends, so we know they are doing well financially). The Parkers invite the eldest Heywood daughter, the level-headed Charlotte, to join them for the summer.

Once in Sanditon, which has fashionably named locations such as Trafalgar House (the Parkers' new home) and a planned Waterloo Crescent, Charlotte meets a large cast of characters who arrive on the scene in rapid succession and in their own episodes, including a student, Miss Lambe, whom Austen provocatively describes as "about seventeen, half mulatto, chilly and tender, [with] a maid of her own."

How this tale with multiple characters will work out is unclear. There have been about a dozen attempts to continue and complete the manuscript, including one by the novelist's niece, Anna Austen Lefroy. The "continuators" tried, unsuccessfully, to emulate Austen's style.

What is clear is that the ailing Austen was composing a broad social satire peopled by many would-be invalids who are reminiscent of the "characters of humours" who dominated the 16th-century genre known as comedies of humours. Playwright Ben Jonson described these characters in the "Induction" (1.108) to his sequel, *Every Man Out of His Humour* (1599), modeled after its successful predecessor, *Every Man in His Humour*:

> Some one peculiar quality
> Doth so possess a man, that it doth draw
> All his affects, his spirits, and his powers,
> In their confluctions, all to run one way.

The *Oxford English Dictionary* defines "confluction" as a now obsolete word that means "the action of flowing together"; Jonson's usage above is the second and final example of the word in print.

The word "humour," as used by the ancient Greek physicians and medieval medicine, refers to the four major humours of the human body, which correspond to the four known elements (fire, air, earth, and water), representing, respectively, the qualities of heat, cold, dryness, and moisture. A person's "temperament" or constitution depended on the proportion of the four humours (fluids) in one's body. A person with a normal personality possessed the four humours in correct proportion. But as Jonson wrote, when "one peculiar quality" or humour predominates or "run[s] one way", the character is "humourous"–not in the sense of cracking jokes, but in behaving in a way that shows the particular humour in an exaggerated way. Such "humorous" behavior gives rise to humor. One wonders about Austen's familiarly with Molière's *Le malade imaginaire*, known in English as *The Would be Invalid* (1673).

This chapter is admittedly a fragment; but so is *Sanditon*.

8. Jane Austen's Popularity and Legacy

When Bill Deresiewicz's book, *A Jane Austen Education: How Six Novels Taught Me About Love, Friendship, and the Things That Really Matter*, came out in 2011, the media boomed with features about a man, a former English professor, who not only read Jane Austen, but also wrote over 200 pages about what he had learned from her novels. For in the last 20 years or so, many persons have viewed Austen as a female author writing exclusively for women, advising them on how to get their own Mr. Darcys. Austen might gasp at this.

Of course, she wrote courtship novels. But before Colin Firth—or actually his double—plunged into the pond to cool down and emerged with his wet white shirt clinging to his abs for the 1995 *Pride and Prejudice* television series, Austen had a largely male readership: while ladies certainly read her novels, her readers and most vocal admirers were predominantly men. The irony is appropriate for Jane Austen, whose stylistic forte was irony.

In addition to Sir Walter Scott, whose review of and laudatory comments about her novels have been discussed, many other male writers commended Austen, and male readers, in general, enjoyed her novels. After Murray published *Northanger Abbey* and *Persuasion* in December 1817, no new editions of her work appeared in Great Britain for 15 years. But she was far from forgotten.

In January 1821, a lengthy anonymous essay analyzing a "new style of novel" and commending Austen's as exemplary of the new style appeared in the *Quarterly Review*. Now known to be the work of the Oxford-educated rhetorician and Anglican cleric, Richard Whately, who in 1831 became the Archbishop of Dublin, it echoes Scott, who in reviewing *Emma* in the same journal had discerned the difference between realistic and unrealistic fiction. Whately stated that this "new" type of novel neither strains our "credulity," nor entertains our "imagination by wild variety of incident or by those pictures of romantic affection and sensibility," found in the early English novel.

Connecting fiction that presents "a perfectly correct picture of common life"—today called realism—to moral instruction, Whately praised Austen for being the best novelist to do this. Rather than indulging in didacticism, her "moral lessons" in the novels "spring incidentally from the circumstances of the story"; hers are novels of "real history." Furthermore, and of great importance, Whately observed that as the narrator, Austen presented "as little as possible in her own person," thus giving "a dramatic air to the narrative, by introducing frequent conversations": Whately recognized not only her use of free indirect discourse, but also her dramatic presentation of the plot as discussed earlier in *Simply Austen*. Commending her "study of human nature," Whately likened Austen to Shakespeare, whom Samuel Johnson praised in the introduction to his edition of Shakespeare's plays for presenting a "mirror of life."

Even before Whately's essay, Henry Crabbe Robinson (1775-1867), diarist, traveler, barrister, and war correspondent for the London *Times*, wrote in his diary on January 12, 1819, of the excellence of *Pride and Prejudice*, particularly its characters and "the perfectly colloquial style of dialogue"; three years later, he recorded his praise for *Emma* for "evincing great good sense" (April 20, 1822).

Among the many prominent male readers and admirers of Jane Austen were Sir James Mackintosh (Whig politician, abolitionist, barrister, and physician); Samuel Taylor Coleridge; William Wordsworth; Robert Southey (poet); Lord Macaulay (who in 1843, in an unsigned essay in *The Edinburgh Review* about the novels of Fanny Burney, whom, he says, Austen has surpassed, wrote that while Shakespeare "has no equal," he had "no hesitation" in naming Austen as the writer who "has approached nearest to the manner of the great master" in terms of her variety of characters and her ability to distinguish among them); George Lewes (journalist who irritated Charlotte Brontë by calling Austen's novels "exemplary" in his *Fraser's Magazine* article of December 1847, in which he was actually the first person in print to use the phrase "a prose Shakespeare" when speaking of Austen); William Charles Macready (actor); Charles Darwin; Edward Bulwer-Lytton, First Lord Lytton (politician and novelist); Allan Cunningham (poet, dramatist, and critic); Edward Fitzgerald (of Omar Khayyám fame; he deemed her novels "perfect"); Alfred Lord Tennyson (who on a visit to Lyme Regis requested to see the steps from which Louisa Musgrove fell); and Benjamin Disraeli (who claimed he read *Pride and Prejudice* 17 times).

Samuel Clemens admired her: in evenings at home, he, his wife, and daughter read Austen aloud. But in his persona as Mark Twain, he sneered at Jane Austen to exasperate his good friend, William Dean Howells, who adoringly called her "The Divine Jane" in *Criticism and Fiction* (1891). Consider Twain's much-repeated statement: "Every time I read *Pride and Prejudice* I want to dig her up and beat her over the skull with her own shin-bone!"–"*Every time*" he reads *Pride and Prejudice*?! (That so many persons for so long missed the dramatic irony of Twain's quip might have amused Austen.)

Rudyard Kipling read Austen to his wife and daughter as they mourned the death of the Kiplings' young son Jack in WW I. Kipling's poignant short story "The Janeites," published in 1924 in *Hearst's International* magazine, deals with a group of soldiers who are Masons and form at the front a shadow Masonic Lodge centered on Jane Austen; they call themselves "The Janeites." Their newest member is a Cockney assistant mess-waiter, Humberstall, whom they introduce to Austen's novels. Reading Austen in the trenches helps "The Janeites" deal with the brutal horrors of the war. "There's no one to touch Jane when you're in a tight place," says Humberstall, the only surviving member, the rest having been killed in a barrage of artillery. He tells their story while helping to clean a masonic lodge. Though Humberstall is now home in London, he suffered severe psychological damage in the war (today called PTSD) and is subject to quiet "fits," having sustained a head injury. He is only alive because he quoted *Emma* to a nurse, also an Austen lover, who thereupon placed the injured soldier on a hospital train, thus saving him. But because of Humberstall's shell shock and fits, his mother has to meet him and take him home from his sweeping job, illustrating the tragic effect of the war on the soldiers who fought in it, including those who survived.

During and after WWI the British army recommended that hospitalized soldiers, especially those who suffered shell shock, read Jane Austen. Her novels were considered as psychologically therapeutic and generally calming by presenting an England of a gentler, more civilized era. After all, it was for this idealized England that they were fighting. Interestingly, shortly after WW I, Austen officially entered the academic canon with a definitive edition of her novels under the editorship of R.W. Chapman and published by Oxford University's Clarendon Press in 1921.

On February 16, 2017, Professor Janine Barchas (Univ of Texas, Austin) published in *The Review of English Studies* a groundbreaking essay, "Why K.M. Metcalfe (Mrs. Chapman) is 'Really the Originator in the Editing of Jane Austen.'" Dr. Barchas shows that while literary history lauds R.W. Chapman as the father of Austen editions, he reproduced Katharine Marion Metcalfe's (in 1913, she became Mrs. Chapman) 1912 edition of *Pride and Prejudice*, published by Oxford University Press. As Professor Barchas demonstrates, Mr. Chapman's edition "mimics Metcalfe's volume in virtually every detail." See

https://academic.oup.com/res/article-abstract/doi/10.1093/res/hgw149/2999313/Why-K-M-Metcalfe-Mrs-Chapman-is-Really-the?redirectedFrom=fulltext

E. M. Forster's review of the Chapman edition in *The Nation* (January 25, 1924) beginning, "I am a Jane Austenite, and therefore slightly imbecile about Jane Austen" reflects the idolatry that had amassed around the novelist.

Leave It to the Women to Discern the True Jane

Austen

But amid all the male readers who admired Austen, it was a female commentator who first called attention in print to Austen's cynicism. Responding to James Edward Austen Leigh's presentation of his gentle aunt in his *Memoir*, Margaret Oliphant, as observed earlier, pointed to her cynicism hidden behind a "soft" and gentle façade that jeers at her world. Austen's depiction of certain characters is "cruel in its perfection" and "unflinching" (think Mr. Collins, John Dashwood, Mrs. Ferrars, Robert Ferrars, etc.). This is a subversive Austen, who presents human quirks and silliness with "consistent remorseless ridicule" (*Blackwood's Edinburgh Magazine*, March 1870).

Likewise, a woman, Sarah Tytler (pseudonym of Scottish novelist Henrietta Keddie), writing in 1880 the first literary biography of Austen not by a family member, describes the novelist as a "brilliant, rather hard girl," who in the patriarchal society in which she lived, is "laughing in her sleeve" (*Jane Austen and Her Works*).

Despite these insights, the gentle Jane Austen sanctified in her nephew's *Memoir* continued throughout the 19th century and even into the 20th century. English author George Barnett Smith wrote of the "gifted woman" who lived a "calm" life untouched by "anger," and whose novels offer "intellectual solace and recreation" (*Gentleman's Magazine*, 1885). William McGuffey included a passage from *Emma*—Mrs. Elton's first visit to Emma (2:14)—to illustrate the moral lesson "that wealth alone is [insufficient] to determine one's social position" (*McGuffey's High School Reader*, 1889). Goldwin Smith's 1890 *Life of Jane Austen* for the "Great Writers Series" reiterates the *Memoir's* emphasis on Austen's "genius" and praises the lack of "hidden meaning" in her work. American editor and author, Oscar Fay Adams, believed Austen was "misconstrued." Aiming to "dispel" the "forbidding" image of Austen as prim and "old maidish," Adams stressed that she was "winsome and delightful" ("Preface" to *The Story of Jane Austen's Life*, 1891). Deeming her considerate "for the

feelings of others," he said that while she "derived amusement from .
. . the vanities and small frailties" of humanity, she manifested it only
to her sister. One wonders how closely he read her novels.

Austen's Novels Widely Available and Accessible Beginning in 1832

Beginning in 1832, Austen's novels would never be out of print. In
1828, London publisher Richard Bentley purchased the copyright
to five of Austen's novels from Henry and Cassandra Austen. In
1830, upon the death of Thomas Egerton, the publisher of *Pride
and Prejudice*, Bentley purchased from Egerton's executors the
copyright for that novel. December 1832 saw the publication of
Sense and Sensibility, and in July 1833 that of the remaining five
novels as part of Bentley's popular "Standard Novels Series." They
were clothbound with paper labels and engraved frontispieces; Jane
Austen's name appeared in the bylines. Her novels were thus
available for the growing reading public's home libraries in what
Bentley advertised as a "Cheap and Complete Edition" (*The Morning
Chronicle*, October 24, 1833). The ad says that these "elegantly"
bound volumes complemented the ones Bentley has already
published of Sir Walter Scott and Lord Byron. From here on in,
Austen's novels were readily available for purchase.

Austen's Literary Influence

While this is a topic of dissertations, Austen's literary influence
is widespread, both on canonical authors and writers of—as I call
them—"Cheeseburger" novels, because every once in a while,
between devouring the classics, we all need a more casual "read,"
just as we need a cheeseburger.

Two of the most prominent canonical authors influenced by Austen were Henry James and Virginia Woolf.

Although James criticized Austen for her narrative intrusions (the "My Fanny" passage of *Mansfield Park*), he admired her novels and her ability to bring readers into the minds of her characters. James's narrative method is more complex than Austen's in its use of stream of consciousness, presenting the thoughts of a character in their randomness, spontaneous associations, and fragmentary quality. Many of his novels are considered comedies of manners, like Austen's.

Woolf admired Austen and wrote memorably about the novels that Austen did not live to write (*The Nation*, 1913). In "Who's Afraid of Jane Austen," scholar Janet Todd showed how frequently Austen surfaces in Woolf's diaries, letters, criticism, and novels (*Jane Austen: New Perspectives*, ed. Janet Todd, 1983). Literary commentators often compare Woolf's novels to Austen's, and on a most general level, Woolf, like Austen, wrote about the common experiences of women.

Cheeseburger Austen

With interest in Austen having reached worldwide proportions, many of her readers become so involved in her characters that they want to know what happens to them after their novels end. This has led to the spinning of sequels—some professionally published, others self-published or done by vanity presses, and some online. Readers seeking information on sequels can go to the Republic of Pemberley website at ww.pemberley.com

Recently, Elizabeth Bennet has fought zombies, and Colonel Brandon has found himself among sea monsters. A film version of "Pride and Prejudice and Zombies" was released in 2016. This is quite a stretch from the 1940 film version of *Pride and Prejudice* adapted by Aldous Huxley and Jane Murfin, and starring Greer Garson and

Laurence Olivier as Elizabeth and Darcy with a helpful, matchmaking Lady Catherine played by the inimitable Edna May Oliver. The women are costumed in mid-19th century hooped skirts as worn by women in America during the Civil War and seen in the previous year's hit film, "Gone With the Wind." The movie's release, with costume connections to America's 19th-century domestic war, was part of the British effort to remind Americans of "Jolly Olde England" and prompt them to come to its aid in WWII—again, we see Austen as part of a war effort as we did in WWI. Garson, the 37-year-old actress who played Elizabeth Bennet—"not one and twenty" as she is in the novel (2:6)—also played Mrs. Miniver in the great 1942 film of that name, thus suggesting the "inter-textuality," as scholars call it, of all three named films.

From Helen Fielding's Bridget Jones novels to dating manuals (*Dating Mr. Darcy*), Jane Austen has been appropriated far and wide, for better or worse. Ever conscious of her finances, Austen would likely deplore the cheeseburger imitators who exploit her, but enjoy enumerating her earnings.

I read neither Cheeseburger Austen nor the Austen-inspired how-to books. When a caller asked me on an NPR radio program what I read after completing Austen's novels, I simply replied, "I re-read Jane Austen because every time I do, I learn something new" ("The Diane Rehm Show: Jane Austen 101" on April 11, 2005).

Sources

Adams, Oscar Fay. *The Story of Jane Austen's Life*. Boston: Lee and Shepherd, 1897

Austen, Jane. *Jane Austen's Letters*. Collected and edited by Deirdre Le Faye. Oxford: OUP, 1995.

Austen, Jane. *The Novels of Jane Austen*. Ed. R.W. Chapman. 3rd ed. Oxford: OUP, 1933-1969.

Austen, Jane. British Library, Cancelled Chapters of *Persuasion* accessible at the British Library.

Austen Jane. *Sanditon* Ms. accessible at King's College, Cambridge.

Austen-Leigh, James Edward. *A Memoir of Jane Austen*. London: Richard Bentley and Son, 1870; second edition, enlarged and revised as *A Memoir of Jane Auden. To which is added "Lady Susan" and Fragments of Two Other Unfinished Tales by Miss Austen*. London: Richard Bentley and Son, 1871.

Austen-Leigh, Richard Arthur, ed. *Austen Papers, 1704-1856*. Colchester, England: Spottiswoode, Ballantyne, 1949.

Austen-Leigh, William, and Richard Arthur Austen-Leigh. *Jane Austen: Her Life and Letters. A Family Record*. London: Smith and Elder, 1913.

Barchas, Janine. *Matters of Fact in Jane Austen: History, Location, and Celebrity*. Baltimore: Johns Hopkins University Press, 2012.

"Becoming Jane," Miramax. 2007. film.

Bigg-Wither, Reginald Fitz-Hugh. *Materials for a History of the With Family*. Winchester: Warren and Son, 1907.

Booth, Wayne. *The Rhetoric of Fiction*. 2nd ed. Chicago: University of Chicago Press, 1983.

Brabourne, Edward, Lord. ed. *Letters of Jane Austen*. 2 vols. London: Richard Bentley and Son, 1884.

Burke, Edmund. *A Philosophical Enquiry in the Origins of our Ideas of the Sublime and Beautiful*. ed. Adam Phillips. Oxford and NY. Oxford University Press, 1990.

Deresiewicz, William. *A Jane Austen Education: How Six Novels Taught Me About Love, Friendship, and the Things That Really Matter.* London: The Penguin Press, 2011.

Fowler, Karen Joy. *The Jane Austen Book Club.* NY: Putnam, 2004.

Hagstrum, Jean. *Sex and Sensibility: Ideal and Erotic Love from Milton to Mozart.* Chicago: University of Chicago Press, 1980.

Heckerling, Amy. "Clueless" film, 1995.

Honan, Park. *Jane Austen: Her Life.* NY: St. Martin's Press, 1987.

Johnson, Claudia L. *Jane Austen: Women, Politics, and the Novel.* Chicago: University of Chicago Press, 1988.

Kaplan, Deborah. "'There She is at Last': The Byrne Portrait Controversy," Accessed 17 November 2016 at JASNA.

Kirkham, Margaret. *Jane Austen, Feminism and Fiction.* London and NY: Athlone Press, 1997.

Lane, Maggie. *Jane Austen's Family: Through Five Generations.* London: Robert Hale, 1995.

Le Faye, Deirdre, ed. *A Chronology of Jane Austen.* Cambridge: Cambridge University Press. 2006

Le Faye, Deirdre. *Jane Austen: A Family Record.* 2nd ed. Cambridge: Cambridge University Press, 2004.

MacKinnon, Sir Frank. *On Circuit 1924-1937.* Cambridge: Cambridge University Press, 1940.

Modert, Jo. *Jane Austen's Manuscript Letters in Facsimile: reproductions of every known extant letter, fragment, and autograph copy, with an annotated list of all known letters.* Carbondale, IL: Southern Illinois University Press, 1990.

Nokes, David. *Jane Austen: A Life.* NY: Farrar, Straus & Giroux, 1997.

Radcliffe, Ann. *The Mysteries of Udolpho.* ed. Bonamy Dobrée. Oxford: Oxford University Press, 1970.

Ray, Joan, ed. *Dictionary of Literary Biography: Jane Austen's Life and Novels,* vol. 363. A Bruccoli Clark Lyman Book. Detroit, NY, San Francisco, New Haven, Maine, London: Gale Cengage, 2012.

Ray, Joan, ed. *Dictionary of Literary Biography: Jane Austen's Popular and Critical Reputation.* vol. 365. A Bruccoli Clark Lyman

Book. Detroit, NY, San Francisco, New Haven, Maine, London: Gale Cengage, 2012.

Ray, Joan. "'The Amiable Prejudice of a Young [Writer's] Mind'": The Problems of *Sense and Sensibility*." *Persuasions On-Line*. vol. 26, no. 1 (Winter 2005).

Ray, Joan. "In Defense of Lady Russell; or, The Godmother Knew Best." *Persuasions* 15 (1993): 207-215.

Smith, Goldwin. *Life of Jane Austen*. London: Walter Scott, 1890.

Straus, Ralph. *Carriages and Coaches Their History and Their Evolution*. Philadelphia: Lippincott, 1912.

Sutherland, Kathryn, ed. *Memoir of Jane Austen: and Other Family Recollections*. Oxford: Oxford's World's Classics, 2008

Todd, Janet, ed. *Jane Austen in Context*. Cambridge: Cambridge University Press, 2005.

Watt, Ian. *The Rise of the Novel: Studies in Defoe, Richardson and Fielding*. Berkeley: University of California Press, 1964.

White, Laura Mooneyham. *Jane Austen's Anglicanism*. London: Routledge: 2016.

Wiltshire Archaeological and Natural History, Devizes: H.F. Bull, 1884.

Wollstonecraft, Mary. *A Vindication of the Rights of Woman*. ed. Miriam Brody. London: Penguin Classics, 2004.

Woolf, Virginia. *The Common Reader*. NY: Harcourt, Brace, and Co., c. 1925.

Suggested Reading

Since the Bentley Editions of 1832-33, Austen's novels have never been out of print. For my Austen seminars, I always used the Oxford World's Classics paperback editions: they are edited by respected scholars and are inexpensive. They also present the novels with appropriate volume breaks: to be clear on this, the novels are single books, of course, but broken into volumes with chapters. *Sense and Sensibility, Pride and Prejudice, Mansfield Park,* and *Emma* are Austen's triple-deckers, comprised of three volumes within one book. Thus, we speak of 3:3 as volume 3, chapter 3. *Northanger Abbey* and *Persuasion* are two-volume novels and were published as such.

The first scholarly edition and still widely accepted as such is R.W Chapman's *The Novels of Jane Austen,* 5 vols. (Oxford University Press), 1st ed. 1923, 1926, 2nd ed., 1932-34, 3rd ed., and many times reprinted with additional revisions, corrections, and additions. See in Chapter 8 the research by Professor Janine Barchas showing that R.W. Chapman based his editing on the earlier work of his wife. In 2009, Cambridge University Press, under the general editorship of Professor Janet Todd, presented *The Cambridge Edition of the Works of Jane Austen.* In some scholarly circles, this has superseded Chapman's edition. The Cambridge edition benefits from modern scholarship. They are expensive, but lovely to have in one's personal library. Besides the six novels, the Cambridge Edition also includes a volume of Austen's *Juvenilia* and one called *Later Manuscripts:* despite the title "Later," this volume includes Austen's early work, "The Watsons" and "Lady Susan," as well as the 1817 *Sanditon,* and other material exclusive of the six novels. Another very helpful volume in the Cambridge edition is Janet Todd's *Jane Austen in Context,* consisting of essays covering a broad array of Austen-related topics.

In 2010, Harvard University Press began printing the over-sized

Jane Austen Annotated Editions, edited by superlative scholars and presented as both aesthetic and scholarly masterworks. Fully annotated and beautifully illustrated with many color plates, this series was completed in October 2016, with eminent Harvard Professor Deirdre Lynch's edition of *Mansfield Park*. I recommend these annotated editions as the best and most responsible fully annotated editions of Austen's novels that owners will appreciate as both coffee table books and insightful additions to the readers' understanding of Austen's novels. Another annotated set of Austen's novels is by a David Shapard, of unknown academic affiliation. His editions, which I have examined, lack the scholarly quality presented by the Harvard edition's wide-ranging current scholarship. I reviewed Shapard's annotated *Pride and Prejudice* on Amazon after observing that particular notes omitted appropriate citations and listening to an interview where he erred in his discussion of entails, omitting Lady Catherine's important announcement to Elizabeth that her late husband's family, Sir Lewis, did not believe in entails. Thus, I question the academic reliability of the Shapard editions.

According to Caroline Austen, her aunt Cassandra Austen destroyed a huge number of her sister's letters—the most recent scholarly editor of Austen's letters suspects Cassandra of burning at least 3,000 (Deidre Le Faye, *Letters*: 33)—but 95 to Cassandra survive, as do a handful of letters to brothers Frank and Charles, nieces Anna, Fanny, and Caroline, nephew James-Edward; and good friends Miss Anne Sharp(e) (the governess at Godmersham for the Austen Knight children), Martha Lloyd, and Alethea Bigg. We have her letters to John Murray II, her final publisher in her lifetime, and to Crosby & Company, who was sitting on her novel *Susan*, later known as *Northanger Abbey*. We also have the letters she wrote to the Prince Regent's Librarian at Carlton House, the Rev. James Stanier Clarke, who was pestering her with his ideas for novels. The manuscript copies of the letters (in her hand) are in collections around the world, but most (13 of them) are in the British Library and the Pierpont Morgan Library in NYC. Some are still in private hands. The Le Faye edition, which is the authoritative edition for scholars, printed 161 letters by Jane Austen in *Jane Austen's Letters*, collected and edited Deidre Le Faye. 3rd ed. Oxford: Oxford University Press, 1995. R.W. Chapman presented the world with the first scholarly edition of Austen's letters: *Jane Austen's Letters to her Sister Cassandra and Others*. Oxford: Clarendon Press, 1932; 2nd ed. 1952. But Deidre Le Faye's edition provides better editing of the letters because Chapman's editions occasionally conflate letters or misdate them. Le Faye also corrected Chapman's numbering of the letters; she conveniently cross-references Chapman's numbers in her edition. The edition has excellent indexes with information about persons and places.

In 1990, freelance writer Jo Modert edited a facsimile edition of Austen's letters (Carbondale: Southern Illinois University Press), but the facsimiles are not high quality and are hard to read. However, she corrected many errors in dates in Chapman's editions. In this edition, one can see how letters were written with blank space for the address so they could be folded and addressed before the introduction of envelopes in the 1840s. Readers interested in learning how Austen and her contemporaries folded letters can go to the website http://toracellie.blogspot.com/2011/11/writing-and-folding-regency-style.html.

A two-volume set of Jane Austen's letters appeared in 1884 under the editorship of her great-nephew, Edward Knatchbull, 1st Baron Brabourne (1829-1893), who in 1882 inherited a cache of Austen papers from his mother, the novelist's favorite niece Fanny Austen Knight. (In 1820, Fanny became the second wife of Sir Edward Knatchbull, 9th Baronet of Mersham-le-Hatch, Kent). From among his mother's papers, he published *The Letters of Jane Austen* (1884), which included 79 letters and voluminous commentary by Brabourne; 14 of the letters have since been removed from collections of Austen's letters as inauthentic. Mary Augusta Ward (1851-1920), a prolific British novelist and book reviewer, condemned the edition for throwing practically "no new fresh light on Miss Austen's personality, and, with half-a-dozen exceptions, . . . had therefore better be reserved for family that use for which it was originally intended. . . . One small volume of these letters, carefully chosen and skillfully edited, would have been pleasant reading enough" (*MacMillan's Magazine*, 51 [December 1884]: 84-91).

Today's scholars recognize the value of Austen's letters. The majority of them are, not surprisingly, to her beloved sister Cassandra, and emphasize in their chatty and gossipy content the strong bond they enjoyed. Nowadays, sisters who are close text each other regularly; Jane and Cassandra kept a constant flow of letters whenever they were apart. While Austen joked in one letter about the "important nothings" (15 June 1808) included in her correspondence, her letters tell us about some of her novels in progress; balls and parties she attended; friends and acquaintances, including her sharp comments about some of them; gowns ordered; food eaten; great houses and small cottages visited–essentially, the world of her novels. In her earliest letter (January 9-10, 1796), she wrote as a 20-year-old about her flirting and dancing with Tom Lefroy. Nearing 40 and in London at brother Henry's to discuss *Emma* with Murray, she met and befriended Henry's young neighbor, the surgeon Charles Haden (1786-1824)–who would later introduce the stethoscope. In a letter to Cassandra on December 2, 1815, she described him as "a sort of wonderful nondescript Creature on two Legs, something between a Man & an Angel"; he was very musical, but as she reported to her sister in an earlier letter (November 24, 1815), "I have been listening to dreadful Insanity.–It is Mr Haden's firm beleif that a person *not* musical is fit for every sort of Wickedness". Notice that at age 40, she still did not respect the "i before e" rule. The letters are an important source of biographical information about the novelist, her personality (often playful), and very significantly, her reading. Letter-writing was extremely important in Austen's day, and her letters flow the way I imagine her tongue did: conversation was also an important talent of the times.

As Austen's novels became increasingly popular in the mid-19th century, curiosity about their author arose: the only biographical material available to readers was Henry Austen's "Biographical Notice" of his sister, first published in 1818 with the four-volume set of *Northanger Abbey* and *Persuasion*, which were slightly revised and enlarged in 1832 for the Bentley editions. Austen's nephew James-Edward and his sisters Caroline and Anna felt the importance of presenting the novelist's life from a family perspective. This was the High Victorian period (c. 1838-1877), which reflected the personal values of the Queen: moral responsibility and domestic propriety. Hence, James-Edward's *A Memoir of Jane Austen* (1869; 2nd ed. 1871) presents an idealized "dear Aunt Jane" perfectly congenial to Victorian taste; the portrait in the frontispiece, which is reproduced and discussed in Chapter 1 of *Simply Austen*, reflects this taste. It is no wonder that Victorian England soon saw sets of lavishly illustrated Austen novels. Biographies based on the *Memoir* soon followed: Oscar Fay Adams wrote *The Story of Jane Austen's Life* (1891; second edition, 1896) and Goldwin Smith wrote *The Life of Jane Austen* (1890). Readers can buy an excellent and inexpensive paperback book that includes Austen-Leigh's *Memoir*, edited by Oxford's Kathryn Sutherland: *Memoir of Jane Austen: and Other Family Recollections* (Oxford's World's Classics, 2008). Her introduction alone is worth reading, and the edition is a valuable source of information.

Austen's collateral descendants returned to the biography business in 1913 when William Austen-Leigh (son of James-Edward) and Richard Arthur Austen-Leigh (William's nephew) collaborated on *Jane Austen: Her Life and Letters, A Family Record* (London: Smith and Elder). In 2004, the great Austen scholar Deidre Le Faye brought out a second revised and enlarged edition of this work called *A Family Record* (Cambridge and NY: Cambridge University Press). Le Faye said in the introduction to that volume that beginning in the 1970s she embarked upon learning "anything and everything which has any kind of bearing upon the life of Jane Austen and her family" (ix). Doing this revision, Le Faye was given access to additional Austen family papers, and this, combined with her own tenacious research, created an essentially new book that is a foundation of biographical and family information on the novelist.

But in terms of the most readable biography that also has strong scholarly credentials is the late Professor Park Honan's *Jane Austen: Her Life* (1987), combining a fully researched biography with serious literary criticism. Academically very sound, it reads like a novel, and I recommend it to anyone interested in Jane Austen.

For those interested in Austen's life and the critical and popular reception of her work through the study of primary sources, I recommend my *Dictionary of Literary Biography* volumes of Jane Austen: vol. 363 *Jane Austen's Life and Novels* and vol. 365 *Jane Austen's Popular and Critical Reputation*. While other collections of critical and biographical essays about the novelist and her works exist, my collection offers endnotes for each entry, explaining references and allusions that go unnoticed and unexplained in other collections of this type. My goal was to assist graduate students and younger scholars in understanding the full scope of these essays.

For astute insights into Austen's work, I recommend Princeton Professor Claudia Johnson's books and essays. I recommend the work of Professor Janine Barchas for historical insights into Austen. For earlier writers' influence on Austen, I recommend the work of Professor Jocelyn Harris. These are three scholars whom I admire greatly.

About the Author

Professor Emerita of English and President's Teaching Scholar at the University of Colorado, Colorado Springs, **Joan Klingel Ray** is the editor of the *Dictionary of Literary Biography* (DLB) volumes on Jane Austen, as well as the author of *Jane Austen for Dummies* and numerous scholarly articles about Austen and other novelists and poets. She has been interviewed on radio and television and appears on the DVDs of the films *The Jane Austen Book Club and Becoming Jane*. Professor Ray is also the only three-term president of the Jane Austen Society of North America.

A Word from the Publisher

Thank you for reading *Simply Austen*!

If you enjoyed reading it, we would be grateful if you could help others discover and enjoy it too.

Please review it with your favorite book provider such as Amazon, BN, Kobo, Apple Books, or Goodreads, among others.

Again, thank you for your support and we look forward to offering you more great reads.

Made in the USA
Coppell, TX
19 March 2023

14442832R00152